Teach Business English

CAMBRIDGE HANDBOOKS FOR LANGUAGE TEACHERS

This is a series of practical guides for teachers of English and other languages. Illustrative examples are usually drawn from the field of English as a foreign or second language, but the ideas and techniques described can equally well be used in the teaching of any language.

In this series:

Drama Techniques in Language Learning – A resource book of communication activities for language teachers *by Alan Maley and Alan Duff*

Games for Language Learning
by Andrew Wright, David Betteridge and Michael Buckby

Discussions that Work – Task-centred fluency practice *by Penny Ur*

Once Upon a Time – Using stories in the language classroom
by John Morgan and Mario Rinvolucri

Teaching Listening Comprehension *by Penny Ur*

Keep Talking – Communicative fluency activities for language teaching
by Friederike Klippel

Working with Words – A guide to teaching and learning vocabulary
by Ruth Gairns and Stuart Redman

Learner English – A teacher's guide to interference and other problems
edited by Michael Swan and Bernard Smith

Testing Spoken English – A handbook of oral testing techniques *by Nic Underhill*

Literature in the Language Classroom – A resource book of ideas and activities
by Joanne Collie and Stephen Slater

Dictation – New methods, new possibilities *by Paul Davis and Mario Rinvolucri*

Grammar Practice Activities – A practical guide for teachers *by Penny Ur*

Testing for Language Teachers *by Arthur Hughes*

Pictures for Language Learning *by Andrew Wright*

Five-Minute Activities – A resource book of short activities *by Penny Ur and Andrew Wright*

The Standby Book – Activities for the language classroom
edited by Seth Lindstromberg

Lessons from Nothing – Activities for language teaching with limited time and resources *by Bruce Marsland*

Beginning to Write – Writing activities for elementary and intermediate learners
by Arthur Brookes and Peter Grundy

Ways of Doing – Students explore their everyday and classroom processes
by Paul Davis, Barbara Garside and Mario Rinvolucri

Using Newspapers in the Classroom *by Paul Sanderson*

Teaching English Spelling – A practical guide *by Ruth Shemesh and Sheila Waller*

Teach Business English *by Sylvie Donna*

Teach Business English

Sylvie Donna

PUBLISHED BY THE PRESS SYNDICATE OF THE UNIVERSITY OF CAMBRIDGE
The Pitt Building, Trumpington Street, Cambridge, United Kingdom

CAMBRIDGE UNIVERSITY PRESS
The Edinburgh Building, Cambridge CB2 2RU, UK   http://www.cup.cam.ac.uk
40 West 20th Street, New York, NY 10011–4211, USA   http://www.cup.org
10 Stamford Road, Oakleigh, Melbourne 3166, Australia
Ruiz de Alarcón 13, 28014 Madrid, Spain

First published 2000

Printed in the United Kingdom at the University Press, Cambridge

Typeset in Sabon 10.5/12pt

A catalogue record for this book is available from the British Library

Library of Congress Cataloguing in Publication data applied for

ISBN 0 521 58557 0 paperback

Contents

Contents

Acknowledgements and thanks

This book would not have been possible if it were not for the many people I have met who have hated Business English teaching or who have been afraid of it! I am grateful to all the people – teachers and others – who asked me about Business English teaching, who asked for my advice, or who expressed their exasperation or explained their frustrations. Without an awareness of the negative side of this work, I would never have got to the point where I actually felt it was necessary for me to write this book. My thanks to all those colleagues who badgered me with questions or who were keen to throw around ideas.

Thank you, too, to my old bosses who were wonderful mentors and guides. Thank you for giving me so many invaluable opportunities to teach Business English or ESP, and thank you especially for leaving me the freedom to experiment. Thank you for listening and for giving me encouragement through your feedback or requests for seminars.

In these acknowledgements I must, of course, also mention my students, even though I doubt any of them will ever read these pages. It was these people who inspired all the solutions you will find in this book. If I hadn't enjoyed teaching them, I doubt I would have been able to motivate myself to keep going. So thank you, students, for being such a great source of inspiration and for giving me such satisfying work!

My special thanks are also due to my mother and late father who supported my work throughout the years. They both recognised the value of Business English teaching so gave me a respect for and a belief in my profession. At a time when many old-time EFL teachers are fighting for acceptance of their work as a 'profession', I think it is particularly important that there are some of us who feel in our hearts that what we are doing really can be called professional.

An enormous thank you, too, to my personal and business partner at Profile Solutions International, Dr Philip B Nathan. His ongoing practical support, stimulating discussion and good, old-fashioned encouragement are constantly appreciated.

Finally, I would like to thank Penny Ur, my series editor, for her valuable comments and everyone at Cambridge University Press who made this book a reality. I won't mention any names in particular because I would be missing out the many mysterious backroom people in the team who are involved in making things a success!

Acknowledgements and thanks

The author and publishers are also grateful to the authors, publishers and others who have given permission for the use of copyright material identified in the text. It has not been possible to identify the sources of all the material used and in such cases the publishers would welcome information from copyright owners.

1 Introduction

1.1 Why this book?

Recent political and economic changes have meant that more and more company employees – or their managers – are asking for English courses which directly address their needs. These so-called Business English courses are becoming more and more popular amongst working adults, who often choose them in preference to General English classes offered by the same language school. At the same time, many teachers working in the field have been trained to teach General English to adults or children, or have no relevant training or experience. New teachers coming into the field from a variety of backgrounds are forced to survive with few guidelines and inadequate support.

This book provides practical help. It is a synthesis of my experience working with a wide range of Business English students of many nationalities who work in US or European companies, or who need English so as to conduct business abroad or study their subject. My work – in the UK, Japan, Singapore, Sri Lanka, Portugal, Italy, Germany, Greece and Morocco – has brought me in contact with many teachers who have appreciated ideas to bring their classes to life or to solve seemingly insoluble problems. My experience comes not only from my training for EFL and state school teaching and my studies of economics and business, but also from working (outside teaching) in a wide range of companies in the UK, France, Germany, Morocco and Japan. The suggestions I make in this book are also strongly influenced by my own experience as a language learner with very practical, work-oriented needs.

After looking at differences between general English and Business English, I give guidelines for teaching and practical suggestions for procedures from the enquiry stage to course evaluation. The book caters for both the novice and the experienced teacher, for the teacher of both mono- and multi-lingual classes, for the teacher with a knowledge of other languages and for those with none. Most of the procedures described will be useful to teachers in a range of teaching situations from extensive courses to short-term intensive one-to-one tutorials. The Glossary will be useful if you are new to the field and the addresses sections will enable you to find out more about relevant support organisations, resources and examinations. Section 10 – Moving towards a better future – gives ideas for follow-up activities. This book, along with the follow-up ideas, will help to provide you with a framework and approach for teaching Business English.

1.2 What is Business English?

Teaching Business English involves teaching English to adults working in businesses of one kind or another, or preparing to work in the field of business. The businesses could be large multinationals (such as Procter & Gamble), small private companies or even state-run concerns involved with providing products or services. Courses may be long or short. Classes may be taught in-company or in a language school or other rented premises.

Business English has much in common with General EFL, but in many ways is very different since the aims of a course may be quite radically different from those of a General English course. Aims – whether broad or narrow for a particular course – will always relate to students' work. Sometimes this will mean developing generalised business skills (such as giving presentations), and sometimes it will mean something much more technical or academic (if the students' work is highly specialised, or if the students need to learn how to take notes and participate in meetings or prepare for a training course conducted in English). Since course organisers often fail to differentiate between Business English and ESP (English for Specific Purposes) or EAP (English for Academic Purposes), you need to be a little open-minded when going into this area of teaching!

The main thing to remember when considering what Business English is relates to expectations – not so much yours, but your students' or their sponsors'. Course organisers will have requested 'Business English' because they want a course which relates to occupational or professional language needs. Investigating, analysing and fulfilling Business English students' needs is, in fact, so important for the success of any Business English course that a great deal of attention is paid to these processes in this book. Even if you see your role as a teacher as being quite well-defined, as a Business English teacher you would do well to consider tasks or concerns which may seem peripheral or beyond a normal teacher's role. Your priority, after all, is to run successful courses, and in order for this to be possible in the field of Business English you may need to consider wider issues, such as those discussed in Section 2 and 3.1, 3.2, 3.3, 3.4, 3.6, 4.6 and 4.7.

The student population

Students on Business English courses might have (or be preparing to have) a wide range of jobs; they could be clerical staff or top-level directors or anything in between; they might equally well have a speciality, such as advertising or patent law. If they are young or still studying, they are unlikely to know much about their work; if they are older and more experienced (which is more likely), they may be experts in their field. Instead of working in an office, they may work in a plant, a lab or out in the field (e.g. in market research or sales). Students may be studying with colleagues or with total strangers in a group, or even on their own if their needs are considered sufficiently urgent or important. If bosses and their subordinates are in the same class, internal politics may affect the learning atmosphere.

Various other factors will also influence the atmosphere of classes, including finance, timing and motivation. In other words it may be very significant whether or not students are paying for the course themselves and whether or not lessons are held inside or outside work time. Motivation will be influenced by the status of English in the students' actual or potential working environment and by the students' own attitude towards both the language and training, quite apart from more obvious factors such as promotion prospects for employees with better English. Sophisticated and stimulating management training seminars or on-the-job training which focuses on tangible, immediate results may have made students a little cynical about what they perceive to be 'traditional' classes. On the other hand, if students have not had any formal training since leaving school, they may be dazzled by your modern teaching techniques!

Whether students are self-confident and assertive (because of their superior knowledge of their work) or apparently unmotivated, you needn't worry! Even students who are tired and preoccupied and apparently uninterested in English can become highly motivated if the need for English in their work is made clear to them and if they are treated as partners in the business of learning. This is perhaps because of the scope in Business English for teaching language which is truly useful to students.

The purpose of a Business English course

The purpose of a Business English course is to fulfil students' work-related needs. These are usually very specific and cover a wide range of language. If students are employed by a multinational corporation their prime need will probably be to be able to use the phone, report to

3

foreign managers, reply to or write faxes and e-mail messages, read periodicals on their subject area and perform other tasks typically associated with the workplace. If students are doing business with companies abroad, their main need might be to survive on business trips, communicate on the phone and by fax, and negotiate contracts. Students who work in an industry whose language is English (e.g. telecommunications or computing) will need to be able to digest large quantities of reading matter in English; they may also need to be able to give presentations or discuss their work in English.

The content of a Business English course

Since courses are set up for many different reasons, the content of individual courses may vary considerably. However, the content of any particular course is usually quite specific and will always be determined by the students' needs and objectives. The most successful courses are the ones which identify appropriate content and which fulfil students' needs most completely in the shortest possible time. Since language training is expensive, both adults who are paying for themselves and companies sponsoring staff will want cost-effectiveness. Needs can usually be fulfilled most quickly if the content is chosen with students' learning and affective needs in mind, and if as much as possible is made job-related. The balance of specific elements will depend on students', or their managers', priorities and the learning process, i.e. some things can be learnt more quickly than others or are more easily learnt before or after other language areas. If you should ever want to violate this principle of needs-directed teaching, you need to be very sure you can justify this both to yourself, your students and to the people you will be reporting to.

Language in class

The language studied is also governed by students' needs. This often means a high technical content, with frequent use of common business terms. It also means a focus on styles of speaking or writing which are appropriate to the students' working environment and to the tasks they have to perform. This means students will need to develop a keen awareness of style – formality vs. informality, directness vs. indirectness. Most importantly, through language study in class students will need to become aware of the cultural context of language use, i.e. national or local cultures, industrial cultures and corporate cultures. As well as the language specifically studied in class, teacher talk (i.e. a teacher's meta-language) can also provide valuable input and exposure for students. In order to capitalise on this opportunity, it is important to make this metalanguage as adult and business-like as possible. See 1.3 and 3.4 for more on this.

Teaching objectives

Objectives for lessons and stages of lessons need to be made very clear to students on a day-to-day basis. If objectives are clear, students will work with enthusiasm and intelligence, which will naturally make your life easier. Decision-making and objective-setting can frequently be passed on to students, who are often used to making decisions, setting objectives and respecting deadlines in their day-to-day work.

Methods used

While objectives are concerned with 'what' one is teaching, activities and techniques focus on the 'how'. Since these can affect whether or not any learning actually takes place, they must be selected and used with sensitivity – according to teaching aims and student response. Variety is often highly desirable and a great range of teaching techniques can be used very successfully. However, it is important to develop personal teaching principles which will give you criteria by which to judge the success or effectiveness of specific methods used and to combine methods effectively so as to provide a coherent course. See 3.2, 4.1 and 4.2 for more on this.

Students will appreciate hearing why certain methods are used for specific language areas. Naturally, if they understand why things are happening as they are, they will usually cooperate with greater enthusiasm.

Student–teacher relationships

On the most effective courses, students and teachers work in partnership to build a constructive learning environment which is appropriate to individual students' professional and personal situations. As well as being a learner, the student is also a provider of information and material, if not also expertise. Above all, he or she is the client and the teacher an agent providing a service. See 1.3, 2.1, 2.6, 3.1, 3.4, 3.6, 4.5, 4.7, 8.1, 8.2 and 8.3 for more on this.

Accountability

The teacher's role as 'tracker of progress' must never be forgotten. Students are often used to working under pressure and they usually take for granted the idea of being accountable to bosses. They will expect promises made in class to be kept and for you to be accountable for the results of the training programme. In addition, students' bosses and supervisors, and/or the person setting up the English training in a company may want to observe classes. Reports may also be expected on a regular basis so that students' attendance and progress can be tracked, especially if the company is paying. See 2.1, 2.2, 2.6, 6.1, 6.6, 8.1, 8.2 and 8.3 for more on these areas.

Since students are basically clients, their level of satisfaction is important. If they are dissatisfied with the language teaching you provide you will soon find yourself without a job! Although business practices and contractual agreements should ensure that you are treated like the professional you are, results-oriented managers are the norm. See 6.6 for ideas on how to cope with bad feedback!

1.3 Why is Business English special?

Business English is special because of the opportunity it gives you to fulfil students' immediate needs for English. In General English classes students' needs are rarely so immediate or urgent. Since work is so central to most people's lives and since Business English relates to students' occupational or professional needs, you have the opportunity to make a real difference to your students' day-to-day experience.

An example of a real-life experience might serve to illustrate how real your link with students can be. A student returning from a trade fair, when asked how it had been, said that there had been one particularly interesting piece of equipment. However, he had written off the possibility of getting this for the company because he had been made well aware of budget constraints for his department! I decided to take a less cynical attitude about budgets and helped this student, who was studying in a class of six students, to put together and practise a short presentation on the virtues of the equipment; it was relatively easy to incorporate this work into the rest of my lesson plan. The next day, having delivered this impromptu and informal mini-presentation to his boss, the student came to class glowing; his supervisor had appreciated the longer-term advantages and cost-cutting features of the equipment and had found a way of approving its purchase.

In order for Business English to become special in this way, you need to build a special relationship with your students ... otherwise you will never hear enough about your students' working lives! Students will be grateful to you if you succeed because in developing a good relationship with them you will be helping them to become self-reliant as learners and users of English. This is an important thing for people who are used to being in control and who may have limited time to attend classes. So what do you need to do in order to build this relationship? Firstly, you need to address your students appropriately so that they will communicate with you openly and informatively. Secondly, you need to give your students more power than is sometimes the case in a student–teacher relationship. See 3.4 and 3.6 for some practical suggestions on how to do this.

When students meet you halfway in a constructive working relationship, Business English is not only special, it can become an exciting and surprising area of teaching. As a result of your efforts to improve a few people's lives you are likely to have interesting classes, increased job satisfaction and a window into other people's worlds. You may also have a springboard into other areas of work, such as those suggested in 10.1.

2 Setting things up for success

Effective pre-course work for in-company or in-house Business English courses will not only make the beginning of courses smoother, it will also help to make courses successful overall. Teachers, students and students' bosses will be approaching the English course with an appropriate set of assumptions and helpful attitudes.

You personally may become involved in some, or even all, of this pre-course work. Roles of individuals vary greatly between organisations, but even in cases where you have no official role it may be helpful – from everyone's point of view – if you become involved. Negotiate your school's political structures carefully though, and make sure that communication channels remain open and are enhanced by your involvement. As long as your contributions are known and well-explained, they are likely to be welcomed and appreciated.

2.1 Customer care

Effective customer care involves listening carefully to what individual students (or sponsors) say and then taking appropriate action. In order to do this, both effective record-keeping and information dissemination are essential. Clear, efficient, consistent and courteous treatment of customers – both inside and outside class – is also essential if students and sponsors are to feel that they are being well looked after.

Record-keeping

Customer care starts at the enquiry stage. At this point records on individuals' requests or expressions of interest can be noted down (per-haps using a form such as the one suggested on p. 10) and then filed for future reference. (A computer database can, of course, make future sorting and access of information even easier.) As soon as a student enrols for a course, either a public course or a private group course, the student's notes need to be transferred to a student record form, such as the one provided on p. 24. This will then need to be kept up-to-date as the student progresses through various courses and examinations.

Information dissemination

Whenever your school offers a course which might be of interest to a student, or potential student, he or she should be informed. For example, if several enquiries were received about BEC3 exam preparation courses which were currently not on offer at your school, as soon as these courses are set up the previous enquirers need to be informed. (To find out more about BEC3, see the Glossary.) As well as showing care for your customers, disseminating any relevant information is, obviously, of great value to a school because it is a kind of advertising and might well result in fuller classes, as well as students who feel they are being kept up-to-date.

Clear, efficient, consistent and courteous treatment

When dealing with students and sponsors, bear in mind the following points:

- Customers will need to know exactly what is on offer to them, at what price and when.
- People will only perceive your service as efficient if they are dealt with quickly and reliably. Nobody likes long waits or unfulfilled promises.
- Potential students or sponsors will probably also be contacting other language schools. Even though you need to take this into account, some people will naturally be offended if you make negative statements about your competitors.
- Courtesy is defined differently by different nationalities so it is a good idea to learn about, then take into account your customers' national preferences.

2.2 Initial contact with clients

Companies and individuals approach schools in various ways, largely depending on local practices. Whether you are involved only occasionally or on a regular basis you may be able to influence the way enquiries are dealt with by providing suggestions or even a form for enquiries – such as the one suggested on the next page. At this initial enquiry stage the client's main concerns might be price, the credentials of teachers and the approach to evaluating and ensuring results. Don't make exaggerated or misleading promises. This is the first stage in a long process in which clients will gradually come to rely on your honesty and expertise. Individual students and personnel managers will have most respect for a realistic approach which looks at real results and probabilities.

During initial conversations with potential clients, irrespective of the country or culture, it is probably best to leave most of the speaking to the client. However, focus on finding out:

- where the real impetus for the course came from, and whose idea it was to contact you
- why the enquirer wants to join or set up a course
- what she or he wants to achieve

If you find out the answers to these questions it is much easier to confirm (and satisfy) clients' needs later on. It is often at the enquiry stage that needs are most clearly expressed.

At this initial contact stage it is often also a good idea to encourage potential students to take a placement test and complete a needs analysis form, such as the one provided on p. 11. Scores and responses (or information on appointments, if it is a telephone enquiry) should also be recorded on the original enquiry form – for ease of reference later on. If tests and forms are readily available at your school's reception desk they can be administered quickly and efficiently. Immediate follow-up oral interviewing – if practically possible – can then quickly result in immediate registration for courses.

Note that placement testing often comes later in the pre-course needs analysis for two reasons. Firstly, different tests might be used for different needs. Secondly, if a large number of new students are involved (e.g. when setting up courses in-company), special arrangements will need to be made. More detailed notes on placement testing are given in 2.4.

A *form for initial telephone or face-to-face contact*

BUSINESS ENGLISH ENQUIRY   Date: Time:

Name: .... Company: ....

Contact numbers: ....

Interested in:

Reasons for wanting English:

Previous courses taken?   Exams already taken?

Placement test taken: Y / N   Score: Date to be taken:

Needs analysis completed: Y / N   Date to be returned:

Suggested / promised:

Enquiry dealt with by: _____

A form for needs analysis

BUSINESS ENGLISH NEEDS ANALYSIS

Name: .... Company: ....

Contact numbers: ....

To help us make the English programme useful, please fill out the form below.
What do you need to do in English? How good are you already? Do you urgently
need to work on improving this skill? Look at the key at the bottom before you start.

Language area	How good am I?*	How urgently do I need this skill?*
talking to clients	0 1 2 3 4 5	now very soon next year don't know
letters or formal faxes	0 1 2 3 4 5	now very soon next year don't know
using the telephone	0 1 2 3 4 5	now very soon next year don't know
dealing with visitors	0 1 2 3 4 5	now very soon next year don't know
talking to colleagues	0 1 2 3 4 5	now very soon next year don't know
reporting to managers	0 1 2 3 4 5	now very soon next year don't know
giving presentations	0 1 2 3 4 5	now very soon next year don't know
attending meetings	0 1 2 3 4 5	now very soon next year don't know
negotiating	0 1 2 3 4 5	now very soon next year don't know
note-taking at meetings	0 1 2 3 4 5	now very soon next year don't know
e-mail, faxes or memos	0 1 2 3 4 5	now very soon next year don't know
report-writing	0 1 2 3 4 5	now very soon next year don't know
understanding the news	0 1 2 3 4 5	now very soon next year don't know
other: _____	0 1 2 3 4 5	now very soon next year don't know

* KEY:

How good am I?   0 = I can't do this at all
                   1 = I try but I'm not very good
                   2 = I can do it but I make a lot of mistakes
                   3 = I'm OK at doing this but I make a few mistakes
                   4 = I'm quite good at doing this – I don't make many mistakes
                   5 = I'm very good at doing this – I hardly make any mistakes

How urgently do I need this skill? Circle the words which are true for you.

Any comments or requests?

Thank you for your time.

© Cambridge University Press

2.3 Needs analysis interviews

It is helpful if interviews can be arranged to confirm initial comments or conclusions about needs. This also applies if needs analysis forms have been filled out by potential students because managers' (or organisers') and students' perceptions of needs may vary considerably. Ideally, you – as the students' future teacher – should attend and/or lead these interviews.

Interviews with in-company course coordinators

Focus on getting answers to the following questions:

- *What does the company want the students to be able to do?*
- *In what specific situations will they be doing these things?*
- *Which of the above are priorities? In terms of percentages? ... e.g. 70% report-writing, 20% replying to faxes and 10% speaking on the telephone*
- *What kind of feedback does the company want from the school?*
- *Have the students had any training before?*
- *Which previous training courses have been arranged in general?*
- *Who attended?*
- *What kind of requests and comments have come from managers and potential students?*

Interviews with students' managers

An even better overview of training needs and requirements can be gained if you can interview your future students' managers. They are the people most directly in touch with students' real needs and they should also have an insight into their company's longer term foreign language needs. Enlist the in-company course coordinator's help in organising interviews with key people within the organisation. Justify these meetings by saying that managers directly above employees taking courses are the people most in touch with their employees' needs and problems. They are the people who can really confirm priorities.

In your interviews, rather than having free-form discussions, focus on these questions:

- *What do you want your staff to be able to do?*
- *In what specific situations will they be doing these things?*
- *Which of these things are priorities? In terms of percentages? ... e.g. 80% speaking and listening – so as to be able to participate in meetings, 20% reading and replying to faxes*

- *How do your staff cope now? Do they get help from colleagues? Do they use an agency? Do they take work home? Do they use a translator or interpreter?*
- *What level of success are you hoping for?*
- *What are your staff's most urgent short-term needs for English?*

When managers are talking, give support through reflective listening and clarifying questions (e.g. *Can they use the phone at all? So you mean you can't understand their memos?*). Since managers have often not given any careful thought to their staff's real English needs, answering these questions may not be easy for them. This is often the reason for the failure of previous training programmes: overly generalised courses may have failed to address their staff's specific needs.

Note that as well as allowing you to confirm the initial needs analysis, these interviews should also help you to 'sell' your courses to students' managers. This is important because when managers believe in an English course, they are likely to make sure that students are freed up to attend classes and may well also make resources more readily available to their staff, e.g. in the form of typical faxes or memos written in-house. The clear focus of your questions will show that you mean to take answers seriously.

Interviews with individual students

As well as helping you to analyse students' precise needs, interviews with students can also help motivation because your clearly focused questions will make it clear to students that you are interested in improving the language they need to use at work. If students are given a very generalised 'chatty' oral interview, they are likely to perceive your language programme as vague and irrelevant to their real-life English needs. Also, determining a student's level of English in a work context will involve more than a 'chat' on general topics. The student will need to be asked very specific questions, such as the following:

- *What do you find most difficult about English?*
- *Which area is most important for your job: speaking, writing, reading or listening?*
- *What exactly do you need to do in each skill area? (What kind of speaking, writing, etc.)*
- *How would you prioritise your needs in terms of percentages?*
- *How have you found training programmes in the past?*
- *What do you think you can do to improve your performance and success on this course?*

If these interviews are part of an oral interview following a written placement test it is also a good idea to ask students to actually perform tasks through role-play after getting answers to these questions. This will help you to ascertain a student's language level. For more notes on written and oral placement tests, see 2.4.

At the end of any interview it is useful to ask coordinators, managers and students:

- *Would you like to make any other comments or suggestions? Do you have any questions?*

2.4 Placement testing

Placement testing can be based on in-house or commercially produced tests. A placement test, as well as material for diagnostic needs analysis, is provided in *Business English Assessment* (Wilberg, P. 1994. Hove: Language Teaching Publications. See p. 334 for their address). Guidelines for designing your own tests are given below.

Written placement tests

If carefully written, these can be quickly administered and should reliably sort students into broad categories. However, because of the likely inadequacies of any written test it is best to adjust your decisions on placement by means of oral interviews. (See next page.)

When preparing an in-house written placement test, note the following:

- The content of your test should reflect the type of programme being offered. For this reason it is useful to conduct your initial needs analysis before administering tests.
- Your test should be 'valid' in testing terms. A test can be considered valid if it gives information on what you really want to test. See Weir (1993) pp. 18–19 for more on this.
- Your test needs to take your potential students into account. If there are quite a few low-level students, your test must enable you to differentiate between the very weak and the fairly weak candidates!
- Items need to be carefully weighted to take your teaching context into account. For example, placement tests for exam courses are likely to be more accuracy-oriented.
- Despite time constraints amongst busy working adults, your test should be substantial enough to give you reliable information. One hour is a reasonable amount of time to expect a student to sit at a placement test.

- Your test should provide a reliable indication of level when administered to different students in different contexts. In the Business English context a test can only really give reliable information if it is confidential and conducted under exam conditions. For this reason, it is preferable to arrange for students in any one company to be tested together. If a Training Manager wants to distribute the test, explain the importance of testing for correct placement. See Weir (1993) pp. 20–21 for more on making tests reliable.
- Your test needs to be easy to administer and mark. When setting up programmes for hundreds of students, multiple-choice may be your only realistic option. With smaller numbers and non multiple-choice test items, marking criteria need to be clear, and possible answers predetermined for quick marking. A clear marking scheme will ensure consistency and more reliable placement when different people mark the test.
- Your test should give you a starting point for oral interviewing. A section which asks students about his or her job, or which focuses on his or her hopes for the course is very useful in this respect.

The sample test on pp. 17–21, which includes guidelines for placement, might be suitable for students wanting to join a course focusing on business writing.

Oral interviews

As well as helping you to fine-tune your placement of students, oral interviews also reveal additional information about students' needs.

You can structure your oral interviews by guiding students through the following questions:

- *What's your job? What does that involve exactly?*
- *How long have you been with … ? Do you enjoy working for … ?*
- *Do you already use English at work? Do you find that easy?*
- *What will you soon need to be able to do? Do you think that will be easy?*

You might also consider adapting the questions suggested on pp. 12–14 if you have not had a chance to have some interviews with course coordinators, students' managers or students.

Next, get students to role-play some key situations:

- *Imagine I'm a visitor to your company. I'm going to ask you a few questions.*
- *Now let's imagine you are at work and I'm a customer. You answer the telephone.*

To round off the interview, after thanking the student, ask:

• *Do you have any special hopes for this English course?*

Make careful notes during oral interviews so that you later have a useful point of reference when preparing your first classes. If you do not have the opportunity to conduct oral interviews yourself encourage interviewers to do this – perhaps using a form such as the one provided below. If oral interviews are considered unrealistic or unnecessary in your particular context (e.g. because of the large number of students or because of the small number of classes being planned), you will need to glean information on students' oral English in the first few sessions of a course.

For ideas on how to find out more about your students' level of English early on in a course, see 3.5 and 4.7. Many of the procedures listed in 4.7 will enable you to find out more about students' language abilities.

BUSINESS ENGLISH ORAL INTERVIEW NOTES

Student's name: .... Position: ....

Details of job:

Time already with company:

Use of English at work now:

Use of English at work in the future:

Student's comments about English:

Special hopes for this course:

> Interviewed by: Date of interview:
>
> Placement decision:

Business English PLACEMENT TEST

Name: .... Company: ....

Position: .... Department: ....

Contact numbers: ....

---

1 **Complete this letter by filling in the gaps.**
Choose one sentence from the box below to fill in each gap.

A: Could you please send me current catalogues, prices lists and technical specifications?

B: I look forward to hearing from you soon.

C: We are a large multiple retailer with outlets in Europe and the UK.

D: These machines are networked through an AppleTalk system.

E: Dear Sirs,

Reasonable Retailers Inc.
RRI GmbH, 71 Karlsdorfstr., 4220 Dusseldorf, Germany
Tel: 77 427 25 Fax: 77 427 26

October 3, 2002

EF Marketing Services
209 Euston Road
London NW1 3DG
UK

1 _____

I am writing to enquire about your video-conferencing equipment. **2** _____
Our associate company, LX Sales, suggested that we contact you.

Our existing data processing system is accessed through Apple LC15s at 27 sites
located throughout Europe. **3** _____ We would like to upgrade one station
at each site for video conferencing.

4 _____ We are also interested in having an on-site demonstration, if this
can be arranged.

5 _____

Yours faithfully,

Jenny Bland

Jenny Bland
Data Processing Manager

(Adapted from: Badger, I. and P. Menzies. 1993/1994. *The Macmillan Business
English Programme: Pre-Intermediate*. London: Macmillan.)

BUSINESS ENGLISH Placement Test – page 2

Name: ....

2 Complete this fax, using one word from the box in each gap.

a explain	e command	i possibly	m message	q possible
b number	f other	j credit	n deliver	r delivered
c can	g able	k bill	o request	s ones
d balance	h creditor	l order	p equal	t delivery

Page 1 of 1

To: Jane P Deighton
Sales Manager
Q & S Electrical Distributors
Tel: 01355 834679, Ext 591
Fax: 01355 834680

QuickStep Lighting
183 High Street
Camberwick Green
Horsham Surrey SU3 9TX
Tel: 01355 783423
Fax: 01355 783424

September 30, 1998

Dear Ms Deighton,

Order No. PK 2173

We received a consignment of light bulbs from you today, against the above **1** _____ .
Could you sort out the following points, please?

1 4 boxes of 100W standard bulbs arrived broken. Could you please arrange a
    2 _____ note and replacements.

2 You delivered 4 dozen boxes of CFL 13 Compact Fluorescent Lamps instead of the 14 dozen
    boxes we ordered. Is this an error or are you out of stock? The despatch note says 4 dozen
    boxes. How soon can we have the **3** _____ ?

3 You delivered 8 boxes of CFB 15 Company Fluorescent Bulbs which we did not order.
    Are they in place of the CFB 20s that were not **4** _____ ?

Could you get back to me as soon as **5** _____ ?

Regards,

J. Jameson.

John Jameson
Purchasing

(Adapted from: Badger, I. and P. Menzies. 1993/1994. *The Macmillan Business
English Programme: Pre-Intermediate.* London: Macmillan.)

BUSINESS ENGLISH Placement Test – page 3

Name: ....

3 Consider the following situation:

Your company has its own cafeteria but you feel the food and service offered
are inadequate. To make matters worse, the cafeteria is always overcrowded and
there were recently also a few reports of food poisoning.

**Write a memo or an e-mail to Alan Starvick, the Human Resources
Manager, complaining about this situation.**

BUSINESS ENGLISH Placement Test – page 4

Name: ....

4 Imagine you have been on a trip to the USA to visit your head office
or main plant. Now you are back in your normal office/plant.
Write a letter, fax or e-mail to someone in the USA, as detailed below.
The beginning has been written for you. You should include the
following:
 • thanks
 • some information on your return journey
 • some comments on your impressions of the USA (especially to do with
   work)
 • some information which you were asked to send on your return
 • an invitation to your US colleague to come and visit when he or she
   is in your area
 • an ending to the letter, fax or e-mail message.

Write between 120 and 250 words.

Dear .... ,

*I've now arrived back in .... after a very productive trip
to the United States.*

BUSINESS ENGLISH PLACEMENT TEST

ANSWER KEY

Part 1: 1E, 2C, 3D, 4A, 5B – 1 mark for each correct answer
Part 2: 1l (order), 2j (credit), 3d (balance), 4r (delivered), 5q (possible) –
1 mark for each correct answer
Part 3: Award points out of 5 in accordance with the following criteria:

Planning & organisation	1	2	3	4	5
Style & use of vocabulary	1	2	3	4	5
Grammatical accuracy	1	2	3	4	5
Clarity of meaning	1	2	3	4	5

You can develop your own detailed scales for these areas or use the following
as a guideline:

1 = None/no awareness of this
2 = A little/slight awareness/slightly effective
3 = Some – but with many errors, misjudgements or inappropriacies
4 = Quite a lot – but with some errors, misjudgements or inappropriacies
5 = A great deal – with very few errors, misjudgements or inappropriacies

Part 4: As for Part 3.

Total possible points: 50.

PLACEMENT

How you place students will depend on the nature of the courses you are
offering. Usually you will be looking for a minimum level of performance,
which you may want to calculate numerically. When considering students'
potential for courses you will, of course, need to take into account the
problems typically experienced by this type of student, the type of 'errors',
the course materials and the teaching approach to be used on the course.
This will affect your judgement about possible progress and therefore the
suitability of students for the course.

The following test breakdown summarises the main focus of each part of
the test.

Part 1: This tests recognition and placement of formulaic phrases. Total beginners
cannot do this. False beginners often can.
Part 2: This tests students' knowledge and/or awareness of vocabulary typically used
in business correspondence. Students with no experience of business writing
are likely to make mistakes in this section.
Part 3: This tests students' ability to write a fairly simple memo. The student's memo
will give an indication of level in terms of the following: use of conventions
and typical phrases, organisation of content, appropriacy of style, range of
vocabulary and grammatical accuracy.
Part 4: This tests students' writing in a broader sense because there is more scope for
error. Appropriate use of vocabulary or formulaic expressions and grammatical
expressions is important here, as is planning and appropriacy of content. A
student who performs well in this section may be quite a proficient writer.

2.5 Decision-making

After the initial needs analysis and testing, appropriate decisions must be made if courses are to have a good chance of success. Decisions about grouping students or timetabling classes might have a significant impact on students' learning.

Grouping students

People have varying ideas as to how students should be divided into groups. While some teachers claim it is impossible to teach groups of students of varying status within a company (e.g. managers, along with their subordinates), others claim it is impossible to teach mixed-level classes (i.e. classes of students with widely differing test scores). In many situations it may be preferable to teach mixed-status or mixed-level classes if the students all have the same needs. For example, if students are to be divided into two groups and half of them only need to develop reading skills, while the other half need to be able to participate in meetings, it would make more sense to divide them according to need. For notes on how to deal with mixed-status and mixed-level classes, see 6.3 and 6.4.

Budgets or internal politics might also influence the way in which students need to be divided up; the in-company course organiser will have inside information on this. The Sales Manager, for example, may wish to have all his or her staff needing English, say a total of four, trained in one small class, rather than have them join a larger class which is being financed from the Human Resources budget. Alternatively, managers or top directors might prefer to be trained apart from lower ranking staff, either for reasons of prestige or again because they might feel their needs will be better catered for in this way.

In dealing with these issues, you must, of course, respect the country or company's culture – even if you do encourage people to be a little more open-minded at times!

Timetabling classes

There is a significant difference between the following 80-hour courses in terms of teaching:

- 2 × 2-hour classes per week, over a six-month period
- 1 × 4-hour classes per week, over a six-month period
- 4 × 1-hour classes per week, over a six-month period
- 4 × 2-hour classes per week, over a three-month period, and
- 4 × 4-hour classes per week, over a 6-week period

Almost anything can be turned to good effect but consider the advantages of the various configurations if you have any say in timetabling. While more intensive courses seem to inject interest and sustain motivation, extensive courses allow for recycling and more relaxed learning. Such longer-term courses might also help students to integrate English practice with their daily work routines. One class per week, however, is often too little for a student to make any progress because of the lack of continuity and lack of time for practice.

Ideally, classes should be timetabled for times when attendance is likely to be high. This usually means holding classes during work time, perhaps contrary to expectation.

2.6 Liaison

Liaison means staying in touch with anyone involved in course set-up, both in your school or in-company. Problems are often averted as a result of good ongoing liaison because issues or possibilities are discovered before they have a chance to become problems.

If liaison between key people before or after pre-course needs analysis seems poor or non-existent, simply supplement it yourself! No system can adequately take account of the vital snippets of feedback that come via teachers. Comments and odd titbits of information will help you improve the course you are teaching. However, negotiate the politics of your own and other organisations with care, always respecting people's professional roles.

In order to establish and maintain a dialogue with key people it may often be necessary to take informal opportunities to liaise – in corridors, cafeterias and other informal locations. Sometimes you will also need to create opportunities to chat by popping your head round people's doors. Don't be afraid to ask managers, or students, if they have noticed any progress or have any comments. Your questions will clearly show that you are open to ongoing feedback or ideas and that you care about the success of the course. Managers will be pleased you are taking an active interest and, in addition, their comments should give you important tips for improving what you do in class.

Keep talking to the coordinator(s) in your school too, because they should have greatest access to any ongoing feedback or inspiration (from students, course organisers or enquirers), as well as information on new exams and materials. Keep them up-to-date on what has been said in your discussions with students or in-company personnel too.

A sample student record form

BUSINESS ENGLISH STUDENT RECORD

Name: ....   Company: ....

Position: ....   Department: ....

Company address: ....

....

Home tel. no.: ....   Work tel. no: ....

Other contact numbers: ....

Best time(s) to call: ....

COURSES COMPLETED

Elem Business Eng 1 [ ]	Int Business Eng 1 [ ]	Adv Business Eng 1 [ ]
Term:	Term:	Term: ....
Elem Business Eng 2 [ ]	Int Business Eng 2 [ ]	Adv Business Eng 2 [ ]
Term:	Term:	Term: ....
Elem Business Eng 3 [ ]	Int Business Eng 3 [ ]	Adv Business Eng 3 [ ]
Term:	Term:	Term: ....
BEC1 [ ]	BEC2 [ ]	BEC3 [ ]
Term:	Term:	Term: ....

Other courses: ....

....

....

EXAMS ALREADY PASSED: (circle as appropriate)

General:	PET	FCE	CPE	Other ....
Business:	BEC1	BEC2	BEC3	Other ....

SPECIAL REQUESTS / NOTES:

© Cambridge University Press

3   Starting up courses

3.1 Confirming agreements and decisions

Before you start planning any new course, check what has already been agreed or decided at the pre-course needs analysis stage. This can initially be done by use of a form which summarises key information, such as that suggested on the next page. Should there be anything which is unclear to you or which you feel may be ambiguous, check with the people who dealt with the pre-course needs analysis or contact key managers again, if necessary. Clarify what is needed by careful questioning. This is vitally important because accurate communication of key points can determine the success or failure of a course.

When you consider the information on a new course, note in particular who your contact person is. This is the person who you will be able to contact in a company if anything goes wrong! If possible, arrange to be taken to the company, preferably using the type of transport you will be using during the course, and make sure you are introduced to this contact person. A personal introduction will get you off to a good start.

You can use this meeting to confirm what you understand from the needs analysis. Since the needs analysis should be more or less clear, it is also useful to confirm practical arrangements at this stage. Check that the contact person will help out if pens run out or if equipment stops working. Ask where you can keep your things; also check where you can sit, whether or not you can use a photocopier and/or a computer, and whether it will be OK for you to use the company cafeteria! Asking about these and other things is better than simply assuming what you can or cannot do, because you will avoid causing offence.

Pre-course panic

As a relatively inexperienced Business English teacher or even as a conscientious human being, you may feel a sense of panic when faced with information on what has been agreed or promised for a Business English course, or when led into a slick business environment to meet an elegantly-dressed contact person. Do not panic! You will soon become accustomed to your new teaching situation, whether the course is to be conducted in-company or in-house (i.e. at your own school). If things go wrong at the beginning or in the middle of courses – as they inevitably will at times – there are solutions! See Section 6 for notes on solving or avoiding a range of problems typically encountered in the Business English context.

A form to summarise information on new courses

BUSINESS ENGLISH COURSE INFORMATION

Start date: _____   Length of course: _____

Days/times of classes: _____

Company: [_____]

Address: _____

_____

Telephone number: _____   Contact person: _____

Travel information: _____

Students: _____

Approximate level: _____

Main course objective(s):

[   ]

Subsidiary objective(s):

[   ]

Materials to be used/not to be used*:   *delete as applicable

Previous teacher(s): _____

Exam or test requirements: _____

Reports to be written for the company: _____

3.2 Planning to accurately reflect needs analyses

After establishing what students need to learn, it is important to plan so that your course reflects those needs. Business English students often expect courses to be planned carefully because they work in a world where planning and accountability are taken for granted. Business Plans are usually necessary for any kind of financial support and shorter range plans are regularly submitted to middle managers. Plans should be realistic and available (in written form, ideally) to both students and managers. Using a course outline, as explained below, makes this quite manageable in practical terms. Sample course outlines are provided on p. 31 and p. 48.

Carefully planning a course in advance has many advantages. Firstly, you will not need to constantly worry about how balanced and appropriate the course materials and focus areas are. Secondly, your students will have a good idea of where the course is going and will feel reassured that they are getting a programme which has been designed to fit their needs. Thirdly, the client coordinators will have increased confidence in the institution providing the language programme. If you produce a course outline which clearly shows your planning your clients (i.e. your students and their sponsors) will easily be able to see how the programme reflects the initial needs analysis; this should make them feel confident that time spent on initial set-up was not wasted.

When planning a course:

- Use a range of planning techniques so as to tap into both your logical and your intuitive mind.
- Check and re-check that your planning reflects the priorities established during the pre-course needs analysis.
- Be realistic about timeframes, i.e. about what can be achieved in a given time.
- Remember that any back-up paperwork you produce, such as a course outline, will act as PR documents.
- Get and take account of any feedback you receive on draft plans from students or colleagues.
- Keep everyone informed of your pre-course planning decisions.
- Update people whenever you make any changes to your course outline.

Notes and tips on all of these areas are provided on the following pages.

Use a range of planning techniques

A few examples of techniques are provided here to give you ideas. Using several of them should help you to tap into both your logical and your intuitive mind.

- Collate the lists of priorities drawn up during interviews in the pre-course needs analysis. Alternatively, consider which one of the lists can be considered most authoritative. Make a pie chart to clearly represent these priorities, as shown on p. 29.
- Collect and review comments made by key managers during the initial needs analysis. This will help you to remember important preferences and pet hates.
- Make lists of sponsors' or students' 'needs' and 'wants', based on information gleaned from the pre-course needs analysis.
- Make a list of performance areas to be covered, with notes about possible materials or approaches. Your list of areas to cover should be comprehensive. Against each item on your list write notes about possible materials or approaches to use. If you're teaching an exam course check what the students will be required to do in order to pass or score well. For non-examined courses, consider what is involved in developing a particular language skill. For an example of this, see the table on p. 29 underneath the pie chart.
- Imagine the course in progress and try to visualise a 'shape' for the whole course, based on priorities which have been established. For example, if most managers interviewed in the needs analysis said the highest priority was to get their employees speaking in meetings imagine a course which includes all sorts of speaking activities. Some activities should coax the student(s) into speaking (via stimulating material) and others should provide a structure for systematic practice of key language. Read through some of the classroom procedures suggested in Sections 3, 4 and 5 for ideas which might activate students with a range of different learning styles.
- Remind yourself which classroom procedures deal with each area of language agreed in the needs analysis. If you categorise classroom procedures in this way, the progression in terms of language learning and practice can be shown on the course outline. This helps to make the final course outline clear; it also helps you, the teacher, to link up language practice in class and show students which language practice relates to which skill area. This is particularly important from a motivational point of view. The course must be perceived as being both effective and relevant to students.
- 'Juggle' the separate elements within the course outline. This will be necessary if certain aspects of the programme appear too dense or if timeframes are unrealistic (e.g. if too little time is allowed for student

practice or review of objectives). Also, check that nothing from the initial needs analysis has been forgotten or marginalised.

Kobe Steel: Lower-Intermediate – small group of staff from Human Resources Dept.

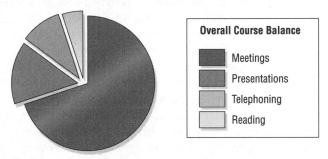

Overall Course Balance

- Meetings
- Presentations
- Telephoning
- Reading

Performance Areas to Cover	% of Course	Additional Details	Materials / Approaches
Meetings	70	with supervisors (one-to-one) daily departmental meetings (5 people)	role-play *Business Interactions*[1] Community Language Learning[2]
Presentations	15	to staff from foreign offices (internal)	in-house materials students work in small groups
Telephoning	10	internal and external giving/getting info taking messages	*Getting Through*[3] 20-min slot periodically back-up lang lab (self-study)
Reading	5	keeping up to date	*Practical Faster Reading*[4] and *In Print*[5] as homework books articles/extracts from company magazine and periodicals

[1] Matthews, C. 1987. Hemel Hempstead: Prentice Hall.
[2] See p. 104.
[3] Parry, M. and L. Weller. 1980. Harlow: Longman.
[4] Mosback, G. and V. Mosback. 1976. Cambridge: Cambridge University Press.
[5] Revell, R. and S. Sweeney. 1993. Cambridge: Cambridge University Press.

Check and re-check your planning in terms of the needs analysis
The percentages that managers assigned to key priorities are particularly important: major areas must be assigned a sufficient amount of class time. If a 30% priority is only assigned 10% of class time, it must be possible to explain why. Sometimes language can be taught and practised quickly, or it can be covered partly through homework or self-study, if facilities are available for the students. Alternatively, course materials may provide a lot more support in certain areas or students may get ongoing, informal training in their day-to-day work.

If the main requirement for success appears to be that students pass an exam, check that there is no subtext, i.e. check the reasons why decision-makers consider this exam to be important. Course coordinators may be hoping that a paper qualification is acquired only as a by-product of the course. Coordinators, for example, who want students to improve their TOEIC score – an exam involving no speaking or writing – may also want courses to focus mainly on these productive skills. If in doubt, check! Then consider whether or not exam practice can be marginalised in favour of practising the core skill(s) really needed by a company.

Be realistic about timeframes
Different facilities and resources may be available in different teaching contexts. How much class time you allocate to each area in your final course outline will depend on the facilities and resources available. For example, if students enrolling at a school automatically pay for ten hours' use of a self-access centre take account of this when planning. If a reference library or language laboratory is available for students' use in-company this may mean that some course items need only be covered briefly in class time. Homework time can accelerate work on writing skills. Make a note of key points on your draft course outline as soon as you find out about them; your notes will remind you to be realistic when finalising plans.

In the case of areas which are particularly difficult to cover it is important that enough time is allowed, even if these areas were assigned a relatively low percentage in terms of priorities. Time allocated must allow for some significant progress to be made or for core objectives to be met. However, don't allocate so much time that other important areas are neglected.

If, for whatever reason, things do not go as anticipated as the course progresses don't be afraid to adjust your programme so that the final balance of training still accurately reflects the initial needs analysis. By the end of the course the most important thing is to ensure that what we actually teach is in fact what we have promised to teach and that the learning which actually takes place matches the learning requested as closely as possible!

A *course outline for a short course in-company*

BUSINESS ENGLISH COURSE OUTLINE
Sony Corporation, English Level 7: May 13 to July 3, 2017

General information:
TEACHER: Sylvie Donna   **TIMES**: 6.00–8.00 p.m.
DAYS: Mondays/Wednesdays   **VENUE**: Sydney Training Centre

Ongoing study programme:
HOMEWORK: Job-related English tasks which are relevant to the programme.
SELF-STUDY: Reading practice using the in-company magazine, periodicals and
In Print (Revell, R. and S. Sweeney. 1993. Cambridge: Cambridge
University Press).

Week	Monday	Wednesday
1	Introduction to course: • Introductions and chats • Needs analysis	Telephoning: • Survival strategies • Chatting to clients
2	Faxes to clients: • Planning and paragraphing • Typical expressions	In-house message-writing: • Introduction to e-mail • Different types of message
3	Problem-solving: • Informal discussion • E-mail messages	Meetings: • Making a point • Taking control
4	Speaking and culture: • Dealing with visitors • Speaking to clients	Day-to-day communication: • Colleagues generally • Bosses and top managers
5	Presentations 1: • Overview/discussion of problems • Planning	Presentations 2: • Preparing visual aids • Using equipment effectively
6	Presentations 3: • Making points clearly and persuasively • Body language	Presentations 4: • Preparing effective introductions and conclusions • Q&A sessions
7	Student presentations and follow-up meetings	Student presentations and follow-up meetings
8	Individual interviews and questions	Review of main points Focus on becoming a more effective learner

Please contact Sylvie Donna if you have any comments or questions.
E-mail: sylvie.donna@profilesolutionsinternational.com

Produce paperwork which acts as PR documents

Anything you produce for your students or their sponsors may be passed around within companies and be considered by important decision-makers. Your paperwork is, therefore, your ambassador in your absence. A course outline can communicate professionalism – or carelessness and lack of commitment. It can also function as a reference point to be used throughout your course and as a motivator to students! Consider the strength of your course outline in terms of both content and presentation. Sample outlines are provided on p. 31 and p. 48.

When you are considering the content of your course outline, you will effectively be writing a syllabus (i.e. you will be deciding what you are going to teach when). (For definitions of different types of syllabus, see 'syllabus' in the Glossary.) A mix of syllabus types (structural, functional, etc.) is often preferable but syllabuses which use only one approach (e.g. a functional syllabus) may be preferable for low-level students who have studied 'grammar' in high school before. If syllabus-writing is a new area for you, simply look at the Contents page in your course materials and there you will usually see a sample syllabus. Copy language points which seem useful and relevant to your course onto your course outline and add others which are needed to make your outline reflect the initial needs analysis.

When you are selecting terms to put in boxes on your course outline, the ideal approach from a PR point of view is probably to label language work in terms of the performance areas which have been prioritised in the needs analysis. For example, instead of writing 'Talking about the past', write 'Presentations 2: progress reports', if you're intending to get students practising past forms in order to improve their presentations. After all, your students and their managers are likely to have very little understanding of syllabusing so the outline will be more user-friendly if it relates directly to the needs analysis. The connection between classwork and the initial needs analysis will then be clear on a day-to-day basis and students will also see exactly how they should eventually be able to use language in their work context. This will help to maximise student motivation – the prime factor, perhaps, in determining a course's success. More detail on language points can be included, if you wish, under performance areas so that the connection between classwork and the real world is still clear. However, giving more detail will mean decreased flexibility later in the course so it is not always a good idea.

When planning your paperwork, the most important thing to remember is that you will be dealing with the learning needs of real human beings. Promises – which might be made by implication on a course outline – must be as reliable at this stage as they were at the initial contact stage (i.e. when clients were merely making enquiries).

If your paperwork does not take the reality of the classroom into account it will soon lose credibility.

For this reason ensure that some areas of language work have been distributed throughout your course because breaking up practice of a specific area allows for:

- regular review and practice, which usually increases learning;
- homework between stages;
- more effective use of materials from the students' own companies.

Breaking up elements within a course may also make classwork on the particular area more interesting for students, thanks to added variety on a class-by-class basis. Note, however, that in some situations areas are most effectively covered all at once, e.g. on short intensive courses. Presentations could be a focus for a week or two during a longer course.

Once you have sorted out the content, computer software can help with presentation and will also enable you to produce clear paperwork quickly. Consider drafting your paperwork straight onto a computer because charts and diagrams which are easily produced by some software may help you to think things through and to see a 'shape' for the whole course. These graphics might later form part of an information pack for students or their sponsors. The chart and table on p. 29 for example, might easily be adapted for a pre-course information pack.

If no computer equipment is available use whatever is available in your particular context. After all, the content of the course outline is more important than its appearance. A well-dressed diplomat who speaks incoherent, irrelevant rubbish will not be saved by his suit and sleek haircut; a person who speaks sense, has an interesting taste in clothes and a careless barber might be more successful when negotiating an international peace settlement!

Whichever way you present your plans, check and double-check that there are no errors in the final course outline and that the content of all supplementary paperwork is coherent and in line with the pre-course needs analysis.

Get and incorporate feedback on draft plans
Some checking or approval of course outlines may be necessary, depending on your teaching context. The best person to show the outline to at this stage is the person who initially set-up the course and/ or conducted the initial needs analysis. This person will be in a prime position to make pertinent comments which may ward off potential problems. Consider his or her comments carefully and make changes to the course outline, if you feel this will result in a more successful course.

Also get feedback from students early on in the course and consider adjusting your outline in line with their comments and their apparent level of English. When you do this:

- Encourage comments.
- Clarify any parts of the outline that students do not understand.
- Focus on getting students to add information on the precise context in which they will be using English, rather than on suggesting fundamental changes. If necessary, remind students that the course outline was based on needs established by their managers.
- Get students to tell you if they have used any materials before.
- Find out if they have any pet hates or preferences.
- Tell students you will adapt your approach and your pace in line with their needs.

However, when getting feedback from students, remember the following:

- Although you will be responding to comments, you will also be 'selling' the programme.
- It is only the outspoken students who will be commenting at this stage and their comments may well not reflect the wishes or needs of the whole group.
- Students often have little understanding or experience of effective language learning so may need some explanation or reassurance.
- Students' comments may reflect their personal preferences, rather than their real needs. Remind them, if necessary, that this is a course specifically designed to improve their use of English at work.

You are the expert in this situation, even if you are still inexperienced. You will have an overview of managers' comments and coordinators' requests and you will have considered a range of possibilities. You may want to quote from research or mention your own experience to explain why certain elements of a course have been arranged in a certain way. Remember too that you will also be accountable for the success of the course so you must be able to justify any changes you make at this stage.

Even if you have not written the course outline yourself, deal with it as if you were responsible for it. It is important that you take responsibility for the course – symbolised by the course outline – and that you show you will continue to do so on a class-by-class basis.

Keep everyone informed of your conclusions
When you have confirmed the course outline, make sure copies are passed to all key personnel, including any in-house and in-company coordinators and your students.

Update people whenever there are any significant changes
This will probably mean amending and reprinting your course outline whenever you make any significant change and copying your new

revised version to students and other key personnel once more. (Date course outlines so as to avoid confusion.) Changes in the course outline which require an explanation for absent students or course sponsors can be explained in an accompanying e-mail or memo, such as the one given below. Minor changes can simply be mentioned on a class-by-class basis.

There are various reasons why you might need to produce a revised course outline:

- Sometimes students, managers or in-company coordinators make a lot of suggestions, either directly or indirectly, which will necessitate changes to the programme.
- Reviews conducted at specific stages of the course (e.g. at the mid-way point and then again two weeks before the end of a course) might necessitate major changes to the programme. (See OBJECTIVES REVIEW on p. 94 for a suggested procedure.) These reviews might show that objectives have changed or that learning needs are not being met. This could be the case if students make unexpectedly fast – or slow – progress or if the students' professional situation changes, e.g. if they are transferred to another department.
- Complaints from students about the overall balance of the course will mean you need to review the entire needs analysis, and consequently the course outline. See 6.6 if this is a problem.

A sample memo to explain more significant changes

| To: Intermediate 4B Students | From: Sylvie Donna |
| cc: P Noyon | Date: June 14, 2001 |

CHANGES TO COURSE PROGRAMME

Following our recent update meeting to confirm your precise on-the-job needs for English, I attach an amended course outline which includes a record of work done so far.

You will notice that more time will now be devoted to presentations and meeting skills. This is partly because of the excellent work done on writing skills in the first half of the course and partly because of your increased need for speaking skills, given the recent joint venture with Speedex Inc.

Please let me know if you have any comments.

3.3 Selecting and using materials

Selecting materials

Appropriate selection of core course materials and supplementary materials, i.e. published books, video or audio tapes and software, is a crucial part of effective pre-course and ongoing planning. Authentic materials – referred to frequently elsewhere in this book (see the Index) – should, ideally, be the core component of courses but are, in reality, not very reliable as sources of teaching material. If selected carefully, published materials can help to give a course structure and direction, precisely because of their predictability! They will also save you preparation time and give you ready-made visual and aural material. Finally, they should also provide the students with a constant source of material for use out of class.

In order to improve your teaching and teach at your best explore the enormous range of materials on offer via your local publishers' representatives. Addresses for major publishers are given on pp. 333–336. If you write to these addresses, introducing yourself and your school, you will be put in touch with your nearest representative. You will then be sent catalogues and inspection copies and be kept up-to-date with new materials as they come out.

Consider and select materials using the following criteria and related questions:

Cost
Will students need workbooks or handbooks to make effective use of the course? Is an adequate budget available to cover the cost? Have materials been included at all in the budget for the course? If not, will individual students be willing to pay?

Availability
Is there a representative for that particular publisher in your area or can supplies be made available by a reliable bookstore? How long will the materials take to arrive? Have all the components of the course (e.g. tapes and videos) already been published?

Content and relevance
Do the materials relate to the students' needs? For example, are discussion skills covered in a general sense or are discussions for departmental meetings specifically covered? Do the materials really do what they claim to do? For example, if the materials claim to develop speaking skills, how much preliminary reading is necessary? Do materials which focus on writing skills focus on areas which your students find difficult or are the exercises simply practising things your students can do already?

Balance
Does the balance of skills reflect that prioritised in the initial needs analysis? If not, how will the materials be supplemented? Does the balance of activities reflect what the students actually need? Is there enough material for practice of relevant areas of language?

Syllabus
What kind of syllabus is used? Is it structural, functional, notional, multi-strand? (See the Glossary for notes on these types of syllabus.) Is the target language divided up in a useful way? Will students easily see which performance area language practice relates to? Are students motivated and confident, and prepared to work at a challenging pace – or discouraged and in need of constant review or consolidation sections? Are review sections included?

Input
Viewed as a primary source of input, how relevant is the language to the students' needs? How much support is given to students? Are students unrealistically provided with lists of key words or phrases, then asked to conduct meetings, present products or write memos? Are models provided through listening or reading comprehensions so that students have something on which to base their own speaking and writing? Are the models provided typical of the type students will need to produce? Are the meetings on similar subjects to those focused on in the meetings students attend in their working life? Are they at a similar level of formality?

Lexis
Is the lexis used in the materials very British or American? (An international slant is usually better.) Is the lexis appropriate to the students' working environment? Are there too many unknown words? Are vocabulary lists provided? Would a bilingual edition be a good or a bad thing? If a lot of business or technical terms are included (letter of credit, pulse code modulation, etc.), are these useful to students?

Student preferences and needs
Will students find the topics interesting? Will the characters be appealing to the students? (It's better if some – or most – are specifically from the students' own culture.) Do the students have any pet hates based on previous language learning experiences?

Presentation
How attractive and clear will the materials seem to students? Are the photos or illustrations modern? Will the layout and design of the materials make a sufficiently serious impression? Do illustrations, photographs or cartoons enhance the material, or might they detract and confuse instead?

Cultural appropriacy and sensitivity

Is the material appropriate for your students' background, i.e. in terms of their religion, political situation or culture? If students work for a traditional company in a conservative industry, will they respond well to materials which constantly provoke controversial discussion? Will students who have never known freedom of speech be capable of discussing things freely and will they be permitted to do so in legal terms? If students work for a go-ahead company which emphasises goal-setting, does the coursebook do this too?

Accessibility and usability

Will students have trouble finding their way round the materials? Are the instructions clear? Is the layout easy to follow? Are there any helpful reference lists of key language or glossaries? Are answer keys and tapescripts provided? Do the materials provide useful and easily comprehensible homework activities? Will the materials be of lasting value to the students for reference or review?

Teacher preferences

Will you, as the teacher, be willing or able to use these materials? Will they limit what you do more than they help? If no answer key is provided, will you be able to work out the answers to the questions? Are model answers given for writing exercises? If not, will you be able to write model answers yourself?

Dates

When were the materials published? Are the examples of corporate problems recent enough to be interesting? Is last year's technology erroneously described as being state-of the-art?

If nothing appropriate seems to be available for a particular Business English course it may be necessary to write or use materials you have written yourself for all or most of the course. If these materials are custom-made so that they really do satisfy the students' language needs in their particular context and if the standard of presentation is high (e.g. black and white, but well laid-out using good word-processing and/or desktop publishing software), the students will probably prefer them to anything available commercially. However, since this option requires time, effort and expertise, consider the advantages of using pre-published materials. They are likely to have been reviewed and piloted by experienced teachers, to be in full colour, with professionally recorded video or audio cassettes, and they are likely to include interesting business stories. They may also provide plenty of reading material or exercises for your students to do outside class time, which students may well appreciate if they become highly motivated. Most importantly, if well-matched to your students' needs, published materials are likely to provide a systematic course of study. Even if not ideal, materials can often easily be adapted to suit your needs.

Using materials

If used well, materials can be a real aid to teaching. Used badly, they can dampen students' enthusiasm, put you out of touch with students and their real-life needs, and turn teaching into a mechanical, unprincipled procedure.

For materials to enhance your teaching they must be adapted to suit your students' needs on a class-by-class basis. Consider doing the following:

Cover items in a different order from that laid out in the course
If students seem bored and under-stimulated move on to a more challenging area (e.g. 2nd conditionals in a grammatical syllabus) which relates to a prioritised performance area (e.g. negotiating). If students consistently make a certain type of error, move on to exercises which cover this. If one student in a class is about to go on a business trip, look at the unit which includes language for this. Students will generally respond much better to material when it appears to be relevant to either their professional or linguistic needs. At all times, however, explain to students your reasons for focusing on these unexpected areas and tell them when, and why, you are returning to the original programme.

Omit certain items
There is no point in covering items which your students don't really need. Particularly on Business English courses, time is money! If students attend one or more classes which appear to offer nothing new or challenging they will soon decide their energy is better used else-where. Don't be afraid to cut short some classwork if students perform better than you had expected when planning; they will appreciate your respect for their time if you explain why you are moving on. Make sure you always have contingency plans so that this is possible! (See 'contingency plans' in the Index for ideas.)

Supplement your course materials whenever students are having difficulty or need extra practice
The course objectives overall can only be achieved if learning actually takes place. As is often observed in language classrooms, input does not always result in 'intake'. Vary your approach until you find that students' performance is actually improving. Consider the notes and suggestions in Sections 4 and 5 and explore as many possibilities as you dare!

Change the focus of activities so as to meet your objectives

For example, if your students need to build their confidence with listening, questions for listening comprehension can be simplified: *How many people are speaking? Where are they? What kind of people are they? What's their relationship? What are they talking about?* Alternatively, writing tasks can be adapted to your students' work situation so that students are practising a form of writing (e.g. faxes, instead of letters or telexes) which is truly useful to them. See SNIPPET INTROS (p. 76) and FOLLOW-UP MESSAGES (p. 253) for more ideas.

Finally, in order to improve your teaching and teach at your best ...

- Think about methods and teaching principles while you are using materials. For example, consider which teaching or learning theory could be behind an activity. Constantly relating theory to practice in this way will help to improve your awareness of how teaching relates to learning and should help improve your awareness of what actually works. (See Richards and Rodgers (1986) for more on this; full details are on p. 331.)

- Note techniques which work well. Develop a special record-keeping system, which works for you personally and which helps you access ideas quickly in emergencies. Techniques which fit easily into your natural teaching style make excellent contingency plans!

- Contemplate reasons behind unsuccessful lessons – the materials may often not be to blame! Adapt your approach and try the same materials again in a different teaching situation if you can see good reasons for doing so.

- Believe in yourself and use materials as a tool to enhance – not dominate! – your teaching.

3.4 Thinking how to address students

As already noted in 1.3, addressing students appropriately is essential in the Business English context. Although using an appropriate style of language is primarily important because it makes students feel they are being treated with respect – which will in turn make them more willing to cooperate with you – it is also important for other reasons. Firstly, your style of language may affect your students' impression of you as a professional, and this will affect the success of a course and the amount of motivation you manage to inspire! Secondly, it is often the language a teacher uses in class (i.e. the metalanguage) which students pick up first, so there is a practical spinoff. In other words, addressing students appropriately – as respected equals – is a key to developing an appropriate relationship with students, as well as being motivating and useful in practical terms.

Even when teaching low-level students, language can be carefully selected so that it seems respectful (e.g. *Could you ... ?* or *If you have time, ...* to preface most requests about homework). More advanced students will have no trouble coping with more sophisticated forms of language (e.g. *Another idea would be ...* or *... by any chance?*). All students should be able to cope with the language you choose if you make a habit of following more sophisticated expressions with simpler versions of the same thing. For example, after saying to intermediate students *I would appreciate it if you could have this done by tomorrow* pause, then say *By tomorrow, please, if possible.* If you do this, students will not only appreciate your efforts to treat them with respect, they will also learn more complex expressions over time. Accompanying the words you select for any level of student with the appropriate paralinguistic features (tone of voice, intonation, facial expression and other body language) will also ensure that your simplified versions of expressions are interpreted as respectful.

With any level of student, it is also useful to 'jump out' of your 'respectful' style:

- at the beginning of a course, when you will need to explain why you are not using oversimplified English with them, why words are run together and why instructions are initially not always oversimplified;
- whenever a student panics because of poor comprehension – such a student needs to be reassured and reminded of the time it takes to 'tune in' and of the need to do this if he or she is to function effectively in the world of business;
- whenever students ask about phrases the teacher is using – students will be reassured when told that they are being addressed in a style which it would be appropriate for them to use themselves with business or professional colleagues.

The 'respectful' style of language you need to aim to use is that which is common amongst adults working together. Note this might be in stark contrast to the style of language often used in the general EFL classroom, even though most general EFL teachers have the very best intentions! The precise style of language you use needs to be adapted according to the students' present or future work environment. Some industries or corporate cultures favour a direct style (for the sake of clarity), while others prefer a less direct, almost deferential style. People in some countries may also have different preferences, so where students use English is also a factor. The key is to make students aware which styles of language are appropriate for different situations. This will involve focusing their attention on whether something is spoken or written, on the relationship of the interactants and on the purpose of the interaction in any particular case. (See STARTER PIX (p. 79),

SITUATIONAL SCRUTINY (p. 119), PREDICTED COMMUNIQUÉS (p. 119), PROMPT CONVERSATIONS (p. 120) and GHOST RECONSTRUCTION (p. 121).)

Note the following, which are all characteristic of most modern business interaction:

- the frequent use of first names – follow the lead of the company with which the students have contact since sensitivity may be required in some countries
- the complexity of language used in some cases
- the interesting mix of formality and directness
- the underlying feeling that the speaker is being 'considerate and respectful'
- double questions, common perhaps because of people's desire to avoid silence and to give other people 'thinking time', e.g. *How's it going? Did you finish that report?*
- the decisive quality of some of the comments, which act as verbal 'signposts' throughout the lesson, e.g. *OK, let's stop there*
- the length of some of the utterances, e.g. when a manager is summarising decisions made in a meeting

Using this 'respectful' style of language as your day-to-day metalanguage should affect the atmosphere of your class, which should gradually become more and more open and more and more focused on the work in hand. When this happens you will probably find that the style of language which you use at some stages of lessons also loosens up. This is a time to be careful because it is important not to become too familiar with students. It is sometimes useful to compare your language with that of a manager chairing a daily departmental or inter-departmental meeting. He or she – as a native speaker of English – would naturally use a more formal style of language whenever 'taking back control' of the meeting, whenever summarising and whenever making requests. This does, of course, mean that there is still plenty of room for humour! However, this, along with all other communication in class, needs to be respectful, considerate, non-sexist and non-racist if it is to be helpful.

3.5 Starting the course

The beginning of a course is an important time because it is then that you set the tone for the entire course. When launching a new course, your main aims might be:

- to clarify practical arrangements, e.g. when and where classes are being held;
- to introduce the class 'rules', e.g. rules about attendance, lateness and homework;

- to motivate students;
- to clarify or communicate objectives, as expressed in your course outline;
- to introduce students to some of the methods you will be using;
- to show students how your approach will help them achieve their objectives;
- to help students relax and use whatever skills they have with confidence;
- to help students get to know each other;
- to get students working together as a group;
- to get students thinking faster, in a more focused way;
- to start getting students to take control in the classroom and share in the ongoing decision-making which takes place in class;
- to embark on the first part of the course in terms of language input and practice;
- to begin making students more self-reliant.

The activities you use will also help you to find out more about your students' level, strengths and weaknesses and, as such, will provide a starting point for further language practice. However, beware of judging students too quickly. Students are unlikely to perform as well as they potentially can in this first lesson because they may be nervous or out of practice. Alternatively, if they did English at high school it is quite possible that their receptive skills will be better than their productive skills so dramatic progress could take place in the first few weeks as language knowledge becomes activated.

Because of the ambiguity of the information you will receive on students' real level in your first few lessons and the importance of getting everybody to relax, beware of over-correcting. Instead of correcting, think in terms of 'prompting' or 'awareness-raising'.

At this stage your primary aim is to build group rapport and positive attitudes towards learning so that students will be more receptive in follow-up lessons. Do, however, include some interesting input so that students feel they are already beginning to do some substantial learning.

Introductions

Before allowing students to introduce themselves to each other (if necessary), using some of the procedures described in this section, give your new students a formal introduction to yourself, your school and the course (as detailed below). It is important to include this introduction at some stage in the first lesson. Adults studying for their work like to be told what's going on! As already emphasised, students will be more motivated from Day 1 if you communicate your intentions and objectives clearly and if you show that you are well-organised and serious about the course as a whole.

In your formal introduction:

1 Introduce yourself briefly.
2 Introduce your school or company, if necessary.
3 Outline the course's main objectives (very briefly).
4 Introduce the class 'rules' (e.g. no homework is compulsory but the company expects approximately three hours per week; lateness to be minimised; absences to be approved in advance – see 6.1).
5 Deal with any necessary paperwork (e.g. attendance forms).
6 Stress that the course aims to fulfil the students' needs and make them better able to use English at work.
7 Encourage students to give you feedback on the course content, methods or materials at any time.

The activities suggested in the rest of this section are designed to supplement your formal introduction and should mostly be used after your more formal beginning. However, if you give this formal, 'serious' introduction after an initial activity, the initial activity will act as a 'taster' for the more relaxed learning which should follow later in the course. Part of your introduction can in any case be made more interesting if it is turned into an activity (e.g. a jigsaw reading to discover the class rules). Don't use too many unusual techniques, though, because students' attention needs to be focused on your message at this stage, not your method or manner of communicating it.

In order to get your message across effectively, speak slowly and clearly, and even consider using the students' own language if you can. Consider the notes on addressing students in 3.4 before you prepare what you are going to say because your style and manner of communicating are also crucial at this stage. Students need to feel that they will be treated with respect, irrespective of their level of English.

□ KEYWORD INTRODUCTIONS

Students introduce themselves and answer questions, focusing only on areas of their choice.

Language self-introductions, questions and answers
Level any except absolute beginner
Time 10 minutes

Procedure

Tell students they are going to introduce themselves using seven keywords or phrases. Demonstrate by writing seven words or phrases on the board which relate to your own life and give a one-minute self introduction which uses all the words. (For example, I might write *London, Japanese, horses, children, calligraphy, spaghetti with tomato sauce, tuna*, then say, *I come from a town near London, I speak Japanese, I have a sister who loves horses*, etc.) Encourage students who are listening to interrupt with questions.

Variation

Ask students to write keywords on paper, then exchange papers with their partner. Student A asks questions about Student B based on Student B's keywords. The student being interviewed can either only answer with *Yes* or *No*, or can be allowed free answers.

□ BALL INTRODUCTIONS

Students learn each other's names or introduce themselves to the group by throwing balls. There is a 'physical shape' to what is said because a ball is thrown each time someone speaks. Students themselves have control over who speaks, when and how often.

Language names, questions and answers
Level any
Time 5 minutes

Procedure

Using soft balls which are unlikely to damage equipment or people, ask students to throw a ball to someone and say their own name. After one ball is circulating well, throw other balls to free students. Be careful not to 'swamp' the group with too many balls!

Variation 1

Students say the name of the person to whom they are throwing the ball. After this has been done successfully, students continue saying the next person's name and also ask him or her a question. Questions and answers alternate with each throw of the ball. This works best if more balls are gradually fed into the circle of students until pairs or threes are throwing balls across the room to each other.

Variation 2

Students say the person's name as they throw the ball and say something about that person, remembered from previous introductions, classes or activities, etc.

☐ ONLINE NEEDS CHECK

Students refine, confirm or reject the initial needs analysis by means of a student-centred needs check and head count. This procedure is particularly useful for courses where course materials form the basis for a course but may be supplemented quite heavily with other activities.

Language any – it doesn't matter if students use wrong terms, as long as they communicate
Level elementary and above
Time 1 hour

Procedure

1 Explain to students that you would like to confirm their precise needs so as to make the course as useful to them as possible. Encourage them to be honest but if they are being sponsored by their companies remind them, either immediately or later on in the activity, that the needs they mention should have something to do with the English they need for their work.

2 Next, draw two intersecting lines on the board, write the words *'Speaking'*, *'Listening'*, *'Writing'* and *'Reading'* in the four quadrants (as below) and ask a student to volunteer to take control: *Who'd like to be the boss? We need someone to write things on the board. I'll listen and help, but I need to copy everything down as you write.* (In cases where you have a photocopying whiteboard it's still a good idea to insist that students take control because more suggestions are likely to be made if students are talking to another student and not their relatively unfamiliar new teacher.)

An example of notes made during ONLINE NEEDS CHECK

Speaking		Writing	
13	public speaking	all	report-writing
2	order canvassing	3	writing marketing plans
9	telephone conversations	all	letters
10	sales presentations	9	project analysis
10	negotiating	5	minutes of meetings
9	discussions	3	diagrams
9	gathering information	0	job description and specification
10	handling enquiries	0	wages (spreadsheet)
8	lecturing	8	writing copy for ads
Listening		**Reading**	
14	foreign accent	1	news items
2	enquiries	9	reading about other businesses
9	presentations	9	diagrams

3 Go and sit at the back of the class, then tell students to call things out for the volunteer to write down. Avoid interrupting and refuse to 'correct' students' language unless their wording is obviously unclear to some of the other students in the class or to you yourself. Sometimes, even when there is confusion in the air, it's a good idea to wait for students to ask for clarification because this usually leads to useful discussion of real needs. Periodically, encourage the student writing to give the pen to someone else so that various students take control. When each quadrant has a list of items (however long or short), tell students that they are now going to check how many students in the group need to spend time during the course focusing on each area. Remind students that they need to be realistic about the time available and also that they may have listed some things (e.g. project analysis and wages (spreadsheet)) which they already do as part of their job and have adequate English for. Ask them to put their hands up only to items which they really need to focus on during *this* course.

4 When each item has a number beside it, go back to the front of the class – thanking students, of course – and make comments about the needs they've prioritised. The example given on the previous page would certainly suggest that presentations need to be a focus on the course, although you may need to clarify what students mean by 'lecturing'. Explain to students that some of the areas – which you will need to specify – will be covered by the course materials (e.g. 'foreign accent', 'discussions' and 'reading about other businesses'). Suggest also that some areas (e.g. 'writing marketing plans' and 'project analysis') can be dealt with if students bring in things they have already written for feedback and comments. Explain further how some items (e.g. 'diagrams') can be included within others (e.g. within 'presentations'). Then agree with students which items will be the focus of the course and which items can be deleted or dealt with when individuals submit items for immediate feedback or discussion in lessons. Finally, promise students that you will prepare or adapt a course outline which reflects the decisions made and distribute this course outline in the next lesson. (See p. 48.)

Notes

1 It is a good idea, when designing or adapting the course outline, to use two columns. The first column should be references to course materials which will be used in specific lessons and the second column should be information about the 'Additional focus' you will have in each session. This will then make week-by-week lesson planning very easy for you, and students will hopefully feel that their collective needs have been taken into account. They will also be able to easily check the focus for each lesson.

2   You may need to get permission to use an amended course outline from the students' sponsors or your own supervisor but you should easily obtain it if you explain how you conducted the needs analysis check. Remember, of course, to copy the new course outline to everyone who has been involved in planning or administering the course.

3   The course outline can be adapted whenever necessary, depending on student feedback and progress made, usually by deleting or adding items or writing an arrow to indicate that items not yet finished will be done the following week, for example.

A sample course outline produced after ONLINE NEEDS CHECK

BUSINESS ENGLISH COURSE OUTLINE
Mitsubishi Electric, Intermediate 2: Jan 4 to June 21, 2019

General information:
TEACHER: Sylvie Donna   TIMES: 0800–1330
DAY: Thursday   VENUE: Opéra Centre, Paris

Ongoing study programme:
HOMEWORK: Job-related English tasks which are relevant to the programme.
SELF-STUDY: Exercises set by the teacher on a class-by-class basis from *Business Class* (Cotton, D. and S. Robbins. 1993. London: Nelson).

Week	Coursebook/main focus	Additional focus
1	Unit 9: Corporate culture Preparation & listening	Introductions: to course and other students Developing your own company
2	Unit 9: Corporate culture (continued) Unit 4: Presentations	Introduction to presentations 1 Initial sales presentations (own company)
3	Unit 7: Negotiations	Telephone conversations Fax-writing workshop
4	Unit 8: Headhunters	Introduction to presentations 2 Letter-writing
5	Unit 10: Caution: People at work!	Using e-mail on a day-to-day basis Writing memos
6	Unit 11: Team-building	Introduction to presentations 3 Report-writing: principles and workshop
7	Unit 12: Meetings	Conversations to gather information Minutes of meetings
8	Unit 14: Japan-globalisation	Presentations by students
9	Unit 15: Corporate strategy	Presentations by students
10	Unit 13: The Entrepreneur	Presentations by students Requests & review

N.B. This course outline may be amended on a class-to-class basis so as to maximise learning or to take account of feedback. Please feel free to make comments or suggestions or give feedback.
E-mail: sylvie.donna@profilesolutionsinternational.com

☐ LETTERS

Students get the opportunity to write a personal message to the teacher. Later, they receive a personalised reply which gives the teacher an opportunity to tell students key information.

Language letter format, free-writing
Level lower-intermediate and above
Time 5 minutes set-up for homework, followed by 20 minutes for the teacher's reply

Preparation

Make sure you're aware of letter-writing conventions. You may find it useful to review these, following the procedure for SKELETAL CONVENTIONS (p. 137).

Procedure

After reviewing basic conventions for business letters with the class, ask students to write a letter to you as homework. Tell them to include information about their job, their company and their hobbies. Collect all the letters in during the next lesson and write a reply to the whole class. Make a photocopy for each student and 'deliver' them in the next lesson. (See p. 50 for an example.) If your class is small, write letters to individual students.

As a possible follow-up, develop a FIND SOMEONE WHO ... warmer activity (see below) based on information in the letters students have written.

☐ FIND SOMEONE WHO

Students ask each other questions so as to find out about other members of the group. This is a good activity for getting people on their feet and chatting freely before a more formal class talk.

Language questions
Level lower-intermediate and above
Time 10–15 minutes

Preparation

Prepare a sheet (to be photocopied for each student) with 7–10 cues (see samples on p. 51). Devise a list of cues which are relevant to the students and the content of the course.

3 Starting up courses

A sample reply to students' letters in LETTERS *(p. 49)*

> The BEC3 Class
> International Communication Club
> 33 Communication Gardens
> London WC1
>
> October 21, 2007
>
> Dear Students,
>
> I was very pleased to receive your letters giving some information about yourselves. I'm glad so many of you enjoyed our first lesson and that you feel the course will be useful. I shall use different methods at different times, according to our particular objectives at each stage. Please do not worry about what you cannot do. You've come on this course to improve your skills and that, unfortunately, means making lots of mistakes! Don't feel embarrassed, just do your best and ask questions if you are unsure of anything.
>
> Many of you seem to have some family involvement in business, whilst others – such as Johannes – are working for huge organisations like the United Nations. Learning English 'on-the-job' is very important so I do hope you will supplement what we do in class by reading English letters and faxes, etc. which are available to you at work, or by asking your colleagues questions about standard practice. This is a very important way of finding out about the peculiarities of your particular field or industry. Mention any differences you notice in class or – even better – bring along some examples of faxes, etc.
>
> There seem to be some very interesting hobbies in the group! Maria paints pots (which, I expect, she may one day be selling!), Johannes likes computer games (which I understand are addictive), Pedro sews, Mahmud speaks Arabic (as well as French and Berber) and sings, Joao plays basketball, Arjuna plays cricket (my favourite spectator sport) and Siew Mei likes travelling to exotic places, like Singapore.
>
> Most of you seem to realise the value of English as an international language. I can say from my own experience that it really is wonderful being able to speak to people from many different countries so as to try and understand their point of view.
>
> I am pleased to have the opportunity to work with you all.
>
> Best wishes,
>
>
>
> Sylvie Donna

Procedure

Tell students they are going to find out about other people in the class, using the worksheet. Elicit questions they will need to ask each other for each cue. Tell them to write down a name whenever they have found someone who answers *Yes*. Then, while students are milling, encourage them to change partners again and again. After a while, get students to report back and comment on the group's experience and attitudes, before leading into a formal introduction about the course (as described on pp. 43–44).

A sample FIND SOMEONE WHO ... *worksheet*
(for business trips)

Find someone who ...

... has been on a business trip _____

... often has to travel on business _____

... speaks more than one foreign language _____

... likes airline food _____

... knows how to deal with jet lag _____

_____

... has to negotiate difficult contracts abroad _____

... has some advice on how to negotiate successfully _____

_____

_____

... likes finding out about other cultures_____

© Cambridge University Press

A sample FIND SOMEONE WHO ... *worksheet*
(for report-writing)

Find someone who ...

... can explain what a report is _____

_____

... loves writing reports _____

... writes one-page reports _____

... writes reports which are over 20 pages long _____

... knows what a visit report is _____

_____

... always makes intelligent recommendations in reports!_____

... has some advice to give about report writing _____

_____

_____

© Cambridge University Press

□ ASKING ABOUT PEOPLE'S JOBS

Students talk about their jobs. The activity will build students' confidence and allow you to give feedback and corrections on pronunciation and appropriacy of language. It's good to get students thinking about these areas early on in a course.

Language conversation with a visitor or new colleague
Level lower-intermediate and above
Time 30–60 minutes, depending on students' level

Preparation

Prepare some cards and laminate them, if possible, so they can be reused later. (Make several sets if you have a large class.) The lettering on the cards needs to be large enough for several students to read at a time. One word should be written on each card, with words to make up the following four questions:

- What do you do?
- What else do you do?
- Which department do you work in?
- What does that involve exactly?

Make sure you prepare four separate cards with question marks on (for each set of cards), and make sure the first word of each question has a capital letter at the beginning.

Procedure

1 Scatter the cards on a table (or tables) and ask students to put the cards in order, making four questions. Get students to decide on the best order for the questions.
2 Establish a context for the questions by getting students to decide who would ask the questions, when they would ask them, etc.
3 Practise the pronunciation (especially focusing on sentence stress and intonation), encouraging students by getting them to focus on the impression they would make (interested, bored, etc.). You may want to drill the questions before asking students to mill around, asking and answering the questions. If students' responses are highly inaccurate or inappropriate, or if they lack the necessary vocabulary to give convincing responses, get everyone to sit down and prepare answers in writing (so that their answers can be corrected or discussed). Focus on getting students to supply answers which are natural and appropriate for a fairly formal first meeting situation. Encourage them to include humorous elements, if appropriate, and to add to the questions if they want to. At all

stages, make sure students imagine a real-life visitor asking these questions and make sure the answers fit together to make a whole conversation.

3 After students have prepared their answers or written out a possible conversation with a visitor to their company, ask them to stand up and role-play the situation. Make sure students practise without scripts and insist they focus on pronunciation, body language and backchannelling (e.g. by commenting *Oh, really? Uhu*).

5 Later, extend the conversation in other role-played pairwork (e.g. starting with introductions and continuing with small talk).

3.6 Encouraging student self-reliance

Making students reliant on their own resources means 'empowering' them, i.e. giving them power. In practical terms, this means putting students in control as far as possible, i.e. allowing them to make minor and major decisions about their learning both in class and outside it, while at the same time remembering our responsibility for the ultimate success of a course. While remembering our students' need for input, we need to strike a balance between teaching and facilitating so that our aim is primarily to make learning possible in day-to-day practical terms and to help students and managers track progress. To do this, we need to take account of both our own and our learners' expertise and use it to maximum effect.

It is important and advantageous to encourage student self-reliance for various reasons:

- As explained in 1.3, empowering students helps us to develop a productive relationship with our students in which learning is maximised and our job becomes more satisfying.
- Students become more motivated, so our job becomes easier.
- We find ourselves getting to know our students as equals, so our relationships with them are likely to become increasingly open and informal – which is good for everyone!
- We find out more and more about our students' work situation and consequently about the world of work in general, which gives us a fresh perspective on day-to-day life.
- Being better informed about our students' work, it is easier for us to make classwork relevant and interesting to students. Materials students bring into class provide a resource for developing new material.
- Individual differences in a class which emerge when students are more active make lessons increasingly varied.
- Given the financial constraints operating in most teaching contexts, it is likely our students will be working alone soon after our courses.

Handing over control early on in a course

A certain amount of teacher control is expected and appreciated early on in courses and, to a lesser extent, later on. Working adults, who are often forced to work under considerable pressure, are usually well aware of the need for a systematic approach, which they hope the teacher will bring to the language learning process. Students may even associate teacher control with professionalism, so they might need to be coaxed out of this expectation into a more active role. Their expectations in this respect may be a hangover from their experience at high school or in other learning contexts.

In order to coax students into a more active role early on in a course, try the following:

- Get students to make seemingly 'trivial' decisions about which colour pens should be used (e.g. on a whiteboard or OHT), how they should sit, or where they should stand during stand-up activities.
- Get them to make learning-related decisions, e.g. whether or not to listen to a recording of a listening a second or third time.
- Get them to decide whether to do listening or reading practice first in a lesson.
- Get them to decide who characters are in role-plays and why people are talking, etc.
- Get them to prioritise short-term learning objectives for their course.

Setting homework

If homework is handled sensitively it can be an invaluable way of handing over control to students because it is one time when students are active on their own, right from the beginning of the course.

In order to achieve good results:

- Establish a routine. If students are always expected to do something outside class, they will get used to allocating some of their personal (or work) time to this end.
- Make as many assignments as possible an extension of work done in lessons.
- Make all homework as work-related as possible.
- Encourage students to adapt homework assignments to their needs.
- Make homework optional. Avoid putting pressure on students to do work outside class. We must assume that if students do not do homework either they consider it inappropriate, insufficiently useful, overly time-consuming, or boring.
- Give students a wide variety of homework 'ideas' (i.e. options). Get them to record these ideas during lessons and have a quick 'recap' of possibilities at the end of a session.

- Provide models when asking students to write e-mails or reports, etc.
- Always respond positively to students when faced with any work they have done outside class, even it appears to be strange or a misinterpretation of what you were hoping to get.
- Write real, adult-to-adult messages on homework, not judgemental and fairly meaningless words such as *Good!* A useful approach is to write descriptions of what was good or bad about the student's work. Add cartoons to illustrate reactions or explain points if you can. In other words, make your feedback both informative and fun!
- Encourage students to buy extra materials for self-study. See SELF-ASSESSED SELF-STUDY (p. 65).
- Expect a lot. When a teacher expects a lot from his or her students, they usually rise to the challenge. On the other hand, when a situation or a person is 'written off', expectations are fulfilled, but with rather depressing results.

Ongoing approaches

There are numerous other ways of empowering students on an ongoing basis:

- Prioritise objectives with students on a session-by-session basis by simply writing up a list of things to do that lesson on the board and getting students to decide what to start with.
- Discuss and review objectives with the class whenever this seems appropriate. See OBJECTIVES REVIEW (p. 94) for a suggested procedure.
- Give students a choice as often as possible on both minor and major issues, while at all times respecting the aims of the course.
- Encourage the use of answer keys, indexes and reference material in course materials.
- Encourage students to use old course materials or to find supplementary materials in libraries, self-access centres (if available to them), local bookshops or the workplace.
- Invite students to lead sessions or parts of sessions, not forgetting you may need to intervene here and there with information, examples or suggestions.
- Review progress, deadlines and priorities with students on a session-by-session basis.
- Give students opportunities to give feedback, and then respond to it. Note preferences, strengths or weaknesses in individual students and adapt your approach as necessary. For practical ideas on eliciting and responding to feedback, see 4.5, 4.7 and 6.6.

Experiment and persevere!

After a few lessons experimenting with each new class, it should be possible to adopt an approach which fosters a cooperative and collaborative atmosphere. Every group of students functions differently not only because of the differences between individuals but also because of the differing classroom dynamics which result and because every group of Business English students will have slightly different reasons for being in the classroom. When you experiment with the suggestions made above and those given below remain receptive to your students' response. Beware of being over-influenced by only the 'loudest' students in a class, though, and at all times remember the needs analysis.

Even if you experience difficulties, persist with the idea of involving students. Passive students who expect English to be administered as a magic potion are unlikely to make progress. The more involved and active students become, on the other hand, the more they are likely to learn. Activating students is undoubtedly the key to motivating them and prolonged focused motivation is usually associated with high levels of success. In other words, encourage interaction about learning, constantly invite and respond to student feedback, and enjoy your livelier, 'empowered' students!

☐ PASSING THE BUCK

Students are encouraged to begin to accept responsibility for achieving goals through a sentence-completion task. This is a useful activity for intermediate or advanced students.

Language any, but can be controlled by cues given on a worksheet
Level intermediate and above
Time 10 minutes

Procedure

Ask students to complete sentences such as the following:

1 During the course I plan to ...
2 My English is now good enough to ...
3 My English should be good enough to ...
4 I am going to improve my rate of progress on this course by ...
5 I shall track my progress by ...

If you feel that students need help with language or ideas for 2 and 3, provide them with sentence endings such as those listed overleaf ... but make sure everyone understands them!

... introduce myself.
... introduce others.
... answer the telephone.
... make telephone calls to ask for information or arrange
    appointments.
... make conversation with colleagues.
... make conversation with visitors.
... give simple instructions.
... give persuasive presentations.
... participate in discussions in meetings.
... report to my supervisor face-to-face.
... write brief work reports for my supervisor.

Help students to fill out sentences 4 and 5 by having a quick
brainstorming session with the class. If students are stuck for ideas,
again suggest a few possibilities. For example:

4 I am going to improve my rate of progress on this course
   by ...
   ... participating more actively in class.
   ... answering and asking questions in class as often as
       possible.
   ... bringing 'work' problems to class, so that my practice can
       be more relevant.
   ... doing more studying out of class.
   ... buying a good monolingual dictionary.
   ... buying a good Business English dictionary.
   ... using the language laboratory at least once a week.
   ... talking to English-speaking staff as often as possible.
5 I shall track my progress by ...
   ... using a homework record sheet.
   ... regularly writing a learner diary.
   ... recording my voice once a week.
   ... filing my class writing carefully so as to get an overview
       of typical mistakes.
   ... using a learning organiser, both in and outside class.

Note that suggestions on how to set up learning organisers and learner
diaries are given on p. 61. Encourage students to discuss their ideas as
and when this seems appropriate.

□ THINK GAPS

After writing down a dictated text, students fill out a gapped version of the same text. The gaps focus students' attention on key points. This is good as a discussion starter.

Language a text about language learning
Level elementary and above
Time 10–15 minutes

Preparation

Write or find a text about language learning. A sample text for intermediate to advanced students is given below. Prepare a second gapped version of the text and copy this onto the back of the complete text, as in the example on the opposite page.

Procedure

Tell students that they are A or B and, after telling all the A students to stand on one side of the room and all the B students on the other, ask everyone to find a partner by walking across the room. Encourage students to sit somewhere comfortable, with their chairs back to back. Then ask one student from each pair to dictate the text to his or her partner. (If you split the text in half, and give out halves of the text, both partners can have a turn at dictating.) When they have finished students can check what they have written down with the original version. Finally, ask students to turn their texts face down before completing the gaps in the gapped version from memory. Follow up with a discussion, asking students if they agree with the points in the text.

A possible complete text

> There are two important steps to improving your English for professional reasons:
>
> 1 identifying the language you need;
> 2 recording what you learn in the most effective way.
>
> Before you begin studying, you need to think about these things carefully. In business you plan before you do anything. You want to avoid wasting time, money and work. It is the same with your foreign language study. You need to plan, to set yourself clear objectives and to work in an organised, efficient and effective way. Planning is not wasting time. It is an important part of your study programme.

(Adapted from Wilberg, P. and M. Lewis. 1994. *Business English: An Individualised Learning Programme*. Hove: Language Teaching Publications.)

A *possible gapped version*

There are two important steps to improving your English for professional reasons:

1 _____ the language you need;

2 _____ what you learn in the most effective way.

Before you begin studying, you need to think about these things carefully. In business you _____ before you do anything. You want to _____ wasting time, money and work. It is the same with your foreign language study. You need to _____ , to set yourself clear _____ and to work in an _____ , efficient and effective way. _____ is not wasting time. It is an important part of your study programme.

Variation

Cut the original text up into phrases (e.g. There are – two important steps – to improving – your English – for professional reasons, etc.). Make enough sets for each pair to have one. Pairs of students put the 'jigsaw' together to make the complete text and then check their version with a complete typed version. Continue with the gapped version as above.

☐ MILLING DISCUSSIONS

Students consider ways to maximise learning by discussing their ideas with other students. The fact that everyone is milling around during this procedure makes everything less intense and formal.

Language free, but based on your predetermined questions
Level upper-intermediate and above
Time 10 minutes

Preparation

Prepare a sheet similar to the one given on the next page. Add any ideas which you think it would be good for students to consider. It is perfectly OK if all the ideas listed are good ideas – the sheet is simply giving you an opportunity to get students to consider them.

Procedure

Briefly consider with students how to maximise learning and then distribute the worksheet. Give students a few moments to consider the following questions:

- *Do you agree with the ideas?*
- *Do you do them? Why/Why not?*

An asterisk can be used for any ideas students find particularly interesting and a question mark for any ideas they find odd. They should mark things they do with a tick and things they don't do with a cross. Next, ask students to stand up and find a partner. After students have discussed their answers to the questions for a while, ask them to find another partner. Encourage students to discuss why they think things are a good or bad idea. (All the ideas listed might be useful to certain people at certain times.) Encourage students to find out what could work best for them and to consider how the ideas could fit into their daily lives, at work or elsewhere.

A possible worksheet for MILLING DISCUSSIONS

BUSINESS ENGLISH THINK SPOT

If I want to maximise learning is it a good idea to … ?

... study English for at least 5 minutes every day
... listen to the BBC World Service
... try not to read the subtitles when watching a movie in English
... watch MTV
... read as much as possible
... use a monolingual dictionary
... guess the meaning of words before looking them up
... use vocabulary cards to focus on and review important words
... think about corrected mistakes
... try to correct my own mistakes before going to a teacher
... learn phrases, not just words
... organise my notes
... think before looking at the answers in a self-study book
... think after looking at the answers in a self-study book
... plan before writing
... plan before speaking
... have practice conversations in my head
... practise pronunciation using pronunciation exercises
... practise pronunciation by reading texts aloud in private
... record my own voice
... experiment with different ways of speaking English on tape
... keep a diary in English
... go to a bookshop to buy other English books
... do other English courses outside class as self-study
... speak to foreigners in the street
... get coaching from senior managers

□ LEARNING ORGANISERS

Students organise notes on English so that they are easily accessible and useful in real life.

Language any
Level beginner and above
Time ongoing (in and out of class); occasionally allocate 10 minutes in class

Procedure

Explain to the class the advantages of keeping well-organised notes, both in- and outside class. Give some examples of how students might use their notes in real life; for example, in meetings they can have their learning organiser on their lap and surreptitiously refer to useful expressions, or they can refer to key phrases when they are writing e-mails. Then ask students to buy a file (e.g. a filofax or notebook) with approximately five sections. Decide with the class what to put in each section, in line with the course's initial needs analysis and the students' personal, work-related, needs. Separate sections might be for questions and answers (for colleagues and visitors), telephoning, meetings, internal e-mail or grammar points, for example.

□ LEARNER DIARIES

Students keep a diary of their experiences of learning and using English. This is useful on intensive courses when students are highly motivated and are prepared to open up a little more.

Language any
Level intermediate and above
Time 5–10 minutes each day or ongoing, for homework

Procedure

1 Remind students of the importance of tracking progress on any project, including English! Then show them an example of a learner diary (see next page). Ask students to keep a similar diary so that you can make lessons as useful to them as possible. Allocate 5–10 minutes to diary-writing at the end of each day of the course. Tell students to write freely because only they personally and you, the teacher, will be reading the diaries.
2 Collect students' diaries in regularly. Write short messages to each student in response to their comments as you read through their entries and don't correct the students' English. When you redistribute

the diaries, make a few comments in response to the whole class, encouraging or making suggestions where appropriate and always respecting the confidentiality of individuals' diaries! Also act on feedback you get through the diaries or through follow-up class discussions, making small changes to the course wherever possible, all the time respecting the initial needs analysis.

3   At the end of the course, get students to write reports on the course using their learner diary as a basis and reminder of what happened. See EVALUATION REPORTS (p. 270).

A learner diary – kept by a student on an intensive course

INTENSIVE 3 ENGLISH COURSE – March 9–13, 2008

Monday
Felt a little shocked when you asked us to use English all the time! Had difficulty expressing my meaning clearly quite a few times this morning. Suddenly, I don't feel like an expert – instead of being a manager, I feel like a little boy! Found the warm-up activities very interesting. I've never studied like this before. They really helped to get us talking! Also found the review of language for faxes very good because I'm often confused about style – is it too informal or old-fashioned?, etc.

Tuesday
Relaxed a bit more today. Was embarrassed that I made so many mistakes but you said mistakes are inevitable if we are learning. I suppose you're right. The meeting we had made me realise how much I need those phrases we were studying! I remember how difficult I found it to make a point in a departmental meeting last month. I hope we're going to be doing more meeting practice this week.

Wednesday
Was horrified when a student from another (more advanced!) class started chatting to me over lunch in English! Realise I must do this in the cafeteria at work whenever I see a foreign manager. Enjoyed writing e-mails in groups but was shocked by how much our group got wrong.

Thursday
Felt our e-mails today were a little better. I'm really glad we did this kind of practice on the course – because I have to write a lot of e-mails. Enjoyed the negotiation this afternoon but was surprised at how difficult it was to score points. How can I be more persuasive?

Friday
Thank you for a very enjoyable course!

☐ PRIORITISING OBJECTIVES

Students say what they feel are the objectives for the course as a whole or for a particular lesson. After prioritising the objectives, students then get feedback from you on how their list matches up with the needs analysis and your own perceptions. This procedure is especially useful for involving students and getting them to share responsibility for what is done in class. It can be used on a class-by-class basis throughout a whole course or periodically, if you prefer.

Language any
Level elementary and above
Time 10 minutes

Procedure

1 Get students to call out the course objectives by saying *OK so what are our objectives for this week/term/year?* Write the objectives on the board. Alternatively, hand (or throw!) a pen or chalk to students, and ask them to write an objective on the board. Coax omissions from students with the odd comment here and there, e.g. *So you don't need to do any listening practice?*

2 Ask students to prioritise the objectives on the board in pairs or in two groups (*Which is the most important? Which is number 1?*, etc.). Ask students to continue changing partners or groups until the class can come up with a final version. Write numbers against objectives listed on the board to indicate the final order and take careful note of this for later reference.

3 Respond briefly to students' priorities by agreeing and/or disagreeing with their choices, or by adding comments on omissions, etc. When doing this, you will need to take account of both the initial and ongoing needs analyses and also progress students have made. It is possible that students may feel, for example, that they need more practice on a particular area when they are already performing at an adequate level. The opposite may also be true! If appropriate, negotiate changes in the prioritisation of objectives.

4 Annotate the list on the board with a timescale (e.g. times or days), if you feel this is helpful. Take care to ensure that all students' needs are given equal value.

Note that instead of objectives, classroom procedures or performance areas can be listed if this seems more appropriate.

Variation

Get students to write objectives on slips of paper. They then put them in order on a table or on the floor. This involves students in a more physical way which might facilitate pair and group discussion.

☐ PANIC PARACETAMOL

So as to assuage students' panic about excessive and difficult reading which they may have to do for their work, help students to build up a file of texts which they have studied or which they can refer to later, and suggest useful study strategies.

Language any
Level intermediate and above
Time ongoing

Procedure

If students are panicking over the number of periodicals, etc. they have to read in order to keep up-to-date in their field, give them the following suggestions. If time allows they can be encouraged to try some or all of the suggestions in class time, making reference to a pile of relevant periodicals, magazines, journals and newspapers:

- Skim through periodicals at speed, only looking at titles to gauge interest. Select two or three titles and predict the content of the articles. Then skim through the actual articles to see if you guessed correctly. (In class you can help students decide if their guesses were correct.) Note that this can be a real confidence booster when guesses are correct.
- Select articles which look interesting, file them in a learning organiser (see LEARNING ORGANISERS on p. 61) and read them on the train, at lunch, or wherever.
- Pick one or two articles per week or per month for intensive study and check all unknown words in the dictionary. Annotate these articles and keep them in a learning organiser for later reference.
- Build up a quick-reference section in a learning organiser of common specialist terms, i.e. compile a personalised vocabulary list. Group vocabulary items topically, not alphabetically, for easier reference and increased memorability.
- Where articles appear bilingually (in parallel periodicals), collect 'pairs' of articles. Read them in tandem, sometimes reading the English version first, sometimes the other one.
- Discuss interesting articles with colleagues or classmates.

☐ ALTERNATIVES

This procedure helps students to get used to the idea of making choices on a day-to-day basis. After listing possible alternatives, students practise mini-dialogues.

Language exponents for making suggestions and taking decisions
Level elementary and above
Time 5–10 minutes

Procedure

1 Give students a real-life choice to make in class (e.g. *Shall we finish this now or tomorrow?*). Then tell students they are going to practise some simple dialogues in which they make similar decisions. Explain that this will help them to negotiate both in class and with colleagues or clients in the real world. To give students the idea, list several alternatives on the board, contextualising them in a question, as follows:

Shall we	finish now speak Japanese play tennis eat sushi take a train practise it again	or	at 12 o'clock? English? badminton? tempura? a taxi? leave it for now?

2 Elicit as many of these 'alternatives' as possible. Elicit possible responses (e.g. *Well, I'd prefer to ... , Let's ... , If you don't mind I'd rather ...*). Then get students to role-play mini-dialogues with several partners (milling around in the classroom). Later, use similar alternatives as often as possible in class so as to hand over some of the decision-making to students. Possible decisions you could ask students to make include:

   • ordering of elements within a lesson (report-writing or telephoning first?)
   • colour of pens to be used (on a board or OHP)
   • listening to a tape again or checking the answers straight away
   • working in pairs or groups
   • standing or sitting for role-played dialogues
   • timing for coffee breaks

☐ SELF-ASSESSED SELF-STUDY

Students consider a list of possible books for self-study in a bookshop and evaluate them themselves.

Language any
Level elementary and above
Time 5 minutes for set-up in class, then ongoing

Procedure

In consultation with colleagues, publishers' catalogues and/or reviews in ELT journals, draw up a list of materials you could recommend for students to use for self-study. (A sample list of books which are useful to many Business English students for self-study is given below.) At an appropriate moment in class give students this list of materials and encourage them to go and seek them out at a local bookshop or library. Tell students that using any of these extra materials for study at home should help their progress, as long as they personally feel that the materials are useful in their particular situation. Get students to evaluate the materials, using the following questions:

- *Are the materials relevant to my language and work needs?*
- *Do I find the content interesting?*
- *Can I understand 80% of the text?*
- *Is it self-contained, i.e. are answers and tapescripts provided?*

If the answer to these questions is *Yes!* (more or less), tell students they should buy the book and use it for self-study.

A sample list of books which are useful for self-study

BUSINESS ENGLISH SELF-STUDY

Check out these books ... See if you want to use them!

For improving your speaking – remember you need to buy the cassettes too!

Adamson, D. 1991. *Starting English for Business*. Hemel Hempstead: Prentice Hall.
Brieger, N. and J. Comfort. 1989. *Early Business Contacts*. Hemel Hempstead: Prentice Hall.
Brieger, N. and J. Comfort. 1990. *Social Contacts*. Hemel Hempstead: Prentice Hall.
Matthews, C. and J. Marino. 1990. *Professional Interactions: Oral Communication Skills in Science, Technology and Medicine*. Hemel Hempstead: Prentice Hall.
O'Neill, R. 1993. *Longman English Works 1*. Harlow: Longman.
O'Neill, R. 1994. *Longman English Works 2*. Harlow: Longman.
Parry, M. and L. Weller. 1980. *Getting Through*. Harlow: Longman.
Viney, P. and J. Curtin. 1994. *Survival English*. Oxford: Heinemann.
Woolcott, L. 1992. *Business Review*. Harlow: Longman.

For improving your reading skills

Revell, R. and S. Sweeney. 1993. *In Print*. Cambridge: Cambridge University Press.

For learning how to write letters, faxes, memos and e-mail

Littlejohn, A. 1994. *Company to Company*. Cambridge: Cambridge University Press.

4　Day-to-day concerns

4.1 Planning on a day-to-day basis

Effective lesson planning involves two things: honouring promises which were made to clients and producing lessons which make a coherent course. When planning, relate everything you choose to do in specific sessions to any promotional material used, the initial needs analysis, notes made and/or course planning. In this way you will be translating the promises made to clients before the course (in brochures, placement procedures and the needs analysis) into practical classroom reality. Also, ensure that activities you use within a course fit together or with materials to make a coherent and effective course.

On a day-by-day basis, adjust your approach in class according to students' response (in terms of enthusiasm and real learning). If things go well or badly, consider the reasons for this, rather than looking for easy excuses. Then consider better ways of planning for follow-up lessons. Always remember, though, that your aim is to teach specific business-related language, as identified in the needs analysis. Doing this should both sustain student motivation and ensure client satisfaction. Generalised grammar or fluency practice is not usually appropriate in the Business English context; work done in class needs to be clearly identified as useful and preferably associated with a performance area.

A suggested procedure for lesson planning

1 Select one or more performance areas from the initial needs analysis as a focus, considering the specific needs and experience of individual students. Use your course outline as a guide, if you have chosen to write one for this course (see p. 31 and p. 48). If no needs analysis was conducted, select procedures which help you to find out about students' professional and linguistic needs.

2 Having selected a performance area (e.g. report-writing, or departmental meetings), break it down into its component parts by considering questions such as the following:

- Which area(s) of lexis will students need to be able to understand or use?
- Which functions will come into play?

- How many exponents will need to be taught for each function?
- How can students be made aware of stylistic differences between exponents?
- Are any pronunciation features particularly important for this area of language? For example, will intonation affect a student's success in meetings?
- Do any grammatical points need to be mastered in order to perform effectively?
- Is accuracy important for this performance area in the students' situation?
- Is fluency particularly important for a student's success in his or her situation?
- Is there a big difference between the receptive and productive skills involved?
- What can students do or understand already?
- What kind of approach will be most useful at this stage?

3 Plan the lesson, focusing on one of the component parts for the performance area you've selected. Carefully consider the following questions at this stage:

- How much can or should be dealt with in this particular lesson?
- Do all students need this area of language equally? If not, what can be done?
- Where can I obtain good models of language to demonstrate what's required? Do I need to produce some myself?
- What should the level of difficulty be?
- What kind of practice will students need?
- Which materials and methods would be appropriate?
- Can the students' own work situation be used to determine the parameters for practice?
- Which students would benefit most from practising which roles?
- Can any other language areas be incorporated into this lesson as a form of recycling?
- Are any particular problems to be anticipated? (Nerves, low attendance, specific linguistic difficulties, etc.)

Your aim is to create the best possible learning environment for your students, while at the same time fulfilling their need for language in the workplace. As well as experimenting with the procedures described in this section, throw around ideas with other teachers.

On an ongoing basis, encourage students to bring in materials (e.g. e-mails, faxes, industrial periodicals) to class. This will help you to plan useful and appropriate lessons and to clarify the initial needs analysis because you will be able to isolate typical errors or problems. The materials will also provide useful reference material, i.e. they will help you find out about appropriate corporate styles or layout; they might even provide material for many lessons, as discussion starters or as inspiration for whole lessons in cases where writing needs to be improved. Keep copies of all materials for inspiration later when preparing worksheets or models of faxes, e-mails, etc., but always respect confidentiality when using these samples.

Periodically review what you're including in the course as a whole, taking special care to ensure that you are teaching what has been promised to students before the course. As well as checking the content of your lessons, also consider the weighting of particular elements in the course. Activities for increasing students' cross-cultural awareness or training students to be better learners can (and must) be included, but not to the detriment of other areas which you have explicitly or implicitly promised to cover.

4.2 Selecting and using methods

The word 'method' is used in various ways by different people in journals and seminars, etc. It can be used to mean an approach which reflects a full-blown, carefully considered theory of learning or it can simply be used to refer to a classroom technique for an activity. The term is used here in its widest sense to mean any way of proceeding in the classroom; it is used to refer to both 5-minute activities and longer-term approaches. This is because any procedure used in the classroom will reflect some perception of how learning takes place.

Business English courses seem most successful when a range of methods are used and when methods are carefully selected to suit individual students. (The classroom procedures in sections 3.5–3.6, 4.3–4.7 and 5.2–5.14 suggest a range of possibilities.) Using different methods at different times might well maximise the learning which actually takes place in class since individuals themselves seem to vary enormously in terms of learning style; even the same learner responds differently at different times, depending on level of difficulty, mood or need.

If we are to select methods appropriately we must remain sensitive to our students and alert to their linguistic, intellectual, social, emotional and professional needs. A certain amount of experimentation is inevitable when doing this, but attempting to 'tune into' students when selecting the methods we use will bring enormous benefits in terms of improved class dynamics and real learning on the part of individual students. This means listening to students and watching their reactions, then responding in a way which seems appropriate.

As well as being alert to students when selecting and using methods:

Give students models of language

With many commonly-used methods students are asked to produce language before they have heard, or read, a suitable model. Students cannot realistically be expected to produce language which they have never seen or heard before. In the same way, they cannot be expected to visualise an entire picture, having only been given a pile of jigsaw pieces; this is why it is very difficult for students to write good business letters – even if provided with a list of suitable phrases – if they have never seen a business letter before. Likewise it is difficult for students to participate in a meeting in a foreign language and culture, armed only with a list of functional exponents. In some cultures both written and spoken communication styles are very different from English.

To overcome this problem, make sure you supplement methods which focus on practice of discrete items with other methods which expose students to models of spoken and written English, i.e. to whole conversations or faxes, for example. See 4.4 and 4.6 for suggested procedures, especially pp. 100–104.

Realistically contextualise language practice

As well as asking students to practise discrete language items out of context, many methods also involve asking students to practise language in contexts which have no relevance to their work. While students will tolerate this from time to time, they – and you, yourself! – may lose sight of the bigger picture (i.e. the course's overall objectives) if these methods are overused. Less real learning might also result from methods which use decontextualised or poorly contextualised practice because it will not always be clear to students how lexis or grammar (which has apparently been well-practised) applies to their real-life contexts; for some reason, their brains fail to make the necessary connections.

If you do use methods which involve decontextualised or poorly contextualised practice of language, make sure you follow up with usefully contextualised practice of the same language as soon as possible afterwards. Also, before and while doing decontextualised or poorly contextualised practice, remind students of the use to which the language can be put. In this way, you will help students to appreciate the value of all language practice in class, which will at least help with motivation, if not with actual learning.

Encourage students to use language to communicate

Since language is intimately connected with communication in real life, non-communicative classroom practice (however good the method) can sometimes alienate or bore students. Therefore, make sure language is practised in a 'communicative' way as often as possible. This will help to make language practice relevant to students' needs because language use will be real; it should also help classroom dynamics and will also fuel students' motivation.

In practice, this means getting students to exchange information, opinions or comments or to formulate sentences which have meaning, i.e. which are true in some sense – in the student's life, in terms of the classroom or in terms of the real world. Allowing and encouraging free comments in English, even during controlled practice, will also facilitate communication generally in class.

Insist that students focus on pronunciation

Improving students' pronunciation is often something teachers attempt to do in isolation but it is usually more effective to make pronunciation a backdrop to most speaking practice activities, i.e. to make it something you consistently focus on. Getting students to use appropriate intonation patterns and to stress key words will help them to develop confidence. Focusing on pronunciation also gives you an excuse to ask students to repeat utterances! Furthermore, a focus on pronunciation before or during role-plays and other language practice makes students' language sound more realistic, which is highly motivating. Most importantly, it helps students to develop a style of speaking which is easily intelligible in business contexts.

Use role-play as often as possible

Getting students to role-play dialogues has various advantages. Firstly, it is enjoyable so it is likely to motivate students. Secondly, and more importantly, it should help students to realise how discrete bits of language 'fit together' in real use; since some classroom practice may involve using less realistic methods, where language is practised out of context, this is an extremely important point. Thirdly, role-play gives students an opportunity to develop fluency and confidence. Finally, students' awareness of cultural differences in the international business environment should increase as you point out inappropriate behaviour for specific situations. In conclusion, since role-play involves simulated real-life language use, it should be the mainstay of classroom practice.

Recycle language using different methods

Repeating language practice using the same method is obviously less interesting and stimulating to students than practice which involves the use of different methods. Look through the classroom procedures suggested in 4.3–4.7 and 5.2–5.14 for ideas.

Balance methods

When experimenting with teaching and learning methods, make sure you provide students with various routes to improving their English.

There are many views on how language is best acquired (or learned!) and overdepending on any one method might mean you close yourself off to some unexpected but pleasant surprises. Allow students to comment on the methods you are using too because their perception may be very different from your own.

Develop your own principles

Don't dismiss methods if you hear them getting a bad press. Some methods are discredited, then readopted as new theories are accepted or when research throws up unexpected results. Many simply remain controversial due to the wide range of theories about how second language learning (or 'acquisition') best takes place.

Instead, develop your own theories and principles by watching and listening carefully to what goes on in the classroom. Remember, though, that the success of any methods will be affected by the teacher and that the response of the students might be due to factors which have nothing to do with the method itself. Preoccupation with work, boredom, confusion as to what's going on, mood, misunderstanding reasons behind classwork and level of difficulty can all affect your students' reactions. Similarly your own mood and attitude, as well as teaching skill or language proficiency, might also affect your ability to use a method successfully on a particular occasion, so use 'working hypotheses' about methods, instead of jumping to conclusions! Often slight adaptations to methods will result in dramatically different student reactions, in terms of both the amount of learning that seems to be taking place and your popularity rating.

Above all, when using any methods ...

- Relate all class language practice to bigger performance areas so that students will be able to see how everything fits together.
- Make your objectives clear to students at all times.
- Tell students what you expect of them so that they will know how to behave. Don't jump from a highly teacher-controlled method like drilling to role-play and expect students to suddenly become active! Tell them when one type of activity has finished and another is beginning.
- Sell methods to students because they will certainly not respond well if you, yourself, have no faith in the methods you are using. Show students how the method can work.
- Be realistic about why methods succeed or fail at different times.
- Adapt methods (or combinations of methods) to suit the situation.
- Elicit feedback from students, then act on it. Remember, as adults on an expensive Business English programme, your students are partners in the learning process – they deserve to be consulted.

4.3 Warming into things

The beginning of a lesson is an important time because it is then that students decide whether or not to give their attention and enthusiasm to the lesson. It is also a time when students might evaluate your effectiveness or the value of what is done in class. In other words, if you do not get your students' attention and commitment at the beginning of each lesson the rest of the lesson is going to be difficult!

When starting a lesson or when moving from one activity to another, your aims might be:

- To wake the students up and motivate them.
- To get students thinking faster, in a more focused way.
- To coax students to go beyond their normal patterns of behaviour.
- To clarify or communicate objectives.
- To show clearly to students how your methods will help them achieve their objectives.
- To teach, practise or raise awareness of an area of language.
- To tap into students' real-life learning needs, e.g. by finding out more about their work.
- To establish a positive atmosphere in class.

When considering how to begin a lesson, you will naturally need to consider your real-life teaching situation. Some students may be late (especially early on in courses), students who have missed several classes may suddenly make an appearance, students with no interest in the lesson you have planned or no need for that language may turn up ... all sorts of things are possible in the Business English classroom. For ideas on how to cope, see 6.5.

However, your selection of procedures from those listed in this section will mostly depend on:

- your objectives for the course;
- your objectives for that particular lesson;
- your students;
- what has succeeded or failed with those students before.

Try to vary your approach, using as many different procedures as possible so that your students get a varied introduction to lessons. Experiment and find out what works for you.

☐ EXPERIENCE EXCHANGE

Students talk about their experience of using language in the workplace before practising in class. As well as motivating students, this procedure also helps you to understand the nature of the problems students face.

Language any
Level lower-intermediate and above
Time 10 minutes

Procedure

Give students a stimulus to remind them of a particular situation they may encounter at work. The stimulus could be a video snippet (e.g. of a meeting), a short newspaper article about an issue (e.g. downsizing after being bought up by a multinational), a short listening (e.g. a telephone conversation about a complaint), or anything else which seems suitable. Focus briefly on the stimulus by asking basic gist and detail comprehension questions, then invite students' comments by asking *What do you think? Is that a familiar situation?* Finally, ask students how they get on in the same situation. Ask *Do you enjoy … ?*, *How do you feel about being in this situation?* After everyone's comments have been heard, remind students of the importance of the area and tell them you'll be practising it in the lesson.

☐ WORDBOARD SPRINGBOARD

This is a good warm-up activity if students are reluctant to talk. Students are provided with a safe springboard for conversation through a guided preliminary task and are then free to talk as they wish.

Language any
Level intermediate and above
Time 10 minutes

Procedure

Choose several words which relate to the topic of the lesson. Write the words on the board, then ask *What do you think of when you see these words?* Write students' initial suggestions around the first word on the board, then get students to continue on paper in pairs, producing 'wordboards' for the other topics. Finally, get students to explain their wordboards to other pairs. When discussion is flowing, lead into the next stage of your lesson, which should be topically connected. Some examples of wordboards to be explained:

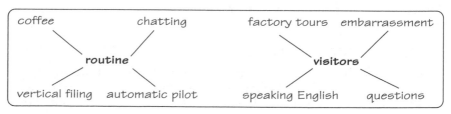

☐ ANECDOTE ACCESS

Stories or news items are a good way of getting students' attention, as long as they are not used too often. This procedure, which essentially involves becoming a two-minute story-teller, is popular with Business English students and appropriate, perhaps, because of the importance given to case studies on MBA courses and in the business press.

Language any
Level intermediate and above
Time 5 minutes

Tell an anecdote about a business situation from your own life or from a business book. Alternatively, tell students about something which you have heard is happening in their company or industry and ask their opinion. Be careful to leave out names and depersonalise information which might offend or turn out to be confidential.

Variation 1

Use news stories as a basis for discussion. Distribute a copy of one or more short newspaper articles or ask students to bring newspaper articles to class themselves. (The articles can be from English or local publications. If they are written in the students' own language students will simply need to explain them in class.) Get students to summarise the article(s) – without looking – before inviting comments and encouraging discussion. Alternatively, give out extracts from business books as extra optional reading material, then at the beginning of the next lesson ask *What did you think?*

Variation 2

Use other published material as a starting point. Take books or magazines into class and simply ask *What do you think of this?* when referring to something you think might be of interest and relevant to language study.

Variation 3

Use extremely easy listening extracts from coursebooks about real-life situations. After playing the extract once or twice, ask students what they think. To get students talking and to ensure that everyone understands the situation simply start with basic comprehension questions. These comprehension questions can then quickly lead into discussion questions. Video clips can be used in the same way, especially if they're easy for the students to follow.

☐ SNIPPET INTROS

Students are introduced to an area of language practice via a listening text which is easy for them to understand. The listening effectively sets the scene and reminds students of problem areas before they are asked to do further practice.

Language lower than the level of the students
Level elementary and above
Time 5 minutes

Procedure

Play students a recorded conversation or an extract from a listening task, then ask simple gist and detail questions. For example, before getting students to prepare presentations, play a short presentation (e.g. Unit 17 of *Early Business Contacts*. Brieger, N. and J. Comfort. 1989. Hemel Hempstead: Prentice Hall), then ask the following questions: *How many people are talking? Where is the speaker? Why is he talking? Who's he talking to? What's he talking about?* It is important that all the questions are very easy for students to answer.

Variation 1

Do the same thing with snippets of video recordings. Many American movies contain scenes of business meetings or other office conversations. Even if they are not very similar to the students' situation, they may provide a good springboard for discussion and language practice if they remind students of cultural differences or if they prompt students to tell you about differences in their own work situation.

Variation 2

Play students a short snippet of sounds from a tape, such as *Sounds Intriguing* or *Sounds Interesting* which both provide sequences of sounds to interpret (Maley, A. and A. Duff. 1975 and 1979. Cambridge: Cambridge University Press). Alternatively, record something from real life or the radio. After establishing the situation, invite students' comments.

Sequence 17 in *Sounds Interesting*, for example, includes sounds from an airport and a plane taking off. This provides an audio lead-in to role-playing conversations between colleagues when one person has just returned from a business trip. Recordings of various sounds from the workplace – telephones ringing, photocopier whirring and a fax emerging from the machine – could also provide the basis for a story and follow-up work. After agreeing on the reason for the phone calls and photocopying, students could write the fax to confirm the agreement.

Variation 3

Photocopy a cartoon or photograph of a business situation onto a transparency. The picture should be connected to the lesson you are planning (e.g. you could use a picture of a woman giving a presentation before a lesson on presentations). Then, at an appropriate moment during the lesson when students have just finished an activity, suddenly dim the lights and flash up the picture. Give students two minutes to write a caption or a speech bubble before inviting comments or simply ask students straight away, *Have you been in this situation?*

☐ DICTATED TEXT HALVES

In pairs, students dictate texts to each other. They then decide if they agree with the comments in the texts.

Language any
Level elementary and above, depending on the texts you use
Time 10–15 minutes

Preparation

Write a text about the area you want to lead into, e.g. about telephoning or talking to colleagues and divide it into two parts. An example of a text you could use with advanced students:

Telephoning in English may mean using a wide range of language because telephone calls can be about a wide range of subjects. However, a lot of the language you need for telephoning is highly conventional and formalised so it is useful to learn these special phrases. Perhaps special, formulaic phrases are often used on the telephone because of the need for rituals and routines in difficult communicative situations.

Using the telephone effectively involves having well-developed skills in exchanging information, clarifying points and explaining. Since speakers cannot fall back on visual support (such as graphics, facial expressions or other body language), the stress on the spoken word is greater than in any other interactive situation. Perhaps this explains why a lot of people who are confident in other areas of life are a little afraid of using the telephone!

© Cambridge University Press

Procedure

1 After putting students in pairs, give students the texts. Ask students to dictate their texts to their partners in turn. (You can stick the texts on the walls and get students to run back and forth if they are young.)

2 After partners have compared their texts with the originals to check for accuracy, ask students to discuss whether or not they agree with the comments in the text. Get students from each pair to report back to the rest of the class afterwards. Encourage students to talk about their own experiences.

Variation

Instead of text halves, get students to dictate lists of questions to each other before discussing their answers. Possible questions you might use for the area of telephoning are as follows:
* *How often do you answer the phone each day?*
* *How often do you need to speak English on the phone?*
* *How often do you need to make telephone calls in English?*
* *What problems, if any, do you experience?*

☐ DEEP-ENDING

Students are asked to actually do something (e.g. write a memo, deal with a visitor, take a telephone message) before the performance skill has been 'taught' or practised in class, i.e. they are asked to jump into the deep end of an imaginary swimming pool before they can swim! Doing this gives students an opportunity to show and become aware of what they can and can't already do.

Language depends on which performance skill you choose to work on
Level any, except absolute beginner
Time anything up to 40 minutes

Procedure

1 Tell students you need to find out more about what they can and cannot do so that what you do in class is totally relevant to their needs. Then ask students to do something which they need to be able to do. Make sure you ask them to do something very practical (e.g. write a fax or a memo). If you want to find out about students' speaking skills, ask them to role-play a situation; clarify the situation and characters before everyone starts so that students know exactly what they're doing. (See STARTER PIX on p. 79.) Before and during students' performance (i.e. when they're in the 'deep end'), make sure that students understand that it doesn't matter how well or how badly they perform.
2 When students have finished, 'debrief' them by asking them how they feel they did and adding your own comments. Set class objectives and follow up. See 4.5 for advice on this.

☐ FLOOR CARDS

Students work on the floor or at tables, and put cards in order. While solving a 'puzzle' as a group, students become aware of discourse elements, in both speech and writing. This can help them to converse in a more culturally appropriate way and plan better letters, memos, e-mails etc. This is an especially useful warm-up activity for classes in which students are often late.

Language any you select
Level elementary and above, depending on the cards you prepare
Time 10 minutes

Preparation

Type or write out questions, a dialogue or a text which you would like to use as a basis for your lesson, as in ASKING ABOUT PEOPLE'S JOBS on p. 52. Use new spoken or written texts, or – better – use ones which have already been the focus of study in a previous class. Each card (or piece of paper) to be put in order should contain either a word or a whole utterance, in the case of a dialogue. Prepare one set for each pair or small group of students.

Procedure

When students come into class tell them to put the cards in order. If there are lots of latecomers move groups round (e.g. simply asking each group to move to the next table) so that weaker students are helped and do not lose face. When the correct order of cards has been established get students to read out the text in pairs. Follow up with more complex role-played conversations or related listening, reading or writing practice.

Note that lesson preparation for this type of procedure won't take long if you build up your own personal sets of floor cards for different dialogues or texts. If you have access to a laminating machine your cards will be both durable and attractive.

☐ STARTER PIX

Students are helped to imagine a situation through annotated 'pix' (pictures), which can be either photos or simple cartoons drawn on the board.

Language any
Level elementary and above
Time 5 minutes

Preparation

Find some fairly large photos of business people or practise drawing cartoons at home! Suitable photos can usually be found in commercially-produced business magazines or in a company's in-house newsletter. Cut out the photos and mount them on pieces of card.

Procedure

1 While students are finishing off another activity, attach your photos to the board or draw some simple cartoons (e.g. faces) of business people. Some examples of cartoons are given below. Tell students one character is going to talk to (or telephone) the other. Ask students questions to establish exactly who the characters are: *Who's this? What's her position? What's her relationship with this man? Why's she going to speak to him? How does he feel about the situation?*

2 When the photos or cartoons have been annotated with the details (as in the example below), elicit and role-play with students the first few lines of the conversation. Then ask students to continue preparing and role-playing dialogues with a partner. Remind students that they will probably need to change the notes around the characters to suit their personal work situation. While they are preparing and practising their dialogues, encourage students to include as many details of their work as possible so that the dialogues are very relevant to their real-life professional needs. Also provide relevant phrases, feedback on pronunciation problems and telephone sound effects whenever necessary! Get pairs to practise their conversations until the language they use is sufficiently accurate and appropriate and the students feel confident. Focus particularly on pronunciation to encourage them to do this.

    Note: Quickly drawn cartoons are most effective, partly because they are a surprise and partly because they can easily be personalised. Details you add may help students to focus on their own work situation more specifically, which will mean that language practised is as relevant to students' work as possible.

An example of some cartoons for STARTER PIX

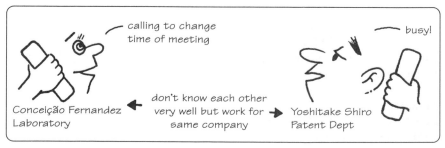

Phonemic chart for use with KEYWORD PHONEMICS

h health	ʌ much	æ match	e get	e another	i happy	ɒ hot	u punctuality	j year
x loch	ɑː forecast	ʊ put	ɪ ring	ɜː first	iː peace	ɔː thought	uː food	w one
p pay	b bay	ʊə poor	eə share	eʊ actual	ɪə peculiar	ɪə here	k cane	g gain
f ferry	v very	aʊ now	eɪ say	əʊ phone	aɪ high	ɔɪ employ	t time	d dime
θ throw	ð the row	aʊə tower	eɪə player	əʊə lower	aɪə higher	eɪə employer	ʃ pressure	ʒ pleasure
s sink	z zinc	r red	l lead	m rum	n run	ŋ rung	tʃ cheer	dʒ jeer

Shaded areas indicate suggested practice groups. Many sounds are placed side by side on this chart to facilitate useful practice.

© Cambridge University Press

□ KEYWORD PHONEMICS

Students are encouraged to familiarise themselves with the phonemic script, which will mean they can check pronunciation for themselves in a learners' dictionary. At the same time, this procedure will give you the opportunity to focus students' attention on commonly mispronounced words which students will be using later in the lesson.

Language words which your students often mispronounce
Level elementary and above
Time 5–10 minutes

Preparation

Make a copy of the phonemic chart on p. 81 for each student and, if possible, also one enlarged copy for the wall. Then write 15–20 words on the board in phonemic script. Take care to follow the dictionary convention of writing slashes at the beginning and end of words so that it is clear that you are using phonemics and not strange spellings!

Procedure

As students come into class hand them a pen or chalk of a contrasting colour and invite them to decode any words they can. Give students some help, if necessary, and/or hand out copies of the phonemic chart so that they can refer to the key. When all the words have been decoded, elicit the word stress for each word. Mark the word stress by drawing a small box above the stressed syllable or by using the marks used in the students' dictionaries. Get students to practise the pronunciation of each word before asking them to use the words in another context.

□ SIMPLE SERIES

This is an excellent activity for students who are tired or lethargic when they arrive for class and usually gets a very good reaction from students. It is also good for reviewing simple series of words or numbers which may need to be used with confidence later in the lesson.

Language series of words (numbers, days of the week, months, etc.)
Level beginner and above
Time 5–10 minutes

Procedure

1 Ask students to stand in a circle. Make sure everyone is standing

close together. Tell the class that you are going to do something to get everyone thinking faster and using English more quickly. Pointing first at yourself, then at each student in turn, with your palm facing upwards and going round clockwise, for example, start counting 1–2–3–4–, etc., assigning one number to each student. After saying a few numbers, pause before the next one until the students start saying the numbers instead of you.

2 As soon as the series is going round fairly fast and rhythmically (with you still pointing to each student before he or she speaks), add a 'chaser', i.e. start another series which is not too similar to the first (e.g. a word-based series, such as the days of the week). Do this by saying the first word and pointing to the second person as you hesitantly say the next word in the series. If the other series falters, get students to start all over again! Change the series if students seem to be finding them either too easy or too difficult.

3 Add a third series, if possible, by changing the original series when it is your turn; this usually causes a lot of good-humoured chaos!

Note: Select series according to what you want to do later in the lesson. For example, if you will later be practising telephone conversations for arranging appointments it would be highly appropriate to practise ordinal numbers for dates, days of the week, months or times. It is not always necessary to explain the pattern behind each series to students in advance because part of the fun is in working out what the pattern is! If anyone hesitates, either another student will come to the rescue or you can yourself.

Variations

Other 'series' which can be used to good effect:

- 10, 20, 30, 40, 50, 60, 70, 80, 90, 100, 110, 120, 130, 140, 150, 160, 170, etc.
- 1,000, 2,000, 3,000, 4,000, 5,000, 6,000, etc. (particularly useful for Japanese and French students)
- 10,000, 20,000, 30,000, 40,000, etc.
- Double numbers: 1, 2, 4, 8, 16, 32, 64, 128, 256, 512, etc.
- Triple numbers: 1, 3, 9, 27, ?!, etc.
  (Note that this exercise is equally useful if you or your students write the numbers on the board first, because then it becomes a fast pronunciation exercise, which is also a challenge.)
- 2, 4, 6, 8, 10, 12, 14, 16, 18, 20, etc.
- 1, 3, 5, 7, 9, 11, 13, 15, 17, etc.
- 100, 99, 98, 97, 96, 95, 94, 93, 92, 91, 90, 89, 88, 87, 86, etc.
- Count up and down by decades, i.e. 1, 2, 3, 4, 5, 6, 7, 8, 9, 10,

100, 99, 98, 97, 96, 95, 94, 93, 92, 91, 90, 11, 12, 13, 14, 15, 16, 17, 18, 19, 20, 90, 89, 88, 87, 86, etc.
(Show students this series on the board before starting.)

- Say numbers 1–100, both ascending and descending. Each time a number is divisible by 3, say *Tom*; when it's divisible by 4, say *Dick*; when divisible by 5, say *Harry*. For example, *1, 2, Tom, Dick, Harry, Tom, 7, Dick, Tom, Harry*, etc.
- 1 o'clock, 2 o'clock, 3 o'clock, 4 o'clock, 5 o'clock, etc.
- five past, ten past, quarter past, twenty past, etc.
- A, B, C, D, E, F, G, H ... Z, A, B, C, etc.
- A, B, C, D, E, F, G, H ... Z, Y, X, W, V, U, T, S, R, Q, P, etc.

□ QUESTION CHAINS

As well as being fun, these question chains can help to bond a group together because individuals will be subsumed under a 'group identity'. The exercise is also a very good way of getting students to repeat new, idiomatic phrases which are appropriate for the situation chosen. Students are encouraged to focus on accuracy and appropriacy of language use, and at the same time they become more confident.

Language appropriate responses to common questions
Level lower-intermediate–upper-intermediate
Time 45 minutes

Procedure

1 Tell students they are going to practise some phrases which are useful and appropriate in a business context and that this practice activity will help them to correct errors that they often make. Get students to stand with you in a circle, then turn to the student on your left and ask, *What did you do at the weekend?* Correct any response he or she makes, in terms of accuracy, pronunciation or appropriacy, and get him or her to repeat the corrected version. This student should then ask the next student the same question and you should correct any mistakes in the same way. The second time round, tell students to imagine they did everything other students have mentioned, so they must repeat the previous students' responses before their own.

2 Insist on the use of words or sounds such as *Well ... , And, er ... !* so as to make students' responses as natural as possible. Also insist on absolute accuracy, on good pronunciation of individual sounds, on good word and sentence stress, as well as on the correct intonation pattern for lists (i.e. up, up, up, down).

3 Change the direction of questions (i.e. clockwise to anti-clockwise)

after a while and keep the pace as fast as possible. Encourage humour and silly answers which will help to make this activity enjoyable but be sure to correct or adapt these responses so that they are appropriate for real business situations.

Variations

Other possible questions to start the question chain:

• *What have you done so far this morning?*
• *What have you done so far this week?*
• (on a Friday evening) *What did you do this week?*
• *What are you doing this weekend?*
• *What are you doing next weekend?*
• *What are you working on at the moment?*
• *What are you responsible for?*
• *What do you usually do in your free time?*
• *How do you think the company could be improved?*
• *What do you like about business trips?*
• *What are your long-term aims?*

☐ GUIDED SPEAKING

This procedure is an extension of the normal chat between teacher and students at the beginning of a lesson. Students are encouraged to ask each other questions which might be appropriate to use with English-speaking colleagues in the workplace.

Language any, but generally work-related
Level elementary and above
Time 10 minutes

Procedure

When you come into class, ask individual students questions such as, *How's it going? Have you had a busy day? Have you heard about the new … ?*, etc. Refer to specific things whenever possible; for example, when you know that someone has just returned from a business trip, ask *How was your trip?* As soon as the first student has responded (with your help, if necessary), gesture to other students to ask each other similar questions. Write possible questions on the board if students need them. Remind students that they will need these questions to build relationships with their foreign colleagues or regular visitors. Make sure students know and practise appropriate responses (e.g. *Don't ask! Oh, not too bad, thanks!*). Consider the level of formality students will need as you provide them with language so that their conversations remain appropriate and internally consistent in terms of style.

Insist that students ask each other these questions on a regular basis when they come into class, even before you're there. To get students used to doing this, send them out of the room as soon as you arrive if they admit they haven't been chatting in English before your arrival! As they come back in they should start up conversations as if they had just arrived by asking their classmates appropriate questions. If you're persistent students will eventually get used to chatting in English, especially if you get them to do this before any meeting role-plays or presentations too.

Variation 1

Elicit an appropriate dialogue. Practise this with the class, then get students to continue practising in pairs or threes, adapting answers as necessary, according to their situation.

Variation 2

Throw a ball to a student each time you ask a question and then gesture to him or her to throw the ball back to you after answering. In other words, each ball throw represents one turn of speaking. When you have thrown the ball to three or four individual students encourage students holding a ball to throw their ball to another student rather than back to you, while asking a question or making a comment. Stand back and listen to the conversations taking place in the room as far as possible and only interrupt by throwing in another ball, accompanied by a question or comment, when you think you can stimulate more discussion or comment. Note that conversation can be amongst the group as a whole or split up between pairs or small groups of students in the class, and that pairs and groupings can be fluid, depending on where balls are thrown. Make sure you use soft balls which will not damage equipment or students!

☐ BODY TALK

Students review parts of the body and idiomatic expressions which include the same words. Doing this gives you a good opportunity to get students doing some physical exercise at the beginning of a lesson or at a sleepy mid-way point and is good preparation for students who go on business trips abroad or who have to work with foreign managers on a day-to-day basis.

Language idiomatic expressions which include parts of the body
Level lower-intermediate–advanced
Time 20 minutes

Preparation

Prepare a worksheet of idiomatic expressions which include parts of the body. Make sure that all the expressions are commonly used in business situations. Blank out the key words to produce a gapfill exercise and provide some paraphrased alternatives for students to match with the 'parts of the body' expressions. A sample worksheet is as follows:

Fill in the gaps, then match each expression with the meaning on the right.

1 Let's *keep an _____ on it*, anyway.

2 I'm afraid I *put my _____ in it.*

3 You've got to _____ it to him!

4 We need some kind of _____-up plan.

5 They're asking *an _____ and a _____.*

6 Let's *do a _____count.*

7 It's a bit of a *pain in the _____.*

8 I'm *up to my _____ in work.*

9 *Put your _____ into it!*

10 You've got to *keep your _____ clean.*

11 Can I *give you a _____ ?*

12 You'd better *keep your _____ to the ground.*

13 He *got his _____ dirty.*

14 I'd *give my eye _____ for that job!*

15 *What's the _____ line?*

a   *very busy*

b   *stay alert for some news*

c   *watch carefully*

d   *keep out of trouble*

e   *contingency*

f   *do anything for*

g   *what does it mean in reality*

h   *became involved in sth. illegal*

i   *said or did sth. stupid*

j   *check how many people*

k   *admire his achievement*

l   *nuisance/headache/problem*

m   *an unreasonable price*

n   *help*

o   *put in more effort*

Answers:

1c eye; 2i foot; 3k hand; 4e back; 5m arm/leg; 6j head; 7l neck; 8a ears; 9o back; 10d nose; 11n hand; 12b ear; 13h hands; 14f teeth; 15g bottom (not exactly anatomical!)

Procedure

Ask students to stand up, gesturing with your hands if students don't respond immediately. Then ask them to touch various parts of their body, frequently asking them to touch their toes after asking them to touch something near their head (e.g. *Touch your neck. Touch your toes. Touch your earlobes. Touch your chest. Touch your toes.*). When everyone has had plenty of exercise, follow up with the gapfill worksheet. Encourage students to use a monolingual dictionary, if necessary. Finally, check students' answers and discuss with the class when each expression might be used.

Some possible 'pix' for PUZZLE PIX

Pedro with his bow tie stuck in the elevator

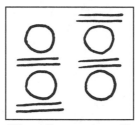

Chinese dinner party … with chopsticks!

Spider watching his new flat screen TV

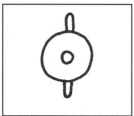

Aerial view of Pedro (who's Mexican) cycling to work

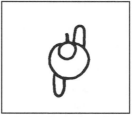

Aerial view of a smoker rushing to work

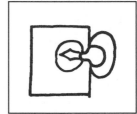

Aerial view of a man whose tie's fallen in his soup

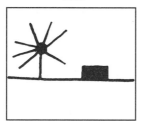

Happy spider – he's just bought a TRX6000!

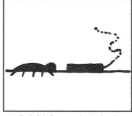

Suicidal ant who's had enough of modern technology

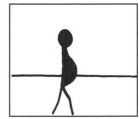

Hungry man – or a businessman – with a swollen stomach

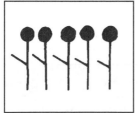

Queue of very thin, hungry people in the cafeteria

Smoker alone in a personalised cloud of smoke

Unsuccessful TR6 sales person with a pile of unsold products

☐ PUZZLE PIX

This is a fun lead-in which can stimulate students to relax and offer off-beat comments. These off-beat comments should be encouraged because they can improve the class atmosphere at any given point!

Language question forms or the language of conjecture
Level elementary and above
Time 5 minutes

Preparation

Select some appropriate puzzle 'pix' (i.e. pictures) from those suggested on p. 88, or make up your own. Three 'pix' seems to be the optimal number because students get a chance to gradually 'warm' to the activity but don't get bored. Adapt pix to individual groups of students and tie the pix in thematically with follow-up activities. Draw the pictures on the board before students come into the classroom or while they are busy doing something else. Note that the descriptions below each picture are provided for your benefit and should on no account be written on the board!

Procedure

Begin by asking, *What's this?* Then invite students to guess what each picture represents by asking questions with a *Yes/No* answer. Refuse to answer until students have asked questions correctly and only accept a guess which is correct in every detail. Encourage students to ask useful questions such as, *Is it made of ... ? Is it used for ... ing?*, which can be written up on the board, if necessary. If students can't deduce what the picture shows, press on with the lesson proper and return to this puzzle at a later point, when questions will come faster!

Variation 1

Use the puzzle pix to start a discussion. In other words, after students have guessed what the picture represents invite their comments with simple questions, e.g. *Do you like Chinese food? Do you have to entertain your clients? Do people smoke in your office? Is it a problem?*

Variation 2

Use pix as a springboard for activities where students are required to think carefully before using language. For example, the last picture (of the unsuccessful TR6 sales person) could lead into product presentations if you use the pix to make students consider why the sales person was unsuccessful and how product presentations can be made most successful. Get students to focus on bizarre details you have included in your pix before asking serious questions which require careful and creative thought. This will help to create the right, relaxed atmosphere in class, which is conducive to focused and creative thinking processes. Bizarre details to include in your pix could be as follows:

- a broad smile on the face of your cartoon to suggest a rather desperate sales person;
- piles of significant shapes to suggest the students' unsold products.

Focus students' attention on these details with questions, such as *Yes, but what's this?*

□ QUESTION STORIES

Sometimes known as 'lateral thinking problems', these stories gradually unfold as students ask the teacher questions. They provide a fun break between other activities and are especially good when started off before a coffee break.

Language any (for the story), then questions using present or past tenses
Level elementary and above
Time 5–10 minutes

Procedure

1 Tell students a brief story which, because of the omission of some important details, does not immediately appear to make sense. Some possible stories, with their explanations:

- *A man who works on the 20th floor goes up to the 18th floor in the elevator almost every morning, then walks the last two floors.*
  Solution: He's rather short so he can't reach the button for the 20th floor in the elevator. When someone tall gets into the lift the man asks him or her to press the button for the 20th floor.
- *A man went into a bar and said, 'Thank you.'*
  Solution: The man had hiccups, which the barman knew. He said 'Thank you' after the barman pointed a gun at him, which made his hiccups go away.
- *A man went into a field with a pack on his back and died.*
  Solution: His parachute didn't open. He was flying to New York on business but something went seriously wrong with his plane.
- *A man picked up the phone and the person at the other end*

immediately hung up.
Solution: It was the woman calling from the next door hotel room. She phoned the man's room because she wanted to wake up her neighbour, who was snoring loudly.

2 Get one or more students to repeat the story but correct any details they get wrong. Ask students if they understand the story, then invite them to ask questions with a *Yes/No* answer. Insist that every question is accurate before answering. This can easily be done by simply saying *Pardon?* whenever a question is incorrect.

Variation

Use an exhaustingly long story which includes the basic 'problem story' along with lots of unnecessary detail! This is especially good when you want students to practise present or past simple question forms. Personalise stories as much as possible and make the setting the students' own company or industry. Prompt students to remember the story with mimed actions. A suggested longer story:

• Norio Watanabe gets up every morning at 6 o'clock. After a shower and a quick breakfast of coffee and toast, he kisses his wife goodbye, unlocks his car, gets into the car, which is a Porsche, drives to work, parks his car in his favourite parking space, says hello to the receptionist, then walks to the elevators. He then goes up to the 18th floor, gets out of the elevator, then walks up the last two flights of stairs to the 20th floor. In the evenings he gets the elevator all the way to the ground floor, says goodbye to the receptionist – he doesn't kiss her! – finds his car (which is still a Porsche) ... etc.!

□ BALL-BRAINING

Students free-associate around a subject while they throw around a ball. This is a good way of leading into a new topic or area of language practice because students' attitudes can be gauged quickly. Throwing balls, rather than writing on the board, means things move faster, there's more eye contact and students have an opportunity to release any pent-up aggression as they speak!

Language any
Level lower-intermediate and above
Time 5 minutes

Procedure

Tell students you're going to talk about a given subject (e.g. giving presentations). Tell them to throw the ball and say any word or phrase connected with the subject which comes to mind. Start off by throwing a ball and saying a word or phrase (e.g. *overhead projector*). Students who catch the ball may then say phrases such as *don't like it, helps with presentations* or *often goes wrong*. Encourage students to contribute more freely by throwing in extra balls and adding different types of words or comments (e.g. *It makes me feel nervous!*). Three or four balls can circulate simultaneously. Encourage students to continue making comments when you have stopped the ball-throwing, before leading into some more serious work on the subject.

☐ QUOTE ZONE

This is another technique to get quiet students talking. It is especially good for groups where participation from students is uneven or where students do not listen to each other.

Language any, plus the language of discussion (agreeing, disagreeing, interrupting, etc.)
Level intermediate and above
Time 30 minutes

Procedure

Write several words from a quotation on the board, then ask students to make a sentence with the words, which they believe in. (Some suitable quotations are provided on the next page.) For example, with the words *business* and *unexpected*, students might write *International business can be exhausting because business people have to deal with the unexpected on a daily basis*. When selecting words to trigger these sentences, aim to choose words which students will understand readily. Then, when students are ready, ask them to compare and explain their sentences in pairs. Invite comments from the whole class before showing and discussing the original quotation (i.e. *International business is fraught with unexpected events*). Follow up with a topically-related activity (e.g. a listening or reading comprehension on the same subject).

Variation

Write a quotation on the board or show it on an OHT, e.g. *I don't want to be a passenger in my own life*. Then get students to write questions about the quotation for other students (e.g. *What would it mean to be a driver instead of a passenger? Do you like taking control?*, etc.).

Some suitable quotations for QUOTE ZONE

International business is fraught with unexpected events.
> Ricks, D. A. 1993. *Blunders in International Business*. Oxford: Blackwell. p. 1.

Cultural differences are the most significant and troublesome variables encountered by the multinational company.
> Ricks, D. A. 1993. *Blunders in International Business*. Oxford: Blackwell. p. 2.

Few things are the same everywhere, and almost no strategy works well globally.
> Ricks, D. A. 1993. *Blunders in International Business*. Oxford: Blackwell. p. 122.

Companies that have cultivated their individual identities by shaping values, making heroes, spelling out rites and rituals, and acknowledging the cultural network have an edge.
> Deal, T. and A. Kennedy. 1988. *Corporate Cultures: The Rites and Rituals of Corporate Life*. London: Penguin. p. 15.

Once it becomes apparent that change is necessary, there are two other tough facts to face: change is time-consuming and very expensive.
> Deal, T. and A. Kennedy. 1988. *Corporate Cultures: The Rites and Rituals of Corporate Life*. London: Penguin. p. 161.

Large organizations exist today because complex tasks require the coordination of many people.
> Deal, T. and A. Kennedy. 1988. *Corporate Cultures: The Rites and Rituals of Corporate Life*. London: Penguin. p. 189.

The world belongs to optimists, pessimists are only spectators.
> *FRANÇOIS GUIZOT, quoted in:*
> Lindenfield, G. 1996. *Self Motivation*. San Francisco: Thorsons. p. 13.

One should act before anyone else has a chance to react.
> *BARON PHILIPPE DE ROTHSCHILD, quoted in:*
> Lindenfield, G. 1996. *Self Motivation*. San Francisco: Thorsons. p. 49.

Nothing can be accomplished without solitude.
> *PABLO PICASSO, quoted in:*
> Lindenfield, G. 1996. *Self Motivation*. San Francisco: Thorsons. p. 158.

I don't want to be a passenger in my own life.
> *DIANE ACKERMAN, quoted in:*
> Lindenfield, G. 1996. *Self Motivation*. San Francisco: Thorsons. p. 130.

□ OBJECTIVES REVIEW

Students review their study objectives informally while throwing around a ball. This is especially useful for a group of students you have taught before or for use mid-course with students whose objectives you feel have either changed or are not being fulfilled. Many new ideas are likely to come from the students themselves.

Language comments about work-related language needs
Level elementary and above
Time 30 minutes

Preparation

Choose three questions and write the words on the board, using a different colour for the words of each separate question. Getting students to do a simple word-ordering activity as you introduce unexciting (but important) questions makes the questions seem less dull and helps students to start thinking in a creative, problem-solving way. Some suggested questions are:

- Is English important for my job? (in red)
- Why is English important? (in black)
- What do I need to focus on? (in blue)

The board might look something like this:

```
                    focus       job

              important     do     why

      what         important     my      I

      need            English    is     to

           Is    on    for    English
```

Procedure

1 Ask students to write down three questions using the words on the board. Don't let anyone speak! When everyone is ready, throw a ball to one of the students. Ask the 'catcher' to say the first word of the red question, and then throw the ball to another student. The next student who catches the ball says the next word of the red question, and so on. If anyone makes a mistake the students have to start the red question again.

2 As soon as the red question is 'in the air' ask students to continue throwing the ball around, but this time saying their answers. If you're teaching on a company programme most of the answers to the first question should be *Yes*. If anybody says *No*, throw the student an extra ball, asking, *Why, isn't English important for your job?* Take students' answers very seriously and take notes on individuals' comments. Note down carefully who said what.

3 Repeat the process for the next question, starting it off by throwing another ball to a student and saying, *OK, the black question.* This time, the answers should be longer.

4 When students are focusing on the blue question help them by supplying possible answers (e.g. vocabulary, speaking fluency, grammar, writing, listening, pronunciation, meetings, body language, learning about Anglo-American culture). Make it clear to students that they don't need to give 'neat', cogent answers. Continue making notes as you listen, recording in detail what is said, by whom, and by how many people. Use a mind map with number tallies. Encourage individual students to ask the group extra questions if they want to. (One student once asked, *How are we going to improve?*) Before moving on, ask students, *Does anyone want to make any other comments before we move on?*

N.B. If there are more than 15 students, divide the class into two and get the groups to brainstorm ideas separately. Sit between the two groups and listen to both of them and/or get someone from each group to report back what was said. Bear in mind in this case that some people's input might not get well-reported.

5 Finally, preferably immediately, give students a formal response to the requests and comments they have made. Suggest how each area can be tackled and comment on any students' suggestions which you disagree with (e.g. lots of exam practice for TOEIC, an exam which aims to test general proficiency). If appropriate, draw a diagram on the board which outlines a suggested approach for the rest of the course. For example:

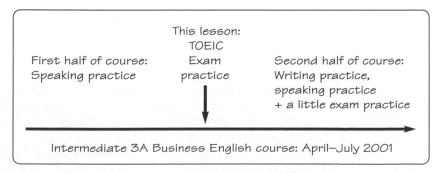

The diagram on p. 95 is a very simple diagram but it clearly shows the suggested work for the second half of the course. Since it is so clear it is more likely that students will give you feedback. If students have specified skill areas as areas to improve (e.g. writing) ask them exactly what they mean. Break the skill area down into types of writing by asking questions. For example, ask students what they need to be able to write. Is it memos, faxes, letters, e-mails, reports, quotations? If you think students are using terms loosely, define each type of writing by asking key questions about it (e.g. *Is it serious writing? Is it handwritten or typed? Who is it sent to? How long is it?*). Identify specific areas to practise by asking students what they find difficult (e.g. the comment *It takes too long to read the faxes I need to reply to* could indicate that students need practice scanning for important information or understanding formulaic phrases, which may be causing difficulty).

4.4 Presenting language

New language needs to be presented to students of all levels, including advanced, although the type of items presented will vary. Having no input or too little on a course is likely to be very demotivating because students will feel that there is little benefit in attending classes. However, since students can obviously only ever cope with a certain amount of input and since too much may also make them demotivated because of the resulting confusion, you need to be careful not to give too much. You also need to take into account the fact that input does not always result in 'intake'. This will mean using your ingenuity in exploiting and combining the procedures suggested in this and other books or in developing alternative approaches so as to maximise real learning. Also, consider the notes in 3.6 for encouraging students to arrange their own 'input' outside class; students will not only select language according to their interests and needs, they are also more likely to be successful if they are collaborating in achieving 'intake'.

Several ways of presenting language are suggested on pp. 100–106. For best results when using these in the Business English context, remember the following points:

Teach relevant language
Although a certain amount of 'frivolity' can be justified and motivating in warmer or filler activities, presenting language which is not directly relevant to the students' needs can waste time and demotivate students in the long run. Courses maintain momentum when the language which is presented can be justified in terms of the initial and ongoing needs analyses.

Teach language in context

Language which you present and practise is most useful to students when it is presented in a realistic context; in this way students will see how and when it can be used in real life. When you depart from this principle, as you may do in warmer or filler activities, always elicit or explain how and when the language will be used in real-life contexts. When planning lessons, take the situation in which the new language will be needed as your primary starting point. Typical situations might be a student reporting back to his or her foreign supervisor after attending a trade fair, or taking some visitors on the train to a branch office.

Use contexts which are useful to students

Get students to explain situations in which they need language so as to ensure that your chosen context will reflect the students' real or probable situation. Encouraging students to make comments about key characters' personalities or likely preoccupations will also help to ensure maximum student involvement and motivation.

Teach patterns of discourse

Point out how language presented fits within conversations or texts. What do people usually say before requests, promises or thanks? For example, before requests people might often give some background information, before promises they might apologise or explain something and before thanks they might give a compliment to the person being thanked. Encourage students to develop their awareness of this because use of language may differ significantly in their mother tongue. See 4.6 for ideas on how to do this, and see 'awareness-raising' in the Index.

Raise students' awareness of language use in real-life contexts

Get students to consider language in its wider local or international context. Some forms, while seemingly 'wrong', may be preferable in countries where English is used as a second language (e.g. Singapore or Sri Lanka) because they will seem appropriately informal to other people from the area. Simplified English which communicates clearly may be useful in an international context where there is a wide range of non-native speakers of English. Non-verbal factors (gestures etc.) may also need to be considered, according to the context.

Teach language selectively

It is better to select a few items that will be of use to students than to burden them with a long list. In other words, when you are teaching a particular function, limit the amount of exponents you teach, selecting them carefully according to the students' present or future work situation. For example, in a fairly go-ahead company you might choose only the following requests:

> — Is it OK if I (do this first)?
> — Do you think I could (leave a little early today)?
> — Would it be OK to (publish this in our next newsletter)?

Obviously, the exponents chosen for any class will depend on many things, including the corporate culture, the students' status, their work and the type of requests being practised.

Insist on good pronunciation
It is important for Business English students to be intelligible internationally and to create a good impression with both clients and colleagues. Getting students to focus on intonation patterns, increasing their voice range (i.e. making their voice go higher and lower) and stressing key words will help enormously.

As far as intonation is concerned, although it is difficult to categorically associate specific intonation patterns with specific grammatical features, some patterns can be said to be more typically or less typically English. Coax students away from intonation patterns which they use in their own language towards patterns which sound more typically English; conspicuously non-English intonation patterns can be confusing, distracting or insulting to people from other places. Use hand or arm movements, a sing-song tone or arrows on the board to indicate patterns. Encouraging students to exaggerate the patterns may make practice more enthusiastic and ensure that students' 'toned down' versions in real life are accurate.

To get students to stress key words, work with some sentences on the board. Elicit which words are stressed and mark them with boxes over the words. Then, drill phrases or whole sentences, encouraging students to speak more loudly and make their voice 'go up' whenever they come to a stressed word. Asking for repetitions of key phrases and insisting on better pronunciation each time will help you to check whether language presented has been well 'heard' before pairwork practice. Repetition of key phrases (ostensibly for pronunciation practice) should also be motivating for students because it will help them 'get into role' and because it's fun in itself!

Teach 'safe' forms of language
So as to help students avoid international diplomatic incidents or unpleasant working relations in multinational corporations, teach them language which is safe! This means selecting phrases which will be acceptable even if pronounced badly. For example, it is much safer to encourage students to use *Could you ... ?* for one-off requests than imperatives! Think carefully when selecting exponents for negotiations or meetings.

Use warmers, fillers and 'enders' effectively

Many smaller language points can be presented quickly in a fun and memorable way at the beginning or end of a lesson or in an interesting 'mid-lesson slot'. Don't lose opportunities to maximise the effectiveness of lessons in this way. However, plan small slots carefully and link them up as systematically as larger slots in lessons.

Encourage students to develop an 'English-speaking personality'

While selecting, prioritising and presenting language, encourage students to develop an English-speaking personality, i.e. a set of behaviours – both verbal and non-verbal, to be used when speaking or writing in English, which are internally consistent and appropriate for the students' situation. (Making 'personalities' internally consistent means ensuring that outgoing students who choose assertive phrases such as, *Hi, let me introduce myself. I'm ... . You're new here aren't you?*, also use similarly assertive language at other times, as in *What can I do for you?*) Students' English-speaking personalities need not relate directly to any specific English-speaking culture but must be acceptable both in an international business context and to the individual students themselves.

Since students will sound very strange in the real world if they use an inappropriate mix of formal and informal styles, or if they use assertive expressions alongside ones which sound more deferential, it is important to give students feedback on any 'discrepancies'. If necessary, discourage individuals from using particular expressions which seem 'out of character' and explain why. Encourage students to make informed choices whenever possible because they are likely to be more knowledgeable about their working persona than you are!

The advantage of using the concept of an 'English-speaking personality' with students is that it will give them 'permission' to behave in a way which is only emotionally acceptable to them when they are using English. (They may cringe at the idea of being so informal or direct in their own language.) It will make participation in role-plays in class more enthusiastic. The concept will also help students to bring together and personalise the disparate elements of a course.

Give students language which empowers them

Consider what the student is left with after the lesson when he or she returns to the real world because language use outside the classroom will have very significant consequences. The introduction of miscellaneous telephone language or language for 'chatting' which can build up relationships with callers is not helpful unless students also have phrases such as *What can I do for you?* which will help them to redirect or hurry along the conversation. Phrases such as *So that's ...* or *Could we just go over that again?* are also a key to enabling students to check or reiterate important details. These phrases are 'empowering' because they give students the power to control or shape conversations, rather than just take part. Also consider ways of empowering students who need to participate in international meetings; teaching a wide range of language for making suggestions, asking for clarification and summarising could have far-reaching consequences.

Use a range of methods

Using a wide variety of presentation procedures will make sessions more interesting for students and will cater to different learning styles, preferences or moods within the class. Teachers who use the same approach every time they present language are likely to bore or demotivate students. Several different approaches are suggested in this section.

Allow and encourage students to 'digest' new language

Students are bound to need a little time to come to grips with new language forms after first being exposed to them; we cannot expect instant success when students start using language which we have just presented. If students are to produce language correctly it is also helpful if they are encouraged to use record-keeping systems which will allow them to refer back to what they have encountered. Getting students to use a learning organiser is very helpful in this respect – see LEARNING ORGANISERS on p. 61.

☐ MODELS THROUGH READING

Students are exposed to new vocabulary and to formats, particularly business conventions, which are unfamiliar to them through reading comprehension exercises.

Language controlled by you, according to your selection of texts
Level elementary and above
Time 5–15 minutes

Preparation

Ask students or in-company course organisers for copies of typical e-mails, faxes or reports, etc. Explain that you are keen to find out about their own company's preferred style of writing. If confidentiality is a problem, ask for documents which have key details deleted. If you have no luck finding a suitable model, write one yourself. Pass your text to your colleagues or to the contact person in-company for editing or comments if you feel in need of support! Note that the text should be a model of the kind of text that students need to produce because grammar and discourse elements function quite differently in different text types. (For example, note the use of the present simple in business letters and faxes.)

Procedure

Distribute copies of the text to the class. Allow students time to read the text quickly, then ask them simple comprehension questions about its content. For a fax, these questions might include such obvious questions as *Who's it to? Who's it from? When was it written?*, as well as more sophisticated questions about its content. Next, draw students' attention to any key features of this type of communication – this is your input – and follow up by asking students to produce a similar e-mail, fax, etc. which includes the same features.

Variation 1

Cut the text up into strips, then get students to put the strips in order. The individual strips can be simply a line of text, probably part of a sentence, or individual strips can each contain a separate sentence. This second approach, although requiring a little typing, is a more valuable exercise because students have to think more about the meaning of the text and about the 'plan' behind it.

Variation 2

Use a photocopier to enlarge a text. Then blank out words or phrases which you want to 'input'. Blanking out parts of a text – even whole paragraphs – focuses students' attention on what is missing, and also acts as a check that students don't already know the language. Put the text on an OHT. When students have guessed at ways of filling in the blanks or completing the texts (by adding paragraphs at key points), get them to compare their own version with the complete text (which you can also put on an OHT). Discuss reasons for the specific language used, taking care to draw students' attention to formulaic phrases commonly used in business writing.

□ MODEL-MENTORING

This is an excellent procedure for helping students to write e-mails, memos, faxes and letters. Early in the course, you write texts for your students with their help, then gradually your roles are reversed. At first students give guidance on content, conventions commonly used in their company and the style preferred, while explaining the situation to you in detail. With later e-mails, memos, faxes and letters you act as a mentor while the students write; you merely provide guidance on style, grammar, use of lexis and conventions common to business writing. The procedure works best with small groups or one-to-one students.

Language determined by the situation
Level beginner and above
Time 15–40 minutes

Preparation

Find out as much as possible in advance exactly what your students need, especially in terms of developing their writing skills. Later you will check this information in class. Note that to do this with beginner level students, you need to speak the students' language. With students of any other level, no knowledge of the students' language is necessary.

Procedure

1 Check with students what kind of writing they need to do in their work. If they need to write e-mails, for example, ask someone to suggest a specific e-mail which he or she will shortly have to write. Ask the student who it is to, who that person is exactly, why the e-mail needs writing, etc. Get as much detailed background information as possible. Focus particularly on finding out what the student wants to achieve in writing this e-mail, or other type of communication.

2 Simply write the e-mail, all the time encouraging students' input. With later e-mails, memos, faxes and letters get more and more input from students until you are eventually offering mere support and comments when needed. Make sure students take control of pens, boards and paper, etc. as early as possible, either individually or in groups. Correct carefully at all times so that students can develop their awareness of appropriate forms, grammar and lexis.

3 When you have finished, draw students' attention to key features (as relevant) and do follow-up work, as suggested in MODELS THROUGH READING (p. 100).

☐ MODELS THROUGH LISTENING

Students are exposed to new language or new ways of using language (e.g. for interrupting or making a suggestion) via a listening exercise. Obviously, for the students to be able to cope they will need to understand most of the language on the tape.

Language controlled by you, according to your selection of video or audio tapes
Level elementary and above
Time 5–15 minutes

Preparation

Find examples on tape of conversations which students will need to have themselves in their working environment. For example, if students need to participate fully in meetings by being able to interrupt or make a suggestion, find recordings of meetings in which this happens.

If you can't find anything suitable, role-play the situation with colleagues and record your conversation. Make a transcript of what's said if at all possible because this will be invaluable to students.

Procedure

Get students to listen to the tape once or twice. Then ask simple questions about the recording to check basic gist comprehension. Next draw students' attention to the specific aspects of language you are focusing on (e.g. ways of interrupting or making a suggestion), before getting students to practise this language in role-played meetings.

Variation

Produce a task which focuses students' attention on certain aspects of language in a conversation – example tasks might be sequencing lines of a dialogue or filling in gaps. After students have completed the task, give them a transcript of the conversation so they can study these features in detail, in their natural context, and act out the dialogue themselves.

□ MODEL-MENTORED DIALOGUES

After students have provided the necessary background information on the kind of dialogues they might need to have, you provide and/or elicit a dialogue which is relevant to the students' work situation. This approach gives the learner a very active role.

Language conversation in the form of a dialogue
Level elementary–intermediate
Time 20 minutes

Preparation

Find out as much as possible in advance exactly what your students need, especially in terms of developing their speaking skills. Later you will check this information in class.

Procedure

Check with students what speaking they need to do in real-life work situations. Ask who they need to speak to, where, why, when, how often, etc. Write on the board the names of two characters the students mention. If you or your students are capable of doing so, add cartoons of the people concerned! (Even poorly drawn cartoons will add to the fun – see p. 80 for some examples of cartoons you might be able to draw.) Next, add notes to indicate who each person is and other details as appropriate, such as a moustache or glasses – so as to add humour and to clarify the situation. Next, write up a dialogue, eliciting as much as possible from students. Get students to practise each line in a very controlled way and focus particularly on pronunciation features. Then get individuals to adapt the dialogue to their own situation and role-play other similar conversations.

Variation

Put students in pairs and ask them to record a prepared or improvised dialogue. Next, get students to listen critically to their own performance. Elicit comments from the 'performers' and also from other students before giving your own feedback. Provide useful language (especially phrases) where necessary, or drill key words or phrases to correct pronunciation errors. Then ask students to record their conversation again, taking the feedback into account. Repeat this procedure several times, depending on your students' level of response!

   Note that this procedure works especially well in a language laboratory which has a pairing facility. Between recording sessions students can change seats and listen and comment on each other's dialogues. The procedure works equally well for presentations which students prepare on their own, followed by Q & A sessions.

☐ COMMUNITY LANGUAGE LEARNING

Students are given new language while they are building a conversation, the content of which they select themselves. This method is great for building the confidence of diffident students or for focusing students' attention on turntaking, appropriacy of language or idiomatic expressions. It works best with groups of no more than eight students. A more detailed explanation of community language learning is given in Stevick, E. W. 1980. *Learning Languages: A Way and Ways*. Rowley, MA: Newbury House.

Language determined mostly by the students – the teacher only corrects or provides language when needed
Level beginner–lower-intermediate
Time 40 minutes

Procedure

1 Get students to sit in a circle. If there are more than eight students, organise parallel conversations, or invite some students to watch or arrange conversations in shifts. Place a tape recorder with attached remote microphone in the centre of the circle so that all students can easily reach the microphone. (A remote mike has a switch on it which allows the tape to be turned on and off. This means that there are no pauses or clicks on the final recording. Whenever a student wants to

speak, he or she simply needs to take the microphone, flip a small switch on it to speak, then flip the small switch off when he or she has finished.) Tell students they are going to have a conversation, that they can say whatever they like and that you will help them to say things in natural English. (A beginner monolingual class, whose language you know, can say things in their own language and you can give them the translation.)

2 Ask who'd like to begin. Move round to that person's left-hand side and listen to what they have to say. Help them to improve it (in terms of grammar, vocabulary or pronunciation), encourage them to practise saying the improved version, then when they're ready, invite them to record their comment by pushing the remote switch to 'on' and then to 'off' again when they have finished.

3 Continue moving to students as they indicate that they want to speak, repeating the same procedure. Make sure that students always turn off the mike when they've finished recording. Let the conversation continue until a natural break or until students show signs of restlessness.

4 Play the conversation to the group. If recorded correctly, the conversation should seem continuous and natural-sounding. Draw students' attention to any new language and write it on the board. Drill or discuss this new language, as necessary.

5 Set up follow-up practice conversations in pairs. One way to do this is by eliciting from students a similar conversation between two colleagues, then getting them to adapt the conversation to suit their own particular jobs or situations in pairs.

6 If you consider the conversation useful enough, type up a transcript and take it along to the next lesson. First, get students to write the names of speakers next to what they said. Then focus students' attention on key language items once more. Finally, get students to read out the transcript. Follow up later with gapfills or sequencing activities, using the transcript as a basis.

Variation

Get students to adopt roles before starting the conversation or to role-play a conversation as themselves but in a particular situation (e.g. a departmental meeting). This is a particularly effective way of improving students' participation in meetings, especially if repeated several times with varied follow-up activities.

□ SILENT WAY

Using coloured wooden blocks, called 'Cuisenaire rods', and sometimes also other equipment so as to make the meaning clear, the teacher models language. Students repeat what the teacher has said and use the language, manipulating the rods according to their comments. In the meantime, non-verbal correction techniques are used so that student talking time is maximised. The rods, as well as other related products, are available from Educational Solutions (UK) Ltd, 11 Crown St., Reading, RG1 2TQ, England (Tel: +44 118 987 3101, Fax: +44 118 987 3103) or from BEBC (by mail order) – see p. 336 for details.

Language controlled by the teacher, but sometimes also 'demanded' by students
Level beginner–elementary only
Time 10 minutes – 1 hour

Procedure

Make statements to the class about the rods, demonstrating with them as you speak. The rods can be described literally (e.g. *The red rod is under the chair*, *The green rod is on the table*, *Put the blue rod behind Anita*) or used to represent things – your imagination is your only limiting factor! For example, if you lay out the rods so that they resemble a plan of a factory and tell students that certain rods are specific people (e.g. the Marketing Manager and a visitor from Brazil), you can model a conversation between the host and the visitor. Make sure students are clear about what every part of the rod plan represents. Then, start modelling language which reflects what the rods are 'doing' (e.g. if the Manager is showing the visitor around the factory you could model *Let's go through to the steam room first*). Get students repeating comments (manipulating the rods as they do so), turn by turn, and expand or reduce what each student has to say according to his or her ability. Insist on accuracy at every stage. Direct and conduct silently, using mime, gesture and finger correction (in which each finger represents a word). Insist that students continue practising until they are confident. Strangely enough, with this method the more language is practised with the help of the rods and the more insistent you are on accuracy and improving student performance, the more fun the lesson becomes.

4.5 Feedback and correction

Why give feedback or correct?

In the Business English context appropriate and correct use of language is often vital if communication is to be successful. It is not difficult to see why the misuse of certain verb forms, which convey impressions of timescales, work done and work to be achieved, can cause so many problems. For example, *I worked in Accounts for ten years* suggests that the person now works elsewhere, whereas *I have worked in Accounts for ten years* suggests that the person still works there. Even a seemingly 'minor' error of a wrong article in the question *Can you give me a report on that?* could generate a lot of unnecessary work if the manager actually meant to say, *Can you give me the report on that?* because the employee might assume that one had not already been written! Meetings, especially, demand extremely sophisticated use of language if speakers are to persuade or explain, object, interject, regale or inspire.

Students who work in an international environment have often been forced to develop the ability to communicate but they are often frustrated with the inadequate results of their 'rough' communication or with the impression they create when they speak or write. They are usually very receptive to feedback because their hope is that we will help them to make their English more effective.

It is therefore essential that we find ways of correcting students' mistakes and helping them to improve in other ways. It is part of our job to tell students when we feel their language is inappropriate or incorrect for a given situation. We must accept the role of 'assessor' and 'corrector' if we are to provide students with a useful programme of study and, indeed, give them what they want.

How to give feedback or correct?

As with all other types of teacher–student communication within the Business English context, it is essential to treat students at all times with respect. Although students will appreciate the fact that we need to take responsibility for assessing and correcting their language, they will respond best if we give feedback or correction in the spirit of offering support, rather than passing judgement.

There are important practical reasons why we should comment, rather than 'judge'. Although we almost certainly have more expertise in terms of language use than our students, there may be limits to our expertise because of the particular language required by our students. We may well be unfamiliar with the particular vocabulary or style of communication considered most acceptable within each student's particular speciality (e.g. Accounting or Law) and may even be surprised by some of the common or preferred styles of spoken and written communication in certain companies or specialities. At the same time, our students may well have been exposed to appropriate forms of language in the workplace and this might give them a keener awareness of what is or is not correct or appropriate in a given situation.

When giving feedback, then, our style of language must show respect and openness towards students' own perceptions. To avoid a defensive, negative, and unreceptive, response to your feedback or corrections, begin by asking students questions such as the following:

- *How did you feel?*
- *What do you think you did well?*
- *What would you like to improve?*
- *So, what do we need to do next?*

There are various advantages in asking students for their comments before you give your feedback:

- The whole feedback session or correction slot is likely to be more open and relaxed because students will not have been put on the defensive right at the beginning.
- You as teacher will have more 'thinking time' and are more likely to be able to give a balanced overview of strengths and weaknesses or 'correct' forms.
- You will have the advantage of knowing the students' own feelings before giving your own comments. This means that you will be able to phrase your comments appropriately, playing down points if confidence levels are low or emphasising the importance of points if students are complacent.
- You will ensure that there is a discussion between yourself and students and will avoid situations in which stunned students simply listen to your monologue. Such discussion and negotiation obviously also improves teacher–student relationships and the overall atmosphere of the class because it ensures that communication is more open and that everyone speaks. If you say everything first and then ask for students' comments, students will probably have very little left to say and may well feel reluctant to contradict their 'teacher'. You may also miss out on the opportunity to find out just how much your students can self-correct.
- You will be helping students to become independent as learners because they will be getting used to evaluating themselves on an ongoing basis.

Having elicited comments from students (using reflective listening, e.g. paraphrasing what students have said), it is entirely appropriate to agree or disagree with what they say. As a language professional, you will have a more objective view of things. In cases where students have been very negative about themselves point out strengths in their performance. In cases where students have over-estimated their performance point out weaknesses so that they can become aware of problems and re-evaluate objectives accordingly. Give your comments with confidence.

The students will appreciate this, will learn to trust you (if you are consistently fair) and will tolerate more 'student-direction' in the classroom as a result. When correcting students, encourage them to view their mistakes or weaknesses in a positive light. You can do this by encouraging them to think of the classroom as a 'safe zone' where trial and error is inevitable and even desirable. Your corrections are a means of helping students to improve, just as a coach's comments help an Olympic swimmer. Conclude feedback sessions and correction slots by discussing goals for follow-up work. Don't simply set such goals for individual students or the group as a whole, let it be a joint exercise. Also make practical suggestions as to how these new goals can be reached, or elicit ideas from your students.

A few methods for feedback and correction common to many EFL classrooms are suggested below. They have been adapted for the slightly different atmosphere of the Business English classroom.

☐ PROFILING

After students have done some work in class, such as a role-play or some workshop writing of faxes, elicit or give good feedback which recognises what is being achieved already. Examples of things to focus on might be clear communication or appropriate, adult, business-like use of language. You can easily do this by asking students, *Did they communicate clearly?* or *Did they sound business-like?* Then, using carefully-phrased questions, elicit some bad feedback on one or two important aspects of the students' performance (e.g. tense body language, poor intonation or inappropriate use of key vocabulary). Questions you can use for these areas might include: *Did they look relaxed? Did they sound like English speakers?* and *Did they use the new phrases correctly?* If possible, make feedback for individuals or pairs link up with feedback given for other individuals or pairs in the same group so that the whole class subsequently has a specific focus for improvement.

☐ POSITIVE IMAGING

As you continue to listen to a student speak, write up the corrected version of what he or she said on the board. This allows the student to continue without losing face and self-correct if he or she chooses. It also provides a record for anonymous future reference when summing up to the class as a whole.

☐ RE-ROLED REPETITION

Give students a reason to repeat phrases or sentences by reallocating roles in role-plays. Make sure that students are given roles which relate to their work situation. Also, adapt role-plays so that students repeat the same language in different situations.

☐ REFORMATTED REPETITION

Reintroduce corrected versions of students' writing in class in other activities – again and again, if necessary, each time in a different guise. For example, if you want students to work with a corrected version of a fax, type out a corrected, rewritten version and use it to make gapfills, sequencing activities (for sequencing sentences or paragraphs) or as a stimulus for other writing. In addition, put the fax on the school computer to form the basis for computer language-learning games. Always ask permission from individual students to reformat their work in private. Then take care not to point out whose work is being recycled unless, of course, the student wants you to and praise is due.

☐ HAND MOVEMENTS

Use hand movements to show and remind students of rises and falls in intonation. Be firm and playful when you ask students to repeat what they have said.

☐ MIME AND MOVEMENT

Correct poor pronunciation of individual sounds by getting students to mime as they speak. For example, to encourage students to make the vowel sound in the word *up* and *cut* get them to mime holding a glass of whisky and throwing it back as they repeat the word. To encourage French students to pronounce the /h/ sound, get them to mime climbing a flight of stairs before letting out a sigh and repeating the word in question. Think up other mimes which force students to correct specific mistakes.

☐ TRIO TRIANGULATION

Put students in groups of three, rather than pairs, when they practise and allocate one student to the role of 'corrector'. The corrector should consult the coursebook or other materials and intervene whenever mistakes are made. Alternatively, the corrector can make notes and give feedback at the end of each mini role-play.

□ QUIZ SHEETS

Compile a list of students' mistakes and make a quiz worksheet. A typical quiz sheet might list sentences or short paragraphs of text, with gaps for the students to fill. The gapped words will be the ones prone to error. So as not to discourage students, include quite a few items which they will get right or which will be relatively easy.

4.6 Awareness-raising

Awareness-raising activities form an important supplement to all other language practice done in the Business English classroom because when adults are consciously aware they can participate more fully in changing their performance. In other words, students who are aware can also be in control; students who are truly in control of their learning take the initiative to fill in gaps in their knowledge and develop strategies for improving in areas where they are weakest. Ultimately, this will result in students who are more effective users of English, which is good for business not only in terms of building good relationships with colleagues and clients but also in terms of getting those all-important contracts. Awareness-raising activities in class can therefore be easily justified to both students and their sponsors.

What do Business English students need to become aware of? Firstly, they need to become aware of what and how they are learning. Doing this will help them to maximise their learning. Secondly, they need to become aware of how culture affects language. Students using English for business will inevitably need to communicate with people from very different cultures and a lack of cross-cultural awareness could lead to all sorts of communication problems. Misunderstandings can lead to lost contracts and soured relationships so it is vital that we raise awareness of any linguistic or paralinguistic behaviour which may confuse or offend in an international forum. Furthermore, if students are to survive in an international corporation they will need to be aware of their company's own corporate culture. Thirdly, students need to understand how English as a language is different from their own; they will need to understand how it functions in terms of effective communication.

Learning processes

In order to get students to consider the best way to approach learning English, use the procedures described on pp. 56–66. Make a point too of discussing any strategies which you, personally, consider useful. As a language teacher you may have more ideas than your students!

Focus students' attention on how well they are functioning as learners as follows:

- First ensure that everyone understands the course objectives, as established in the initial or ongoing needs analysis, perhaps using a course outline as a reference point (see p. 31 and p. 48).
- Encourage students to monitor how well they are meeting these objectives personally on an ongoing basis. Performance areas which have been covered to a student's satisfaction can be 'ticked off' on the course outline. Periodic achievement tests (as described in 7.2) will also help students to keep track of the amount of progress they are making.
- When progress appears to be slow suggest reasons for this and help the student concerned to discover strategies which are effective for his or her particular situation.
- Encourage a discussion in class about the best or preferred ways of studying and try to accommodate all students' preferences, while maintaining a varied programme of study.

Culture

Raise students' awareness of cultural factors in communication in the following ways:

- Encourage students to become aware of any behaviour or language which is distinctive of any particular culture by pointing this out whenever appropriate. Remember that our job is not to encourage students to adopt a British or American style of communicating. Instead, we need to raise their awareness of what is considered acceptable or preferable in English in a particular situation, as far as we have information on this. Students can then decide for themselves how they should speak or write. They may even choose to use a non-standard variety of English, such as Sri Lankan English, so as not to alienate other non-native English speakers from the same part of the world; alternatively, they may opt for a kind of English bilingualism where they use standard and non-standard varieties of English according to the situation.
- Raise students' awareness of their corporate or industrial culture by commenting on or eliciting differences between formats used in standard memos, etc. and those preferred in the students' corporate or industrial culture. If you are unsure yourself, talk to more advanced and experienced students and with English-speaking managers. Note that even 'departmental' culture may be significant; for example, sales personnel may behave and speak very differently from marketing personnel. For more on this interesting area, see

Deal, T. and A. Kennedy *Corporate Cultures, The Rites and Rituals of Corporate Life*. Harmondsworth: 1988.

- As well as focusing on students' choice of lexis (i.e. words and phrases), focus also on how they use language in larger chunks of written or spoken discourse because this will have a significant effect on their success at communicating.
- If students use inappropriate behaviour (e.g. if they ask offensive questions) during any class activity, alert them to this and suggest alternative behaviour (or questions), which would be more acceptable.
- Make students more aware of their own body language by commenting on it whenever it is particularly good or particularly inappropriate and by including a rating for body language in any assessment you give students (e.g. when doing presentations). (See the marking scales on p. 300 for an example of this.)
- Help students to select and combine words, phrases and sentences consistently in terms of a cultural (or sub-cultural) style. In other words, help students who want to appear professional in business negotiations to develop an 'English-speaking personality' (as described on p. 99).

Language

In order to make students aware of key points about language which they don't seem to have grasped, use sensitive feedback and correction (see 4.5) and give examples of the target language yourself. Raising students' awareness of how English functions in real-life contexts inevitably involves the use of models of language because students will normally need to have seen or heard language operating in a realistic context before they can understand or produce it. Models of spoken or written texts can be any of the following:

- Listening and reading comprehension texts from course materials.
- Taped discussions on the radio and videoed meetings in films or soap operas.
- Materials from students themselves, i.e. e-mails, reports, faxes, etc. written by their colleagues or bosses. Assure students that you will respect confidentiality by editing out any sensitive information.
- Dialogues elicited from students or written with their help. (See MODEL-MENTORED DIALOGUES p. 103.)
- Corrected or rewritten versions of dialogues, faxes, etc. originally written by students either in class during workshop activities or as homework.
- Transcripts of language previously practised in class in role-plays or workshops. Note that this is a particularly useful way of providing a

113

model because students have a correct 'final version' and you are able to recap important points or recycle language.

- Material you have written from scratch, taking into account what you know about appropriate and typical use of language in a particular context.

Procedures which involve the use of models are given on pp. 100–104.

You can use the procedures in this section at any point in a course, as you feel appropriate, in order to:

- Make individual students aware of areas of strengths or unusual proficiency. Stress what they are already accomplishing in English so as to help them track their progress.
- Focus students' attention on areas of weakness. Be sensitive when drawing attention to weak spots – eliciting points from students themselves is much more effective than stating them yourself! Consider the comments in 3.4 and 4.5 before using any of the procedures in class.
- Develop your own awareness of how language is really used by effective speakers or writers. Since there is, as yet, little published material on this area, you will need to make your own observations and notes on key points either alone, or with others in private groups or at conference workshops. Develop your awareness of how language operates in business contexts on a lesson-by-lesson basis. You may observe, for example, that requests are often preceded by apologies and background information and that promises are often preceded by apologies and explanations. Teaching students patterns is important because patterns might be very different in the students' own culture and these are likely to be automatically transferred when students use English. Developing an awareness of how English is used in business contexts will help you to teach appropriate language.
- Become more aware of how strong you are personally in terms of being an effective communicator. Honesty is important in this respect! Try to become aware of your real-life use of English in work situations on a daily basis by constantly analysing and critiquing your use of language in terms of the response you receive.

At all times encourage your students to take notes as they notice important features. These can easily be incorporated into a learning organiser – see LEARNING ORGANISERS (p. 61).

If your own confidence levels are a problem when you approach the area of awareness-raising, remember that you will have access to more information than your students. As a native or proficient speaker of English you will also be much better at adapting or correcting language than your students and will be more capable of picking out salient features, simply because you will be less bogged down by detail. Don't be overly dogmatic about your conclusions, though, because language use varies enormously according to its context of use. The following are all important in a Business English context: the company and its corporate culture, the industry (e.g. telecommunications vs. computing), the speciality (e.g. patent law vs. logistics) and the country in which English is used.

While continuing to make observations about students' use of language, make it clear to students that you are all exploring together and that you are only offering opinions which may help your students to communicate more effectively in English. Whenever students challenge anything you say about language in class take their comments seriously; exploring why something is different in the students' context will often help you to understand the reason for differences. Remaining open to new perspectives will enable you to build your own expertise as well as enhance your relationships with students.

□ FOREIGN PERSONALITY CHECKING

Students focus on the impression they make when using English. If their use of intonation or lack of word linking makes them appear 'stupid' or unhelpful to listeners this is pointed out to them either by the teacher or by other students. This is one way of focusing students' attention on important details in pronunciation, which might otherwise be regarded as unimportant.

Language any spoken language
Level intermediate and above
Time 10–15 minutes

Procedure

At the end of practice of a particular type of language (e.g. giving presentations), when students are interacting quite freely, ask students to record what they have been practising in pairs. When they have done this, tell them you are going to do a quick self-awareness exercise so that students can consider the impression they might make on people when they are using English. With students working in small groups, get them to critique each other's performance by using questions such as the following: *Does the speaker sound intelligent? Does he or she sound good at his or her job? Does he or she sound interested? Does he or she sound hard-working? Does he or she sound serious?*

Encourage students to give each other frank evaluations and to re-record, aiming to correct the wrong impressions they might create. If students are unaware of the impression they might make, tell them! Correct students' evaluations of each other by saying *Well, actually …* You are doing students a favour in telling them these things! Focus on reasons for impressions created, before encouraging practice and re-recording. Pronunciation, non-verbal and other paralinguistic features (e.g. tone of voice) are important things for students to learn about if they are to use English effectively in the world of work.

Variation

Either before or after students comment on their own conversations, get them to rate native speakers recorded on tape, either video or audio. Make an effort to select a range of speakers, some good, some bad! There are plenty of examples of both types in published materials or on news programmes.

The following procedures will also help you to raise students' self-awareness:
MIMED ARRIVAL (p. 168); CULTURAL MIMING (p. 128); TRIO REFLECTIONS (p. 218).

☐ DOUGHNUT DIALOGUES

Students analyse their own learning problems using 'doughnut' diagrams, which they explain to a supportive partner. This is based on an idea by Julian Edge, explained in his book *Cooperative Development*. 1992. Harlow: Longman. pp. 35–40.

Language free speaking
Level intermediate and above
Time 20 minutes

Procedure

1 Provide students with some blank paper, if necessary, and ask them to find a partner. First one student writes a word which encapsulates a learning problem in the centre of the piece of paper, draws a circle around it and the student explains the problem briefly to his or her partner. After a few moments' reflection, the same student notes down three subdivisions of the problem and explains what these three subdivisions are. An example of a possible first doughnut is provided on the opposite page.

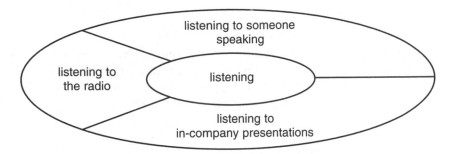

2 Next the same student takes any one of these three aspects of the original problem and, again, using it as the centre of a new 'doughnut', divides it into three parts elsewhere on the page. Once more, the student should explain the subdivisions.

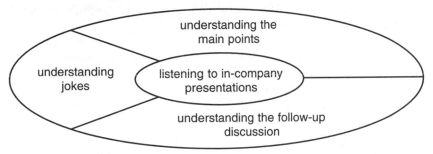

3 Following through one aspect of the problem each time, the student continues drawing doughnuts until he or she starts thinking of solutions. The non-doughnut-drawing partner must at all times listen supportively, using phrases such as *Uhu, I see* to show interest and supportive body language, such as eye contact, turning towards the speaker, nodding, smiling. (To get students to practise being good listeners in advance, use a procedure like NOISY LISTENING on p. 153.) The student who is listening should only interrupt when he or she truly doesn't follow what the other person is saying. At no time may the listener ask provocative questions which subtly attempt to push the speaker towards a particular solution or view of the problem. However, the listener can ask constructive questions to help the speaker focus his or her thoughts, e.g. *What are the practical implications?*

4 After students have changed roles in their pairs, they then report their conclusions and insights to the rest of the group and decide what a good course of action might be for each 'learning problem' that was considered. As the teacher, feel free to offer some additional suggestions while you are listening to this final review given by students.

☐ GRAMMAR WORKSHOPS

Students become more aware of how particular areas of English grammar operate by consulting a range of grammar reference books. They present their 'findings' to each other. You provide corrections, whenever necessary, during the students' mini-presentations.

Language any
Level upper-intermediate and above
Time 1 hour

Procedure

1 Bring several reference books, a selection if at all possible, into the classroom. Grammar books, grammar practice books and dictionaries might all be useful. Put them in the middle of the floor or within easy reach of the students.
2 Elicit or give students a list of three or four key grammatical areas or tenses which are in need of revision. Ask students to volunteer to take responsibility for each area. If there are enough students in your class, one student can be responsible for the 'formation' of a tense, another for its 'use', and another for example sentences used in a real-life context (e.g. an e-mail).
3 Allow students a reasonable amount of time, say 20 minutes, to prepare mini-presentations on their area. Then ask them to present their findings one by one, using the board or OHTs, if they have prepared these. Before the presentations begin reassure students individually and as a class that you will step in and help if they get anything wrong or if they need extra or more realistic example sentences. Both audience and presenters will be able to relax more, knowing that they have your support and that discussion is possible at any point.
4 Finish off by dealing with any questions from students or by adding any comments about major omissions in their presentations. Follow up with writing tasks which require students to use the grammar points reviewed in class.

The following procedures will also help you to raise students' awareness of grammar: TRIO TRIANGULATION (p. 110); SPOT THE ERROR (p. 140); FLOOR WORD JIGSAW DICTATION (p. 275); DEEP-END RECORDED MEETINGS (p. 205); TEXT REBUILDING (p. 230).

☐ SITUATIONAL SCRUTINY

Students who are already using English at work consider a situation in which they have to use English and the problems they encounter. They then consider, with the help of your feedback, what they need to learn or improve in terms of their communicative skills.

Language any
Level intermediate and above
Time 10 minutes – 1 hour

Procedure

Tell students which work situation you are going to focus on. Then ask them how they usually get on when using English in that situation. Use careful questioning to draw out problems. If students are oblivious to problems, get them to role-play the conversation or write the memo, etc., recording conversations if possible. Then elicit problems from students or give them feedback, based on your impressions of problems they are likely to experience. Consider the effect students' use of language will have on a wide range of native and non-native speakers of English and focus especially on cross-cultural problems. Make the problems the focus of follow-up work.

The following procedure will also help you to raise students' awareness of culture: CARD CONCEPT EXCHANGE (p. 171).

☐ PREDICTED COMMUNIQUÉS

In this procedure students predict a follow-up conversation or written text (e.g. a memo) using a spoken or written text – a 'communiqué' – as a starting point. 'Communiqués' to use as starting points can be any kind of business communication (e.g. a recorded telephone call, a fax or an e-mail).

Language any
Level intermediate and above
Time 30 minutes

Preparation

Select a 'communiqué' and find or write the response to it. This will later be used as a model.

Procedure

Give students time to study the 'communiqué' and discuss the probable follow-up. Then give them a fixed amount of time to produce this follow-up (i.e. a fax or script for a telephone conversation), either alone or in groups. Finally, get students to compare their follow-up texts with your model.

□ PROMPT CONVERSATIONS

This procedure allows students to check how well they can predict the kind of language that is likely to be used in a particular type of conversation.

Language any work-related conversation
Level intermediate and above
Time 30 minutes

Procedure

Explain or elicit a situation which students are likely to encounter in their working lives and write notes on the board. Check that students all understand the background for a conversation, then get them to prepare and role-play the conversation in pairs. Give feedback on each pair's conversation and allow students time to correct or rewrite the conversation, as appropriate, before getting students to role-play their conversations to the rest of the class. After each 'performance', encourage students to comment to the class on how their initial conversation differed from their final corrected or improved version.

□ PATTERNING

You elicit the pattern behind a conversation from students. Students then use this pattern as the basis for follow-up role-plays of conversations.

Language conversations, especially those involving requests, apologies or complaints
Level intermediate and above
Time 10 minutes

Procedure

Select a conversation on tape which seems natural and effective in terms of communication. After using gist and detail comprehension questions with the recording, elicit a summary from students of the conversation. Start by establishing the main message of the conversation (e.g. an apology). Then ask students where this occurs – at the beginning, middle or end? Elicit what went before and after the apology. Write the pattern on the board in diagrammatic form. Using the diagram on the board as a basis, elicit a similar conversation which includes an apology, or get students to write a conversation in pairs.

The following procedures will also help you to raise students' awareness of expected styles of communication which may not apply in other languages: EMPOWERING PIVOTS (p. 152); ADDING INFO (p. 183); GIVING INFO (p. 183).

☐ GHOST RECONSTRUCTION

Students carefully study a text and then attempt to reconstruct it. They compare their reconstruction with the original and note any differences. They then write a parallel text.

Language any
Level elementary and above
Time 20 minutes–1 hour, depending on the text

Procedure

1 Distribute a text to your students which is a good model of a text type they will need to produce (e.g. a memo containing a request or a fax confirming some information). Give the students time to understand the text, letting them use dictionaries where necessary. Ask gist and detail questions about the text and focus students' attention on any important linguistic features. Get students to review in their mind what the text is about, either by annotating the text itself with its underlying plan (e.g. paragraph 1 = thanks for fax, paragraph 2 = information about stock levels, etc.) or by discussing the content in pairs.

2 Ask students to turn over the text so they can no longer see it, before asking them to reconstruct it. Students should attempt to make their reconstruction of the text as similar to the original as possible, making no changes or seeming 'improvements'.

3 When everyone has finished, get students to compare their reconstruction with the original, noting any differences. (Pairs can exchange texts to check that all differences have been noticed.) It is a good idea to get pairs to discuss how their own version differed from the original before discussing this as a class. Bear in mind the importance of consistent use of vocabulary and the frequency and appropriacy of formulaic expressions, and give students feedback on the 'correctness' or appropriacy of any differences which they consider valid.

4 Finally, ask students to cover up the original and reconstructed versions of the text and write a similar text containing different information.

5 When students have finished writing, get them to check carefully that

they have used key expressions appropriately and that they have organised their points as clearly as in the original, model text.

6 As a follow-up, give out texts to be studied alone for homework or ask students to follow up with their own selection of texts. Encourage students to focus on any important features of the text themselves by thinking through the answers to simple questions such as the following:
  • Who's it to?
  • Who's it from?
  • Why was this written?
  • What response does the writer want?
  • Is there a deadline?

Variation

Explain the background to a situation to the class. Then ask students to write a text before looking at a model. Students compare their version with the model after they've finished writing to see if there are any significant differences.

□ CUT-UP TEXTS

This fun procedure allows you to recycle language previously encountered in class and at the same time make students aware of how language is organised within a text.

Language any
Level elementary and above
Time 20 minutes

Preparation

Take any text which has already been used in class and cut up the text either line-by-line, sentence-by-sentence or paragraph-by-paragraph. (If you include salutations and other routine features, such as the date and reference number on a letter or fax, you can encourage students to become more aware of typical layout and conventions used.) Make several sets of the cut-up text for pairs or small groups of students.

Procedure

Put sets of 'pieces' on tables or the floor and invite students to piece together the text. If you are using a taped conversation you can play the tape when students are having difficulty; if you are using a written text (e.g. a fax) copies of the complete text can be stuck up on the wall for students to consult. Committing details to short-term memory, as is necessary if listening or reading in preparation for the sorting of text, and physically manipulating the pieces of paper will help students to focus on key details.

As you will see from studying the following procedures in other sections – all based on the same idea – this basic procedure can be adapted in various ways to suit your objectives: ASKING ABOUT PEOPLE'S JOBS (p. 52); FLOOR CARDS (p. 79); OBJECTIVES REVIEW (p. 94); MESSAGE PUZZLES (p. 249); JUMBLED PHRASES (p. 250); FLOOR WORD JIGSAW DICTATION (p. 275).

☐ FOCUSED GAPFILLS

Either you or your students make gapfill exercises based on students' typical errors or areas of difficulty.

Language selected by you or the student(s)
Level elementary and above
Time 10 minutes

Preparation

Get model texts from students or write these yourself, taking the students' particular work needs into account. Having made a copy of the complete text, select an item for focus (e.g. use of definite and indefinite article or past tenses) and blank out any words or phrases in the text, as appropriate, substituting a line for each blank.

Note that it is better if this is done on a wordprocessor so that blanks can all be of equal length (e.g. 20 spaces). Using a wordprocessor will also allow you to add a number of 'unnecessary' blanks, which is especially useful for testing students' awareness of when the definite and indefinite articles should be used.

Procedure

Ask students to complete the blanks. Then get them to compare their answers with the original text. Finally, discuss reasons for errors.

Variation 1

Encourage students to make their own gapfills after doing homework on a wordprocessor. (A 'Find and replace' function will make this a fast procedure if students replace specific words with 20-space lines.) When students have got your corrections they simply gap any words or phrases which they got wrong, substituting a line for each missed word. Carefully filing the original, the gapped and the fully corrected versions together will provide a useful reference and self-testing task later in the course if gaps are always filled in in light pencil.

Variation 2

Instead of making gapfills in which the gaps need to be filled by individual words or short phrases, prepare worksheets of texts with whole lines of text missing. The lines of text can be sentences of any kind. (In a dialogue, for example, the lines may be simple comments such as, *Oh, I see.*) If you wish, make a separate list of sentences which students will need to 'slot' into the text at the correct point. You can also include a few additional incorrect lines of text to make the exercise more challenging. Selecting appropriate lines for each gap can help students to become aware of how specific phrases are used in real-life conversations or texts.

The following procedures will also help you to raise students' awareness of linguistic and cultural details which appear to be going unnoticed: DEEP-ENDING (p. 78); MODEL-MENTORING (p. 101); MODEL-MENTORED DIALOGUES (p. 103); COMMUNITY LANGUAGE LEARNING (p. 104); SPOTLIT ROLE-PLAY (p. 313); MIMED ARRIVAL (p. 168); MONDAY MORNING CHATS (p. 168).

Other procedures are listed under 'awareness-raising' in the Index. These will help you to raise students' awareness of language features generally and students' own language use. See also the following Index entries if you want to raise students' awareness of any of these specific areas: conventions used in letters, phone calls, etc.; cultural differences; discourse; grammar; interjections and non-verbal language; planning or organisation of points; pronunciation. See the Glossary (pp. 338–346) for clarification of terms if necessary.

4.7 Ongoing adjustment of the needs analysis

Although the process of needs analysis should be started before a course begins, it should certainly also continue throughout a course if students' needs are to be identified correctly and satisfactorily filled. A great deal of this ongoing adjustment of the initial needs analysis can be done at or after the beginning of a course by the teacher alone.

Try the following so as to refine the initial needs analysis:

- Use specific needs analysis procedures, such as OBJECTIVES REVIEW (p. 94), EXPERIENCE EXCHANGE (p. 73), ANECDOTE ACCESS (p. 75) and DEEP-ENDING (p. 78).
- Ask students about their real-life use of English on a day-to-day basis.
- Ask students' opinions before telling them about things. Even 'standard' conventions (e.g. in letter-writing) may not be considered standard in the students' company. Find out what happens in the students' 'real world'.

- Get parameters for language work from students. See STARTER PIX (p. 79), MODEL-MENTORING (p. 101) and MODEL-MENTORED DIALOGUES (p. 103) for suggested procedures.
- Ask students to bring in brochures and other literature on their company or industry.
- Get copies of real written work (e.g. e-mails, reports, faxes), and use them in lessons.
- Edit students' reports, e-mails, faxes, etc. whenever possible.
- Encourage students to bring language problems to class. These can then form the basis for classwork (e.g. on developing reading skills or giving presentations).
- Talk to students in their breaks.

Trying out these suggestions will not only make you more aware of your students' real needs, it will also increase your awareness of your students' working environment. An enhanced perception of your students' perspective – of their 'real world' – is likely to mean you develop better rapport with students which is, of course, a useful spin-off.

When developing an awareness of your students' working environment, stay open-minded about 'how things are done' in the business world. While there are often standardised ways of doing things, there is also a lot of variety. The more up-to-date you are on modern business practices in general, on common approaches used within a particular corporation or speciality (e.g. computing), and on your students' practices in particular, the more accurate your final needs analysis is likely to be.

5 Developing students' skills

5.1 Tips for success

Developing students' skills in the Business English classroom is most effective if very specific areas of weakness are identified, e.g. dealing with the question and answer session after giving a presentation. If specific areas of weakness are identified in terms of performance skills (i.e. in terms of specific language use in work contexts), students' on-the-job performance is likely to show a marked improvement. Generalised notions of 'speaking skills', 'listening skills', etc. are usually *too* general in the Business English context, unless of course managers specifically request that work be done on these areas. (In case you do have to do this, lists of useful procedures are given in the Index under 'speaking skills', 'listening skills', etc.). When developing students' *specific* skills for performance areas, as you will need to do most of the time in the Business English classroom, note the following:

- Students' ability to achieve a task (e.g. give a presentation) is ultimately more important than more generalised notions of accuracy or fluency, although these are vital too in certain situations (as explained on pp. 106–107). Appropriacy is a more useful concept than accuracy for the Business English classroom because it can relate to both grammatical accuracy and lexis, which also needs to be appropriate for a given business situation.
- Decontextualised practice, although sometimes necessary, must always be linked to more contextualised practice if it is to be perceived as useful. If, for practical reasons (e.g. lack of materials) you sometimes have to decontextualise language practice, tell students how it relates to performance areas and follow up with contextualised practice immediately afterwards. In this way, students will constantly be aware of the reasons for language work in class.
- Using authentic materials or real-life situations will help you to make practice in class relevant to real life, especially if materials are sourced from the students.
- Ongoing assessment is as important as end-of-term tests because of the difficulty of writing useful and helpful formal tests and because of the need for ongoing reporting. See 7.2, 7.3 and 7.4 for some ideas of test formats.

Listing performance areas at the beginning of a course (as on p. 29) will help you to keep track of what you have covered and what still needs work. However, don't expect perfect performance before moving on to the next performance area! Ongoing recycling is more effective and more motivating for students. Sudden improvements or backsliding seem common in the Business English classroom; this is not only because of the nature of learning but also because of students' varying confidence levels, erratic attendance and because of the possibility that students might be getting practice opportunities outside class, in the workplace. Finally check performance areas off your list when both you and your students feel enough work has been done on that particular area. Sometimes, of course, you can surprise your students with review spots later on in the course so as to keep them on the ball!

5.2 Talking to clients

Only some Business English students will need to deal directly with clients as part of their normal job. However, students should all be capable of introducing themselves and their company in case they ever meet a potential client (e.g. on a plane, at a bar, at a conference). In addition, students should all be able to put clients at ease, if necessary, so as to avoid embarrassment and 'keep a conversation going'. The procedures in this section may therefore be useful to most students. Those which focus on sales techniques will, obviously, be of most interest to those students who are in direct contact with clients as part of their job.

☐ SELF-INTRODUCTIONS

After making notes, students mill – as at a conference welcome party – and introduce themselves.

Language self-introductions
Level beginner and above
Time 5–10 minutes

Procedure

Elicit what students say about themselves when first introducing themselves to others. (With low-level students, simply model a teacher-to-student dialogue, then do open- and closed-pair practice.) Make notes on the board. For example:

> name – job/position – company/industry – reason for participation in the conference

Then, elicit a self-introduction, using these notes. For example:

> Hi, I'm ... from ... . I work in the ... division.
> I'm here to check out the new technology. I don't think we've met ... .

Next, give students an opportunity to prepare a suitable text for themselves. Check each student's dialogue before encouraging private or paired practice. Then after role-playing your own self-introduction with a student, get students to give similar public performances, using appropriate body language (e.g. shaking hands and smiling) and first meeting phrases (e.g. *How do you do? Nice to meet you*), as appropriate. Finally, ask everyone to stand up and introduce themselves to other people in the class. Every few minutes, ask students to change partners. Get students to continue their conversations for as long as possible. Interrupt as often as necessary to encourage better use of intonation or voice range or to give other feedback.

☐ CULTURAL MIMING

Students mime a conversation with a visitor, all the time focusing on making their body language appropriate.

Language all non-verbal
Level lower-intermediate and above
Time 10 minutes

Procedure

Explain to students that they are going to have a conversation with a client – without saying a word. Explain or elicit the reasons for doing this, perhaps by role-playing a conversation with a student in which you speak English, using body language which is acceptable in the students' culture but strange to Westerners' eyes. Continue by role-playing silent conversations, in other words miming, with volunteer students. After each mini-performance, get students to rate other students' performance; you can add to the fun by insisting that they rate your performance too! Help them to do this by repeatedly asking key questions: *Did we look friendly? Did we look business-like? Do you think we're good at our job? Did we make a good impression? Did we look strange?* (If students are unused to body language associated with English speakers, perhaps the answer to this last question will mistakenly be *Yes!* You might need to reassure students about what looks normal in English.) When everyone has the idea, get students to work in groups of three – two students mime, then the third student 'rates' the performance of the other two students. Encourage comments and protestations from students before continuing with some spoken role-play practice.

☐ COMPANY PRESENTATION

Using cue-cards as a basis, students prepare and practise a brief description of their company. All students – even if not in sales – should be capable of doing this because many occasions might arise where it might be necessary.

Language any
Level elementary and above
Time 10 minutes–1 hour

Preparation

Prepare cue cards, either using your own cues or those suggested on pp. 130–131. When selecting cues consider the statements which might result and how useful they might be for your particular students. Include several blank cards for statements students might later suggest are useful.

Procedure

1 To help students imagine the situation in which they might use the language you are going to practise, simply ask the students: *What would a potential client want to know about your company?* Encourage students to visualise a real-life situation by saying: *Imagine you are talking to someone at the airport while waiting for your plane.* Then, after agreeing on some possible subject areas (e.g. products, turnover), elicit sentences on the same areas (e.g. *We manufacture a wide range of low-priced household appliances* or *Our annual turnover is 4 billion DM*). Make corrections or improvements where necessary. Next, show students the cue cards you have prepared and ask students to prepare complete sentences for each card in pairs, using the cues. While they are doing this, add any statements you elicited which you had not anticipated, reducing them to cues on the blank cards.

2 Check students know an appropriate and correct statement for each cue card and drill each one as much as you feel appropriate, focusing on both accuracy and pronunciation. Then get the students to practise the sentences in a logical order, such as the one suggested on pp. 130–131. A particularly effective way of practising the sentences is to use cues on numbered cards, with students standing in a circle. Cards can be redistributed several times and students can say their

129

'line' when their number comes up. Call out the numbers so as to spur students on! More advanced students will obviously need much less guidance and repetition than lower-level students, unless they are making a lot of grammatical errors.

3 Put students in small groups and ask them to prepare and deliver mini-presentations on their company (using several or all the sentences they have practised). Allow about five minutes for preparation and two minutes for each presentation.

Variation

Elicit questions, instead of statements, for each cue card and ask students to practise them. Note that you can again use numbers to prompt questions and appropriate answers from students if you have chosen to number the cards. After students have practised short answers for each question and adapted their answers according to their own work situation, get them to role-play a conversation with a stranger – a potential client – who asks about the students' company. Encourage individuals to admit ignorance, if indeed this is the case, and to add other questions or comments which might be made in a real-life conversation. Obvious examples of additional comments to teach students would be: *Let me give you my business card, I could fax you some more details on that if you like, I'll get someone to send you a brochure.* During the feedback session after the role-played conversations it might be amusing and useful for students to consider who in the class might best represent the company in this type of situation.

Sample cues, text and questions for COMPANY PRESENTATION

1	people employ	We employ 2,500 people.
2	head office	Our head office is in Nagoya.
3	branches	We have branches in Osaka, Taipei, Singapore and Jakarta.
4	factories	We have two main factories: one in Osaka, the other in Taipei.
5	main product	Our main product is the TZ400 microwave oven.
6	other products	We also manufacture other types of oven and a range of food mixers.
7	turnover	Our turnover last year was around 26 million yen.

8	market products	We market our products all over Asia, but mostly in Japan.
9	president	Our president is Takiyuki Yamamoto.
10	join company	I joined the company in 1999.
11	department	I work in the Sales Department.
12	other training	Apart from English training, I'm also doing a Sales Techniques course.

1	How many people does your company employ?
2	Where's your head office?
3	Do you have any branches?
4	Where are your factories located?
5	What's your main product?
6	What other products do you manufacture?
7	What's your annual turnover?
8	Where do you market your products?
9	Who is your president?
10	When did you personally join the company?
11	Which department do you work in?
12	Are you doing any other training at the moment, apart from English?

☐ CLIENT QUESTIONS

Students think of a particular product or service (preferably one offered by their own company) and answer questions from other students, who imagine that they are clients. This activity gives good practice for both questioners and information-givers and is surprisingly engaging for students.

Language questions and answers about products or services
Level intermediate and above
Time 15 minutes

Procedure

In order to set the scene for this activity tell students that you are thinking about a particular business (e.g. a floristry business, which you should explain, if necessary). Then tell students to ask you questions to find out as much about the products and services of this business as possible. Next, ask students to do the same in pairs, one person thinking about a specific company, the other asking questions. Encourage students to answer questions on their own company's products or services and encourage students who are asking questions to behave like difficult clients! Finally, get students to role-play a conversation in which a potential customer is making enquiries.

Variation

Get students to role-play conversations in which they have to reassure clients. After students have asked about each other's products or services get them to prepare some especially difficult questions for their partners. Before getting students to role-play the conversations, elicit or give them the language that they might need when they respond. Some language you could encourage students to use might include the following:

> Well, we always, ...
> I'll make sure you get ...
> If ever that were a problem, we would ...
> Don't forget, there's a ...

For other procedures which you can use to help your students practise language for this area, see the Index entry for 'clients, talking to'.

5.3 Snail mail and formal faxes

Letters – now fondly known as 'snail mail' – are still used, although in most countries they are fast being replaced by faxes or e-mails, which, if formal, are often simply the same text faxed or e-mailed! However, real letters are likely to survive for some time to come for various reasons:

- They seem particularly appropriate for formal introductions to companies, confirmation of contracts and thank you messages, possibly because they can seem appropriately formal, caring or impressive (if printed on good paper).
- They can be a useful back-up to important e-mailed or faxed messages.

- They can be used to send bulky material, such as brochures or samples.
- They can be used when there are problems with the technology required for faxes and e-mail.
- They can be sent to or from companies which have limited technology.

Letters are, of course, only used to communicate with people in other companies, not in one's own company, so they are likely to be more consistently formal than other types of correspondence. Their relative slowness, compared to faxes and e-mails, adds to this sense of formality, perhaps because everyone is aware that there is time to express things more carefully. It is very easy for students to achieve the right level of formality, though, because many formulaic expressions (e.g. *I look forward to meeting you next week*) have become standard in letters. Students will benefit enormously if they learn these formulaic expressions because as well as helping with their letter-writing, these same expressions can usually be used in other types of correspondence too. Varying the style so as to make letters to long-term contacts more friendly is, of course, relatively easy to do.

Conventions and layout for letters vary to some extent but the following are widely accepted:

- Block layout (i.e. no indented paragraphs) with open punctuation (no commas, etc. in addresses) is the most common layout used nowadays worldwide. See p. 135 and p. 136 for sample letters which use these formats.
- Initials must always be included with the surname above the address of the recipient. In other words, *Mr Jennings, Sales Manager, Dynaco Ltd, ...* is not acceptable; you have to write *Mr K Jennings, Sales Manager, Dynaco Ltd, ...* .
- Letters beginning *Dear Mr Jennings* (i.e. using a name in the salutation) end *Yours sincerely* (or even *Sincerely yours* or *Yours truly* in the US). Letters beginning *Dear Sirs* or *Dear Sir/Madam* (i.e. letters to companies or people whose name we don't know) end *Yours faithfully*. *Gentlemen:* is an exclusively American beginning (and very sexist) so not recommended for international communication.

For notes on less formal faxes, which are more common in business, see p. 241.

Common layout for letters

Our ref	Company logo
Your ref	
	Company address
Name of addressee, including initials	
Position	Tel, fax and e-mail nos.
Company's name and address	
	Date (e.g. May 2, 2000)

Dear Mr/Ms X (no initials)

Subject line (e.g. Order No. PQ733)

Introductory paragraph, referring to last communication or introducing self or company and introducing reason for writing

Main body of letter, perhaps divided into several paragraphs

Polite ending (e.g. I look forward to hearing from you soon.)

Yours sincerely (if you have the name of the addressee)

Signature

Full name typed out
Position

Copies to ... (e.g. cc P Jameson)

Enc (if there are any enclosures)

A typical letter

✿ SPICE MARKETING LTD

49 Galle Road
Colombo 3
Sri Lanka
Tel: 00471 885 639
Fax: 00471 885 638

Ms P Pereira
24 Jurong Park Road East
Singapore 2084

January 24, 2000

Dear Ms Pereira,

Thank you for your letter of January 15, enquiring about our products. I am writing to give you the information you requested.

We were initially established in 1877, so have many years of experience of collecting and storing spices. This ensures they reach your kitchen in the best possible condition. Our workforce has expanded from just three staff in 1877 to 1,237 in 2000. The last few decades have seen many organisational changes as a result of technological advances and we are now able to offer the best possible service for spice users worldwide.

As you will see from the enclosed brochure, we offer a very wide range of products and services. Our prices are also competitive and our delivery procedures state-of-the-art, which guarantees that our spices reach you in the best possible condition. I also enclose a copy of our price list for your reference.

Please do not hesitate to contact me if you would like any further information. I can be contacted on the above number on extension 373. I would be pleased to arrange a tasting party for your office, at your convenience.

I look forward to hearing from you soon with your first order.

Yours sincerely,

PETER JONES
South Asia Sales Representative

Enc

© Cambridge University Press

135

Another typical letter (which could also be faxed)

CLEARVIEW WINDOWS LTD
49 Southampton Street
Watford, Herts, WD7 4PQ
Tel: 01923 679356
Fax: 01923 679357

Mr J Smithson
21 Cranfield Road
Caversham Park Village
Reading
Berks RG4 6RZ

June 20, 2002

Dear Mr Smithson,

Thank you for your letter of June 12, informing us of the problems you have experienced with our Clearview double-glazed windows. We sincerely regret that these windows have not been to your satisfaction and were, in fact, surprised to hear this since we receive so many letters from satisfied customers who all report improved protection from draughts and lower electricity bills.

We shall send our representative, Mr Philip Green, to visit you and discuss this problem further. Mr Green will also be able to check the windows which do not completely insulate against draughts. There may be some simple explanation for this.

We would be grateful if you could telephone this office at your earliest convenience to arrange a suitable time for Mr Green to visit.

In the meantime, we would like to assure you that we will do all that we can to ensure your satisfaction with our products.

Yours sincerely,

J MORRISON
Customer Service Manager

☐ SKELETAL CONVENTIONS

This procedure focuses students' attention on a typical layout for letters and on important conventions used. See p. 134 for the answers!

Language minimal
Level intermediate and above
Time 5 minutes

Procedure

Give students a copy of the diagram on p. 138 or photocopy this onto an OHT. (Note that this diagram is simply the one on p. 134 without the text.) Tell students that the boxes represent different parts of a letter, and get them to decide what goes in each box (recipient's name, position, company name, date, introductory reference to previous communication, body of letter, polite ending, *Enc* if there are enclosures, etc.). Encourage students to ask questions about the different elements or conventions. Also encourage them to express surprise – because it is important that they realise that conventions for writing letters in English may be quite different from those for letters written in their own language.

Variation

If you think that your students will have no idea what goes in the boxes, give them a model letter before asking them to fill in the boxes on the worksheet. The model letter will help students to decide what goes into most of the boxes.

☐ SETTING LETTERS

Put students in at the deep end by asking them to write a letter or fax for a particular situation.

Language any
Level ideal for classes whose real level (for letter- or fax-writing) you don't know
Time 35 minutes

Procedure

Describe a situation to students in a lot of detail, drawing cartoons of characters on the board if you can or showing previous correspondence, as appropriate. Then, setting a time limit (e.g. 30 minutes), ask students to write a letter or fax to deal with the situation. Explain that you want to find out how much the students can already do before focusing on areas to improve. Reassure students that it's OK if they make a lot of mistakes, or even if they make no mistakes at all.

An example situation: Mr H Watanabe ordered 25 Regal Red executive chairs from President Furniture Ltd but they are currently out of stock. The chairs will not be available until the end of the month. Students imagine that they work in Sales at President Furniture and write to Mr Watanabe.

Worksheet for SKELETAL CONVENTIONS

a
b

c

d

e

f

g

h

i

j

k

l

m

n

o

p

q

r

s

t

© Cambridge University Press

☐ SENTENCE LOCATION

Students are made more aware of discourse patterns common to letters by simply deciding whether sentences would typically occur at the beginning, middle or end of a letter or fax.

Language preselected sentences common in letters or faxes
Level intermediate and above
Time 30 minutes

Preparation

Type out a list of sentences which are used in the type of letters or faxes common in your students' line of business. (This can be a general list if you have a mixed group of students or if you want to give a general introduction to the modern style used in letters.) Make sure the sentences are all mixed up. Alternatively, copy the general list given below.

Procedure

Ask students to decide where each sentence would typically occur in a letter or fax – beginning, middle or end? When going over the answers, elicit or explain the reasons behind the positioning of certain phrases and allow for certain variations. For example, the third sentence in the list below would usually be found in the 'middle' of a letter because most writers would finish the letter with a polite ending, such as *I look forward to hearing from you soon* and possibly even more text. However, if a writer chooses not to use a polite ending, the sentence would appear at the end of the letter.

Some possible phrases: (B = beginning, M = middle, E = end)

B	Thank you for your letter of October 7, 2001. (A very typical beginning.)
E	Many thanks in advance. (Because you've made a request earlier in the letter.)
M	I would be grateful if you could look into this problem as soon as possible.
B	Further to our recent telephone conversation, I am writing to confirm details of your forthcoming factory tour. (Another common beginning.)
B	Many thanks for your letter of July 7, requesting more details on our pricing structure.
M	We regret to inform you that we are unable to supply the chairs you ordered because this model is temporarily out of stock. (You wouldn't usually **start** with bad news.)
E	I look forward to hearing from you soon. (A typical ending.)
E	We apologise for any inconvenience caused. (A typical ending in letters containing bad news.)
M	Might I suggest you call my secretary to arrange an appointment?
M	I would appreciate it if you could fill in the attached form and return it to me by November 2.

After going over the answers, ask students to write a letter or fax, using or adapting at least three of the expressions.

☐ SPOT THE ERROR

Students find deliberate errors in a 'model' letter. This procedure is useful for reinforcing what you have already taught students about layout and conventions used in modern letters.

Language letters
Level intermediate and above
Time 5 minutes

Preparation

Copy out or write a model letter, then 'add' ten mistakes. Examples of possible mistakes you can include are as follows: wrong ending (e.g. *Yours faithfully* when the letter has been addressed to a specific person; *Dear Bradburn*, omitting *Mr*; mistakes in key set phrases, such as *I look forward to hear from you*). This activity is especially effective if you include mistakes students have been making.

Procedure

Simply get students to spot the mistakes in the letter, after saying how many mistakes there are. Encourage students to look back at any notes they made in previous lessons or to look at other model letters in their coursebook if they can't find the mistakes.

Variation 1

Add mistakes to pairs of letters (or faxes), each 'pair' consisting of a letter and a letter which answers it. It's useful to make the first letter of each pair contain mistakes relating to misused conventions and the other letter contain mistakes which relate to inaccurate information. As before, students have to find the mistakes.

Variation 2

If you prefer, make 'mistakes' more sophisticated. Examples of 'mistakes' you could use include the following:

- Wrong layout (see p. 134)
- Bad or unclear organisation of information or ideas – so that misunderstandings or negative reactions are likely from the reader
- Old-fashioned style or spelling mistakes
- Inappropriate selection of key vocabulary

- Inappropriate use of common expressions (e.g. *I look forward to hearing from you soon* when the reader is not required to reply)
- Sentences which are too long or inappropriate in style (too formal/ informal)
- Elements which are likely to cause offence because of cross-cultural differences (e.g. handwriting letters in red ink, which is offensive in some cultures because it is associated with 'being in the red')
- Wrong or inappropriate use of materials (e.g. using scented, personal stationery instead of headed notepaper)

Since it is difficult to 'quantify' some of the above mistakes sometimes you will simply need to ask students to improve their letters and give them an indication of the items to improve.

□ SCRAMBLED LETTERS

This is a good activity for focusing students' attention on planning and appropriacy in letter-writing, taking into account the reader's reaction and needs.

Language any
Level upper-intermediate and above
Time 40 minutes

Preparation

Using a well-written letter as a starting point (e.g. the one on p. 135), prepare a letter similar to that on the following page. Note that as well as mixing up the paragraphs in the original letter, you also need to change the style and add lots of unnecessary, irrelevant comments. If these are amusing, all the better!

Procedure

Give students the scrambled letter and get them to put the different sentences or elements in order. Then ask them if anything can be improved; students can consider this in pairs. In groups, students then rewrite the letter on an OHT (if available). Finally, one individual from each group uses the OHP to present their version of the letter to the rest of the group. Other students should be encouraged to comment or ask questions. Give the students feedback before providing them with a model answer. (See 4.5 for guidance on giving feedback.)

Variation 1

Ask students to unscramble a letter which is well-written if you simply want to focus attention on planning.

Variation 2

Simply ask students to rewrite a bad letter in which the elements have not been mixed up if your objective is simply to focus students' attention on improving certain elements. Limiting the number of elements to be improved will help to focus students' attention.

Variation 3

Get students to evaluate each other's or their own rewritten letters (or faxes), using an evaluation worksheet, such as the one on p. 260. Ask them to consider the letters from the point of view of the reader and to focus on both accuracy and style. Use students' feedback or comments about general difficulties to inspire follow-up work!

A letter to unscramble and improve for SCRAMBLED LETTERS

Very best wishes for good eating and a satisfying 2000!

Dear Spice-Eater,

I, personally, am responsible for dealing with enquiries from new customers. I also handle most of our UK and US accounts so I will be your contact person as you place your orders over the coming months.

SPICE MARKETING LTD

I enclose a brochure and price list for your information. As you will see, we offer a very wide range of services, catering to both wholesale and retail customers. Our brochure is also well-produced so will make an attractive addition to your coffee table.

I look forward to hearing from you soon with your first order for our excellent and tasty Sri Lankan spices. Spice up your life with us! You'll never regret it.

Further to your recent enquiry, I am writing to give you some information on my company. I hope this information will inspire you to order our spices and incorporate them into your daily cooking.

We were initially established in 1877, so have years of experience of collecting and storing spices so that they reach your kitchen in the best possible condition. At first, we only exported cinnamon because other spices proved to be difficult to store. We soon expanded to include cardamom, coriander and cumin when our researchers discovered the new dry-storage method, still used today. Our workforce has expanded from just three staff in 1877 to 1,237 in 2000. There have been many happy weddings between staff members over the years. The last few decades have seen many organisational changes as a result of technological advances and we are now able to offer the best possible service for spice users worldwide.

Yours faithfully,

© Cambridge University Press

A worksheet for the procedure SENTENCED OR NOT?

BUSINESS ENGLISH THINK SPOT

Sentenced or not?

Are the following complete sentences or not?

Tick the ones which are complete.

1   I am writing in response to your advertisement in today's *Observer* to apply for the post of Accounts Clerk.

2   I am writing in response to your advertisement in today's *Observer*.

3   As advertised in the *Daily* on 21 October.

4   With reference to your advertisement which appeared in the *Daily News*.

5   I am writing to apply for the post of Network Administrator, as advertised in the *Daily* on 21 October.

6   In response to your advertisement in today's *Evening Post* for the position of Sales Manager.

7   I am writing in response to your advertisement in today's *Evening Post* for the position of Sales Manager.

8   After graduating, I followed a professional training course in accounting.

9   After graduating.

10   As you will see from the attached CV.

11   As I have considerable experience in this area.

12   I have considerable experience in this area.

13   Although I enjoy my present job.

14   I enjoy my present job.

15   I enjoy my present job but am looking for new challenges.

16   If you need any further information.

17   Please do not hesitate to contact me.

18   Please do not hesitate to contact me if you need any further information.

19   To arrange a convenient time for interview.

20   I look forward to hearing from you soon.

Answers:

The following are complete sentences:
1, 2, 5, 7, 8, 12, 14, 15, 17, 18, 20

© Cambridge University Press

143

☐ SENTENCED OR NOT?

Students consider whether or not 'sentences' are complete. They then write a letter of application, adapting phrases from the initial exercise and adding information as necessary. This procedure is especially good for students who have 'picked up' English but not done much formal study.

Language formulaic phrases for letters of application
Level intermediate and above
Time 30 minutes

Procedure

Briefly elicit from students ideas on what might be included in a letter of application. Students then do the worksheet on p. 143. (As well as helping students to use formulaic phrases in complete sentences appropriately, this exercise will also expose students to up-to-date phrases for letters of application.) Next, get students to write a letter of application, using as many of the phrases in the worksheet as possible. Encourage them to attach an appropriate CV as well. If done for homework, this letter can refer to a specific job advertisement.

☐ PLAN DETECTION

This is a good procedure for students who do not organise information well or who do not appear to have understood standard planning principles which are used for letters or faxes written in English.

Language any
Level intermediate and above
Time 10–15 minutes

Procedure

Show students various letters or faxes and get them to work out what the plan is behind each one. Help them to annotate the letters with notes such as intro/reference to previous contact, polite ending and reminder, background info, etc.

Variation 1

On strips of paper, prepare notes (such as those above) which go with different sections of letters. Students have to decide which letter and which section of that letter each note refers to. (Providing students with notes on underlying plans will, of course, make their task slightly easier.)

Variation 2

Students sequence unlabelled paragraphs, then explain why they have sequenced them in that way. Doing this forces students to explain the basic plan which underlies the text.

For other procedures which you can use to help your students practise language for this area, see the Index entry for 'letters'.

5.4 Telephoning

Non-native English speakers need to be able to use the telephone effectively if they are to survive in an international office environment. Since many students suffer from nerves when using the telephone, the first aim of skills practice must be to simply help students to overcome their fear. A second focus is helping students to understand how telephones are typically used in British or American corporations because telephone etiquette can be very different in different parts of the world. It may, for example, be normal for anybody to pick up the phone or for very direct, or indirect, forms of speech to be used in the students' home country. Students may also find it difficult to have a casual chat over the phone before getting down to business. Thirdly and equally importantly, we need to help students to improve their pronunciation and audible non-verbal language; these aspects of communication obviously become so much more important on the telephone because of the absence of the visual image which is present in any face-to-face conversation.

Also note the following when preparing to practise telephone skills with students:

- In companies the telephone is usually answered in one of the following ways:

  - *Good morning/afternoon! Mitsubishi Electric* (= company name).
  - *Hello, Sales Department* (= name of department).
  - *Moore* (= name of manager in own office).

- There are many ways of finishing telephone conversations, for example:

  - *Bye.*
  - *Goodbye.*
  - *OK, 'bye.*
  - *I'll get back to you later on.*
  - *See you on Thursday, then ...*
  - *OK, thank you for calling. I'll make sure you get a new price list immediately. 'Bye.*

145

☐ IMPROMPTU CALLS

Students get an opportunity to show what they can do in fun, impromptu phone calls. This is a good way of finding out how proficient and confident students already are with telephone language.

Language any, entirely determined by students
Level elementary and above
Time 5–10 minutes

Procedure

1 While another activity is drawing to a close, suddenly – without warning – start making the noise of a telephone ringing. The more realistic your telephone sounds, the better! While you are making these ringing sounds, look surprised that nobody has answered yet. If students still fail to respond, say, *Could someone answer the phone?*, while still keeping the ringing sounds going! As soon as a student replies, ask the class *Who's calling?*, so as to get a second volunteer. Leave these two students to improvise a telephone conversation, only looking at them enquiringly if they hesitate. The only intervention or correction necessary might be to say, *OK, now imagine you're at work* if students have improvised a call which is too general.
2 Continue with three or four calls performed in open pairs (see Glossary). Note that students will self-select – there's no need to decide who's going to speak in advance. (For the first call you can be the caller yourself, if you prefer, but leaving it up to the students is much more fun for the whole class, and students usually rise to the challenge!)
3 Debrief students, using the approach suggested in 4.5. Then lead into further role-played telephone practice (using plenty of closed-pair practice to allow students to get used to any language you introduce), grading the practice in accordance with what students already seem to be capable of. (See the other procedures suggested in this section for ideas).

☐ ANSWERING MACHINES

Students practise recording messages for answering machines or voice mail.

Language any
Level elementary and above
Time 5–10 minutes

Preparation

Record a simple message which callers might hear on a company's answering machine when calling out of office hours. A typical message might be as follows:

> Thank you for calling Metallix UK. The office is closed at the moment but you can leave a message after the beep if you wish. Otherwise, please call back between 9 a.m. and 5 p.m. Monday to Friday. You can record your message after the beep. (BEEP!)

Procedure

1 Play your simple recorded message to the class and ask students when they might hear this. Next, elicit possible responses to the message. If students have no idea what an appropriate response would be or if their suggested responses are full of errors or inappropriate language, give them the following message:

> This is Jane Browning from Pipeline. I urgently need to speak to Ben Freeman. Could you ask him to call me? The number's 423706. I'll be in my office on Monday from 8.00 a.m.

You could perform this message, then write it up on the board (or put it on an OHT in advance, if you have a projector in class) so that it is possible for students to analyse and note the type of language used.

2 Ask students to prepare their own message for the same answering machine. After you next play the recorded message to the class, each student should respond with his or her own message. (Note that everyone speaks at the same time!) If you have a language laboratory, get students to record their voices so that they can listen to how they sound. Repeat the exercise in pairs so that partners can listen to each other and give feedback.

□ PHONE FORMULAE

Students practise phrases which are commonly used on the telephone.

Language routine phrases commonly used on the telephone
Level elementary and above
Time 10 minutes

Preparation

Copy each phrase listed below onto a separate slip of paper or prepare a handout which includes them.

Hello? Purchasing.
Tom Brown here.
Speaking.
Could you hold the line, please?
Just a moment, please.
I'll just put you through.
I'll see if I can find him/her.
I think he/she may have already left.
It's a very bad line. Do you think you could call again?
I'm afraid I can't transfer you. You need to dial another number.
  Have you got a pen?
I'll give you his/her extension.
I'm afraid we got cut off.
The line's busy at the moment.
I'm not getting any answer at the moment.
I'm afraid he/she's not at his/her desk at the moment.
I'm afraid he/she's away on business.
I'm afraid he/she's in a meeting.
Would you like to try again later?
Would you like to leave a message?
Can I give him/her a message?
Sorry I can't help.
It's my pleasure.

Procedure

Give students the slips of paper or the handout. Then ask students to decide when and why each phrase is used in a telephone conversation. Next, ask students to select at least seven phrases and include them in role-played telephone conversations. This can easily be turned into a game if pairs score points each time they succeed in incorporating a phrase into a conversation in a realistic way.

Variation 1

Provide a transcript of a telephone conversation from which some of these phrases have been deleted. Students complete the conversation with the phrases.

Variation 2

Provide a transcript of a telephone conversation from which some of these phrases have been deleted but don't indicate to students where the gaps are. Students need to decide how the conversation could be improved in terms of customer care.

□ SURVIVAL STRATEGIES

Some students have great difficulty understanding what is said to them on the phone. This procedure involves getting students to practise phrases which will help them to survive.

Language phrases which help students to survive when in difficulty
Level beginner and above
Time 20 minutes

Procedure

1 Tell students that they are going to make telephone calls which include some detailed information, e.g. sales figures or times of meetings. Encourage them to imagine they are phoning to confirm details of a conference or to discuss the company's performance. Get students to plan what information they are going to give. Make sure each student has listed ten items of information to be included in their telephone call.

2 Ask students if they ever have trouble understanding detailed information on the telephone. Elicit or give them phrases which will help them to survive. With higher level classes this can simply be done on the board or OHP. With lower levels, consider giving students phrases on slips of paper, which they can sort through and discuss one by one, considering when and why they would use each phrase. Some phrases you might use:

> Could you hold on a moment?
> OK, let me just get a pen.
> Could you speak a bit louder? I'm afraid it's a very bad line.
> I'm afraid I didn't quite catch that.
> Sorry, could you repeat that, please?
> Are you saying ... ?
> Could you spell that please?
> Is that ... or ... ?
> Do you really mean 'three zero'?!
> So that's almost a third of total sales! (i.e. paraphrasing the information)
> Let's just run through that again. The first one was ...
> Can we go over that again? That's ...
> So that's ...
> There seem to be a lot of figures involved here. Do you think you could fax me this information, then give me a call again later on? I'm afraid I'm a bit busy at the moment.
> OK, but do you think you could confirm these figures/dates/times by fax?

3 Divide the class into pairs, then get students to role-play telephone conversations. (It's best if students sit back-to-back and don't compare notes until the end of their conversation.) Get everyone to change partners once or twice for extra practice and at all times encourage students to give each other a hard time!

□ TAKING MESSAGES

Students practise noting down and passing messages to other members of the class.

Language any
Level elementary and above
Time 15–20 minutes

Preparation

Copy each line of the conversation below onto separate strips of paper or OHT (which has been cut up). Alternatively, write the lines in the wrong order and label each line with a letter.

> Good morning. Electric Angel Inc.
> Good morning. Could I speak to Ms Geneva, please?
> I'm afraid she's not in the office this afternoon. Can I give her a message?
> Er, yes please. Can you tell her John Marnie rang? Tell her I'll call back later.
> Mr Marnie. OK. Which company are you calling from?
> Jennings Furniture.
> And could you give me your number please?
> Yes, it's 743208.
> 743208. Fine. I'll make sure she gets the message.
> Thanks.
> You're welcome. 'Bye.
> 'Bye.

Procedure

1 Ask students to put the lines of the conversation in the correct order.
2 Having put students in groups of four and allocated each student a letter (A, B, C, D), explain to students the following procedure:

- A calls B, wanting to talk to C.
- A leaves a message because C is out.
- B tells C the message. (*John Marnie rang from Jennings Furniture. He said he'd call back again. If you need his number it's 743208.*)

- C then calls D, asking to speaking to A, but A is out so C leaves a message.
- D tells A the message.
- A then tries to call back C, but C is still out so A leaves another message.

These calls can be represented on the board as follows:

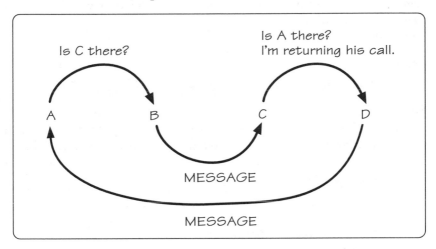

3 Tell students to make telephone calls until they manage to speak to the person they are calling. Encourage them to continue the process for a while before they find the person in! It doesn't matter if students get extremely confused ... that's all part of the fun!

□ BONDING CHATS

Students practise chatting with regular callers before getting down to business.

Language phatic communion (see Glossary)
Level elementary and above
Time 5–10 minutes

Procedure

Tell students that they are going to receive a call from a colleague or client they know well. Elicit possible conversation beginnings and write any key phrases on the board. Insist on good use of sentence stress and intonation (especially wide voice range) when students are saying these phrases. Next get students to role-play mini-chats, making telephone ringing sounds to start. Possible subjects for these mini-chats could be health, the weather, family or current news.

151

☐ EMPOWERING PIVOTS

This procedure provides essential follow-on practice to BONDING CHATS (on p. 151) since students may find that they are caught in long, time-wasting chats which they are unable to draw to a close!

Language empowering phrases for use on the telephone
Level elementary and above
Time 10–15 minutes

Preparation

Copy the chart below onto the board or an OHT.

Procedure

1 Ask students how they will move from the first part of the conversation to the second, i.e. what they will say in Section B.

A Hello and initial friendly chat:
   Oh hello! How are things going your end?

B [   ]

C Main message/information/request from caller:
   I'm afraid I'm having a bit of a problem with the ...
   Is there any chance you could ... You see ...

D [   ]

E End of conversation – goodbyes:
   Thanks a lot. Speak to you again soon.

Provide the phrase *What can I do for you?* if students don't already know it. Similarly, ask students what they can say in Section D if the conversation is going on too long, they have got the message and want to ring off – maybe they have a visitor waiting or an important report to finish. Give them: *Anyway ... I'll ...* .

2 Next, tell students to imagine they are on the telephone talking to a colleague or customer, for example, and tell them they are going to role-play this conversation with a partner. Give them a few moments to make brief notes on the call they are going to make or receive and to note down any phrases which might be useful during the call.

3 Having asked students to find partners, get students to explain their situation to their partner before role-playing the entire telephone conversation. While you are monitoring, elicit or give students further empowering phrases as needed, such as the following:

> Let's just go over that again
> Don't worry, I'll get it off to you today
> I'll need to get back to you on that
> Can I call you back later — I'm a bit busy right now?
> I'm afraid I'll need more information
> Could you fax me your request?

4 Ask students to find new partners before repeating their role-played telephone conversations.

☐ NOISY LISTENING

Students make noises while listening to lengthy monologues within a conversation so that the caller knows that they are still there! This is a fun but useful procedure which gives students an opportunity to practise appropriate English sounds.

Language backchannelling sounds (see Glossary) and phrases for use on the telephone
Level any, even false beginner
Time 5–10 minutes

Procedure

1 Introduce the idea of backchannelling (see Glossary) to students. To do this, ask for a volunteer to talk to you about their work. Ask *How's it going?* to get them talking, then look at them stony-faced and silently while they talk! (Obviously, it's best if you encourage a confident, talkative student to volunteer.) Then emphasise the need for backchannelling when using English on the telephone, simply so as to indicate understanding and continued listening. Next elicit sounds or phrases that can be used in English. Reject any sounds which are peculiar to the students' own language or culture, which would not be familiar or acceptable to a proficient speaker of English. Some sounds and phrases to encourage students to use:

Uhu ...	No.
Oh, I see.	Ah ...
Mmm.	That sounds like a real problem!
Oh, that's interesting ...	That's one good thing at least.
Hmm ...	OK, I've got that.
Yes, well ...	Yes.
OK.	OK, fine.
Yep.	Of course.

2 Drill these 'noises', insisting on good pronunciation. (Students usually enjoy repeatedly practising a two-tone *Uhu*!) Then get students to sit back-to-back to practise using these sounds in pairs. The speaker in each pair can speak about anything connected to his or her work. (Beginners can speak in their own language.) The listener shows continued interest and comprehension with the sounds and phrases practised. As you monitor, focus especially on how appropriately students are using particular sounds or phrases. Stop pairwork if some students are misusing one or more 'noises' and focus their attention on how to use the noises appropriately before letting pairwork continue, saying OK, *carry on. Sorry to interrupt you!*

Note that using this procedure with beginners or very low-level students is good for raising their confidence and helping them to survive the difficult phase of language learning where native or proficient non-native speakers of English don't bother continuing to speak in English because of the poor feedback they are getting. Warn students, however, of the potential dangers involved in over-using this backchannelling; students may sometimes offend people who feel their time is being wasted and misunderstandings which go unnoticed by the more competent speaker may have important consequences.

□ TIME DICTATIONS

Students listen and note down times which are all embedded in longer comments. This activity is good for helping students to practise listening for key information, or it can be useful as a warmer for higher level students.

Language times and naturally pronounced comments
Level elementary and above
Time 10 minutes

Preparation

Make a list of ten times and ten spoken contexts for these times, or use those listed on the opposite page.

Procedure

Dictate the ten times to students, each one in a natural spoken context. Make sure that you speak fast and as naturally as possible, making no effort to slow down as you say the times. Students only write down the times they hear. Repeat the sentences as often as necessary, never slowing down for students!

5.00	I'll see you at five, then.
11.30 a.m.	How about half past eleven in the morning?
12.00	Noon would be fine.
3.25	Can we make it before half past? How about twenty-five past three?
9.00	OK, so that's nine on the dot.
6.15	Well, I usually get back at about quarter past six.
3.50	OK, so I'll call at about ten to four in the morning ...
12.15	I usually finish lunch at about twelve fifteen.
5.30	Is half past five too late?
5.45	Let's make it quarter to six instead.

When going over the answers, write out the full sentence. Then say each sentence again so that students can understand the correct answers.

Variation

Embed other numbers (e.g. percentages, decimals, fractions or large numbers) in sentences which could crop up in a telephone conversation. Days of the week, place names or names of people could also be embedded if students find any of these a little difficult. You can also ask students to differentiate between similar-sounding names (of places or people). In order to do this put a list of possibilities on the board or on an OHT, arranged in two columns (A and B) before reading out the snippets.

☐ ELICITED TELEPHONE DIALOGUES

The teacher helps students to build up a telephone dialogue which students then practise until they know it by heart. The dialogue provides a useful model and acts as a springboard for the practice of adapted dialogues which are useful to individual students' own work situations. Note that this procedure is especially useful when only two or three students turn up to class or when students want to practise language for a specific situation.

Language determined by the teacher and students together
Level elementary–lower-intermediate
Time 40 minutes

Procedure

1 Establish a situation for making a telephone call using photographs (e.g. on OHTs) or cartoons on the board. If you use photographs, you might consider using photographs which depict whole situations as well as only people.

2 On a line-by-line basis elicit and practise a telephone conversation with students. Elicit lines by asking *What would he say? And then?* An example dialogue is as follows:

A: Good afternoon, ABC Research.

B: Good afternoon. This is Ken Tan. Could I speak to Mr Shiamon, please?

A: Sorry, which department is he in?

B: He's in the Patent Department.

A: Er ... we have two Patent offices: one in Jurong and one in Raffles Quay. Do you know which office Mr Shiamon works in?

B: I think he works in Jurong.

A: OK. Hold the line, please. I'll connect you.

B: Thank you.

C: Hello, Shiamon speaking.

B: Hello. This is Ken Tan. I'm calling about the outstanding patent.

C: I'm sorry, Mr Tan. Could you tell me which lab you're calling from?

B: I'm calling from the Metalwork Research Lab.

C: Uhu. Could you give me the invention number, please?

B: Yes. It's A123.

C: OK. What's the problem?

B: The other day I asked you if you could check the patent application.

C: Yes, I checked it this end and now I've sent it to the Patent Attorney.

B: Oh, thank you. When do you think you'll get the report from the attorney?

C: Probably by the end of March. Are you going to give a presentation on A123? If so, I'll ask him to get it back to me earlier.

B: Yes I am, actually. I'm giving a presentation in April. It would be a great help if I could have it before the end of March.

C: OK. I'll see what I can do.

B: Thank you very much. Goodbye.

C: 'Bye.

Write only notes or symbols on the board to remind students of each line, amplifying the notes only if students have difficulty with specific parts. Get students to repeat and practise any phrases which cause difficulty. Practise the conversation in sections initially (e.g. six lines). As you go through the dialogue, alternate between whole class practice (i.e. choral drilling – see Glossary), open-pair practice and closed-pair practice (again, see Glossary for an explanation of these terms). At all stages insist on good pronunciation (especially intonation and sentence stress). During closed-pair practice regroup pairs frequently.

2 Ask students to write a similar conversation which is relevant to their work either in class or for homework. To stimulate students to write conversations themselves you might make some suggestions about possible reasons for phone calls (e.g. phoning to check on an outstanding payment or phoning to remind someone to send in a summary of sales figures). You can later give students feedback on how appropriately and accurately they have used telephone language in these conversations.

Variation 1

Build up and record this conversation as in COMMUNITY LANGUAGE LEARNING (see p. 104). As a follow-up, cut up individual speakers' sentences and get students to sequence them. Alternatively prepare a gapfill exercise so as to focus students' attention on key phrases.

Variation 2

If you have the equipment available, students can practise their conversations privately and record them so that other students in the group can listen to their conversations. (If no tape recorders are available, students can practise and then 'perform' their dialogues to the rest of the group.) After everyone has listened to each conversation, the appropriacy of language can be discussed (as described in 4.5). Students can then re-record, or continue practising, their conversations, incorporating improvements.

For other procedures which you can use to help your students to practise language for this area, see the Index entry for 'telephoning'.

5.5 Dealing with visitors

Nearly all students have to deal with foreign visitors to their company occasionally, if not on a regular basis, so this is an important skill area to practise. Chance or planned introductions and chats with visitors can be the first step to building relationships with people who matter, so can affect career prospects!

Students practise language for this area most enthusiastically when you help them to imagine a situation, e.g. a day when they're suddenly introduced to someone by their boss. You can help your students to practise common beginnings, useful questions and typical responses so that they have a good 'springboard' for a freer conversation in real life. Since intonation, voice range, sentence stress, backchannelling (*Uhu*, etc.) and body language (especially eye contact and body space) are all extremely important if students are to make a good impression, realistic role-play is essential.

☐ INTRODUCTIONS

Working in groups of three, students practise introducing each other.

Language introductions and preliminary chats
Level any
Time 15 minutes

Procedure

Ask students to get into groups of three. Get them to check that they all remember each other's names! Alternatively, give every student a new name – written on a card, with brief notes about the person (e.g. Clare Williams, Marketing Manager, Taipei office). Standing in clusters, as if at a welcome party (e.g. before a conference), students then introduce each other using appropriate language, such as the following:

> Peter: Hello, John! This is Clare Williams from the Taipei office. She's the Sales Manager there. Clare, this is John Benn. He's your counterpart, here in Paris.
> Clare: (Shaking hands and smiling) How do you do?
> John: It's good to meet you at last. Have you just arrived from Taipei?

© Cambridge University Press

If students are using language inappropriately (e.g. *How do you do? I'm fine, thanks*) or incorrectly, both of which are highly likely, stop everyone and do a quick language focus, eliciting appropriate phrases and responses and writing these up on the board. Role-play a few conversations with volunteers before getting students to continue practising in their groups of three. Insist on appropriate, 'interested' intonation throughout.

☐ QUESTION QUANDARY

Students select and practise questions typically used by people when they first meet.

Language selected by the teacher
Level elementary and above
Time 10–15 minutes

Preparation

On index cards, write ten questions which would typically be asked at a first meeting and ten questions which would be inappropriate for use with near strangers. Some questions you might use are as follows:

Appropriate questions
How long will you be here?
What line are you in?
Which department are you in?
What do you do exactly?
What does that involve?
Have you been to this part of the world before?
Is this your first visit?
Where are you staying?
So what do you think of it so far?
What do you plan to do while you're here?

Inappropriate questions
How old are you?
Are you married?
What's your position?
How much do you earn?
Do you have any children?
What are your qualifications?
Which university did you graduate from?
When did you graduate?
Do you like your job?
I hear your company's about to go bankrupt. Is that right?

Procedure

Spread the index cards out over the table and get students to decide which questions are appropriate for use with visitors. Having discarded the inappropriate questions, elicit and drill suitable responses. Get students to put questions and responses in a possible order. After private pair practice (if necessary), get students to mill around the room and role-play casual conversations that they might have with visitors.

☐ EXCHANGE FORMULAE

Following on from the previous procedure, students match formulaic responses to formulaic comments or questions. This is essential practice if students are to sound 'normal' in casual conversations with visitors or colleagues and if they are later to become capable of appropriate witticisms or departures from formulae.

Language formulaic comments, questions and responses selected by the teacher
Level elementary and above, especially if used as a warmer
Time 10–20 minutes

Preparation

Select about twenty formulaic comments or questions for different situations, and prepare responses which would be acceptable in an international business setting and in particular, in the students' work setting. Write the comments, questions and responses on strips of paper. It may be a good idea to write the responses on strips of a different colour. (Prepare several sets for different groups of students to use.) Some formulaic exchanges you might use are as follows:

Question/Comment	Response
Did you have a good flight?	Oh, not too bad, thanks. It's good to be here at last.
How do you do?	How do you do? / Pleased to meet you.
Is this your first visit to … ?	Yes, it is. It's quite different from what I expected.
What are your first impressions?	That's a difficult question! Well now, let me see …
How are you finding the climate?	Too hot! It's much cooler back home.
Do you travel a lot?	Yeah, quite a lot. It's just part of the job.
Congratulations on your transfer!	Thanks. It's good to be here.
How are things going in New York?	Oh, pretty well, I suppose …
Everything must seem very strange.	Yes, it'll take a while to get used to everything.
How long are you staying?	Just a few days. I fly back on Wednesday evening.
How about some coffee?	That'd be nice. Black, no sugar, please.
Will you be joining us for lunch?	Oh, thank you. That would be nice.
Can you join us for a drink tonight?	Yes, I think so — thanks, that'd be great.
Let me know if you need any help!	Thanks very much.
Let me know if I can do anything.	OK! I know where to find you!
I look forward to seeing you again.	Yes. Thank you for giving me such a warm welcome.

Procedure

1 Start by giving students the comments or questions and ask students to consider suitable responses.
2 Then, having mixed up the strips, ask students to match the response strips with the comments or questions.
3 Go over the 'answers' by asking some students to read out questions or comments and others to read out the appropriate responses. (Note that students can improvise who says what when.) Insist on appropriate sentence stress and intonation, and good use of voice range (i.e. wide voice range). As each pair of strips is identified, students can put them to one side.
4 Give students time to copy down and/or ask about any exchanges they are unfamiliar with.
5 Get students to improvise their own conversations in pairs, using these exchanges and adding comments as necessary to make the conversation seem natural.
6 Finally, get students to role-play the conversations standing up, with other partners.

□ MINI-CHAT MILLING

Students mill and chat, imagining they are at a get-together with visitors after work.

Language elicited dialogue, including language for socialising
Level elementary, or above if used as a warmer
Time 20 minutes

Preparation

Prepare students for this activity with ASKING ABOUT PEOPLE'S JOBS (p. 52), SELF-INTRODUCTIONS (p. 127), CULTURAL MIMING (p. 128), NOISY LISTENING (p. 153), QUESTION QUANDARY (p. 158) and EXCHANGE FORMULAE (p. 159). If you are not confident about scripting a dialogue for socialising, script a suitable dialogue in advance or put separate lines of the dialogue below on strips of paper for sequencing. Make enough sets of strips for students to work in pairs. (Alternatively, you can elicit a dialogue in class.)

Procedure

1 Tell students to imagine that there are some visitors at their company and that they have been invited to join them for drinks after 5 p.m. Although they know which company the visitors are from, they know nothing else about them. Elicit or give students a suitable dialogue, such as the following:

A: Hello! Can I get you a coffee?

B: Oh, thanks.

A: By the way, I'm Jo Bloggs from Design. How about you? What line are you in?

B: I'm in Brand. Actually, I was hoping to meet some people from your department.

A: Ah, well … you're talking to the right person!

B: I was wondering why you chose such bright colours for your new Career Man range. Most of your other products are pastel shades.

A: Yes, that's true. Of course, we did a lot of market research before we settled on red and yellow. Somehow people seem to associate those colours with success …

B: Interesting. Where did you do your research?

A: Mostly in South Korea. We also did small-scale surveys in China and Japan – but the results came out more or less the same. Enough about me … what about you?

B: Oh, I'm responsible for the Shavers line. We use very subdued colours for that line … mostly browns and navy blue. You've probably seen the products.

A: Not only have I seen them, I use them every day! You've got a loyal customer here!

B: Well, that's good to hear. No need to give you any free samples, then!

A: You can buy me a drink sometime instead!

© Cambridge University Press

2 Allow students time to prepare adapted dialogues of their own. Encourage them to anticipate questions they might ask 'visitors' in the class and to think of suitable comments to make about their own present or future work.

3 Finally, get students to stand up and mill around, as they might at a party for visitors. Encourage students to improvise and extend the conversations, as appropriate. Be prepared to stop students many times so as to encourage them to use friendlier intonation, a wider voice range or more appropriate body language.

□ COMPANY RUNDOWN

Students practise explaining or discussing some of their company's products or services, using authentic materials as a starting point.

Language any
Level intermediate and above
Time 1 hour

Preparation

Ask students to bring in copies of their company's sales literature. As well as bringing in brochures or leaflets, they should print off any web pages their company may currently use or even try and obtain copies of responses to customer enquiries about specific products or services. (Note: You may prefer to obtain some authentic material yourself, if this is feasible.) If your students are not yet working, obtain a range of sales literature which you think may interest your students. Obtain all this material in advance of your lesson and make copies for all your students.

Procedure

1 Tell students to imagine some visitors are coming to their company. Ask them to decide precisely who the visitors are (in pairs or groups of three) and what they might want to know or discuss. Suggest, perhaps, that they might imagine visitors coming from their company's head office or from a potential partner for a joint venture.
2 Using the sales literature for inspiration or information, students should then write out a possible dialogue with a visitor. They can continue working in their pairs or groups of three. While you are monitoring, encourage students to use less formal language than that used in the sales literature (or other material) and to imagine and include interesting 'background' details which their visitor might want to discuss. Correct and provide language as necessary.
3 Ask students to extract from their script a list of questions the visitor might ask. Get them to write these out on a separate piece of paper.
4 Finally, ask students to role-play their conversations with various partners, having first given their 'visitors' a list of questions to ask.

□ ADVERBIAL BALLS

Students throw a ball around and make sentences using time expressions. If you dislike throwing things around the classroom you can use a more conventional approach – but balls work better!

163

Language time expressions, plus present simple statements
Level elementary (or above, if used as a warmer)
Time 10 minutes

Preparation

Write various time expressions on the board or put these on an OHT.
Some expressions you could use:

always	occasionally	sometimes	generally	frequently	often
usually	normally	on a regular basis	once a week		regularly
every year	every two weeks	twice a year		once in a while	
from time to time	never	seldom	rarely	hardly ever	

Procedure

1 Ask students to imagine they are explaining things about their job and department to a visitor. Throw a soft ball to one of the students and give them an example by talking about yourself (e.g. *I come here to teach twice a week*).
2 Tell the student who caught the ball to make another true sentence about him- or herself, using one of the time expressions on the board. As students continue, correct any errors (in terms of facts or grammar, making sure the present simple tense is formed correctly).
3 After students have warmed up and got the idea – in particular, the idea that their statements must be true! – tell them you are going to check to see how often they use each expression. Then, as students continue to throw the ball around and make statements, put a tick beside each expression every time it's used. This will, of course, encourage students to try out some of the expressions they are not used to using.
4 No longer using the balls, ask students to continue in pairs, making a response to their partner's comment each time, e.g. *Oh, that's a lot more often than we do* or *Why's that?*
5 Ask students to continue with different partners, role-playing an entire conversation with a visitor.

□ GUIDED TOURS

Using 'Cuisenaire rods' (see pp. 105–106 for information and stockists) or simply drawing plans on paper, students imagine that they are showing a visitor round their offices or factory.

Language any
Level elementary and above
Time 10–40 minutes

Procedure

1 Get students to build a plan of their offices or factory using Cuisenaire rods; alternatively ask them to draw a plan on a large sheet of paper. If you can get hold of an official plan of the company's offices, so much the better!

2 Review appropriate language with the class, then get a volunteer student to act out a conversation with another student, as they imagine walking around.

3 Next, get pairs of students to draw plans of their departments and to prepare similar conversations with visitors. Encourage students to make questions 'chatty' (e.g. *How many people work here then?*) and to include invitations (e.g. *Would you like to stop for some coffee?*).

☐ INTERVIEW INTERROGATIVES

Students prepare questions, give interviews and write summaries. This procedure should help you gauge the level of your students and spot problems relating to grammar, vocabulary or pronunciation.

Language determined by the students
Level elementary–advanced
Time 40 minutes

Procedure

1 Explain to students that they are going to interview each other, imagining they are interviewing someone for a job. As a class, decide which position is vacant.

2 Elicit and write question words and phrases on the board, e.g. *What, Who, What kind of, How long*. Then get students to write one question for each word or phrase, remembering that they will be using these questions to find out if an applicant for a job is suitable. Monitor carefully while students are preparing their questions, correcting as much as possible (i.e. grammar, use of vocabulary, etc.). This is important because students will then practise 'correct' questions in the next stage. Encourage students to avoid intrusive questions, e.g. asking too much about people's background.

3 Ask students to choose partners and interview each other, role-playing a real job interview. Insist that students use 'interested' intonation patterns. Stop them if necessary and model a 'bored' questioner and an 'interested' one, getting students to comment on the differences, i.e. wider voice range, stressed words, livelier facial expressions.

4 Next, ask students to give their partner a false name and to write up an anonymous summary of the information they have discovered about him or her.

5 Finally, get students to exchange summaries with other students and decide who would be the best person to recruit for the position. Only allow students to guess the candidates' true identities when a decision has been made!

Note: With a mixed-level class, students can work in groups during the question preparation stage. Weaker students in each group will get support from stronger ones. If you monitor carefully, you will still be able to get an impression of individuals' problem areas.

☐ HUMAN CHATS

Students focus on making conversations with visitors more 'human'. As well as using interjections and comments, students ask questions which aim to make a visitor feel cared for.

Language interjections, comments and questions
Level intermediate and above
Time 20 minutes

Procedure

1 Show students the following conversation or use one which you have scripted yourself:

> **I haven't seen you around before ...**
>
> No, I'm from the Kyushu Technical Centre.
>
> **Oh, I see. By the way, I'm Hiroe Hatano. I'm in Accounts.**
>
> Nice to meet you. I'm Yoko Ohto.
>
> Pleased to meet you. **What do you do at the KTC, Ms Ohto?**
>
> I'm in Patents.
>
> **Hmm, what does that involve?**
>
> Well, I research new inventions and check out the patents.
>
> **Oh, that sounds interesting.**
>
> Yes, it is, actually.
>
> **How long will you be over here?**
>
> Oh, only until Wednesday afternoon. I've come over for a few meetings.
>
> **Well, maybe see you around again.**

2 Ask students to consider what makes this conversation seem warm and 'human'.

3 Focus students' attention on the phrases and questions marked with bold script. Emphasise the importance of this type of language. You can easily do this by asking a strong student to explain something long and complicated to you and making no response while he or she does so!

4 Give students some time to prepare or plan dialogues, then ask them to practise 'human' conversations in pairs. Encourage students to include open questions which encourage long, complicated responses (e.g. *What brings you to this part of the world?*).

5 Ask students how they could make their conversations with visitors even more 'human'. Elicit possible questions they could ask the visitor when standing at the photocopier, or when showing a similar visitor round the office. Some possible questions they could use are as follows:

> What are you planning to do for lunch?
>
> By the way, have you met the Marketing Director yet?
>
> Is there anything in particular you'd like to see?
>
> Will you be going round the plant while you're here?

6 Finally get students to practise their conversations again.

For other procedures which you can use to help your students to practise language for this area, see the Index entry for 'visitors, dealing with'.

5.6 Talking to colleagues

For some students, chatting to superiors or foreign colleagues is a bizarre idea which involves a big conceptual leap! However, since students' relationships with superiors and foreign colleagues might have a great effect on their career, this is an important area of language to practise.

Practice will mean considering three main areas. Firstly, since acceptable subjects of conversation, turntaking and topic management may differ dramatically from culture to culture, students may need to be sensitised to the cross-cultural angle of 'casual chatting'. Secondly, students will need to be made aware of any body language they use which might seem conspicuous or inappropriate in an international context. Thirdly, they will need to consider what specific language they can use in this seemingly relaxed situation.

☐ MIMED ARRIVAL

Students mime their arrival at the office (or factory, etc.) so that they can become aware of the impression they make through their body language.

Language imperatives
Level elementary and above
Time 5 minutes

Procedure

If students are already working, find out from them what they usually do when they arrive at work. (If students are not yet working, get them to imagine what they will do.) Insist on plenty of detail! Make notes on the board so as to help students to remember the cues or key vocabulary; they will need this language later on in the activity. Next, ask for a volunteer and get this student to mime in response to your commands. Some possible commands:

> Walk through the door. Smile at a colleague. Take off your jacket. Hang it up. Put your briefcase on your desk. Open it. Take out your newspaper. Open it ... Pick up the telephone.

After this volunteer has finished, ask him or her – then the rest of the class – if he or she did anything which foreign colleagues might consider strange (e.g. look serious, bow or look over-enthusiastic). Add your own comments, being as tactful as possible, and miming a more 'acceptable' version in terms of international business. Finally, get students to continue in pairs, one person giving commands, the other miming. Encourage students to make bizarre or outrageous suggestions (e.g. *Look miserable!*) and to give honest feedback.

☐ MONDAY MORNING CHATS

Typical formulaic questions – often used on Monday mornings! – are elicited or given, then practised. If repeated often enough (e.g. every week), this exchange of questions can become quite natural to students, who will benefit from better relationships with foreign colleagues.

Language formulaic questions
Level elementary–upper-intermediate (if used as a warmer)
Time 5–10 minutes

Procedure

Get students to visualise the situation where they come into the office on Monday morning and see one of their foreign colleagues. What do they say? Elicit or give students some of the following questions, typically used on Monday mornings by people working together:

> Did you have a good weekend?
> How was your weekend?
> Did you do anything interesting?
> Did you see that movie on Saturday night ... ?
> Did you go away anywhere?

One way of giving students these phrases is to jumble up the questions and ask students to put the words in the correct order. (This is also a useful way of recycling question formation, as well as giving students something fun to do in the initial stages of this activity.) Next, get students to consider possible, appropriate responses and get pairs to write down or improvise dialogues.

Variation

Elicit a different dialogue at the beginning of each week. Drill pronunciation and insist on accuracy. Then get students to practise in pairs and adapt the dialogue to their own, personal situation. Encourage the use of idiomatic expressions.

If this kind of informal chat is very unusual in the students' own culture and students are reluctant or uncomfortable with it, get them to consider cultural equivalents in their own culture, alongside literal translations. For example, *How are you?* translates as *Have you eaten?* in Chinese, and *Fine thanks* as *Thanks be to God* in Arabic. Discussing these may help students to understand why English speakers say such strange things!

☐ DIALOGUE CHAINS

This is a fun way of focusing students' attention on their typical errors and/or appropriate responses in typical conversations with colleagues, either face-to-face or on the telephone.

Language any (especially idiomatic responses to questions)
Level lower–intermediate
Time 45 minutes

Procedure

Ask students to stand up and form a loose, but even circle. Turn to the student on your left and say, *Hi, how are you?* Allow the student to answer but correct any errors of grammar, pronunciation or appropriacy. It is essential that all the utterances practised are appropriate for real-life, adult business situations if this activity is to be useful. Next, use verbal or non-verbal feedback if appropriate. A typical exchange might be as follows:

> – *Hi, how are you?*
> – *Well, OK but I've got a bit of a headache.*
> – *Oh dear ... sorry to hear that.*

Allow the conversation to continue naturally, then at a suitable point indicate that the student you were talking to is to ask the next person in the circle the same question. Again, allow the new conversation to continue until a suitable point, then get the responding student to begin a new conversation. When everyone has practised 'in public', get students to continue in closed pairs, milling and changing partners every few minutes.

With all students at all times, be ready to correct even tiny errors or supply more appropriate language because the focus in this activity is on accuracy. Try hard to get every student working to improve in some area or other by providing stronger students with more appropriate or idiomatic expressions. Also insist that students only say what is true. In this way, they will learn how to express things they may have been wanting to say. At every stage of this activity students will have been focusing on eliminating minor errors which they typically make, on improving their pronunciation, and on making their language more appropriate to their working contexts.

☐ STRUCTURED RELAXATION

Students practise mini-conversations with colleagues, using structures in a very controlled way.

Language a selected structure (e.g. present perfect continuous)
Level elementary–intermediate
Time 10–15 minutes

Preparation

Select a structure which you would like students to practise and which is commonly used in an interchange between colleagues. Think of several drill cues. An example is as follows:

I've got a terrible	1 make/photocopies	... all morning!
headache!	2 type/letters	Oh, well, why don't
Why? What have	3 telephone/clients	we go somewhere
you been doing?	4 work/computer	special for lunch?
	5 write/report	
	6 help/new trainee	
	7 deal with/complaints	

© Cambridge University Press

Procedure

Use the cues you've selected to elicit a dialogue. A dialogue for the above would be:

> A I've got a terrible headache!
>
> B Why? What have you been doing?
>
> A I've been making photocopies all morning.
>
> B Oh, well, why don't we go somewhere special for lunch?

Get students to practise this dialogue in a very controlled way before role-playing the same conversation with variations and additions. Make sure that students use natural pronunciation at all times (e.g. using the contractions, *What've*, *I've* and *don't*) and that they stress key words (e.g. *What've you been doing?*).

□ CARD CONCEPT EXCHANGE

This is an activity which will help students to practise explaining key concepts from their own culture. This might frequently be necessary when students are working with foreigners in a multinational corporation, or when they are talking to colleagues in foreign branches.

Language explanation of concepts which are important in the students' own culture
Level upper-intermediate–advanced
Time 20 minutes

Preparation

Make a short list of words or phrases which you think your students might need to explain at some point while working in an international business environment. Write these words or phrases on cards or pieces of paper, either in the original language or in translation, as seems most

171

appropriate. Finally, prepare sets of blank cards for students to use in your lesson; students will write other words or phrases on these cards.

Some key words or phrases which you might select for certain nationalities:

Japanese:
tatami shoji Golden Week after-work drinking set meal trains
tea ceremony Tokyo earthquakes typhoons ofuro kimono
Western dress universities

Singaporean:
courtesy campaign CBD district chewing gum
housing development board (HDB) compulsory savings scheme (CPF)
durian mass rapid transit system orchids

Indian:
beef eating cleanliness modernisation equality/the caste system
saris bureaucracy trains animals flooding karma spices
vegetarianism cars

Spanish:
siesta mañana paseo Madrid tortilla fish tourism
bullfighting dubbing dancing flamenco the sea religion
food working hours Argentina olives

Greek:
Athens relationships trolley buses cafés cinema coffee frappé
the sea archaeology Acropolis mountains dancing taverna
fish ouzo contracts

© Cambridge University Press

Procedure

1 Tell students that they are going to practise explaining important words or concepts from their own culture so that they can do this with colleagues at work when necessary. Place the cards you have prepared in advance face down on a table. Turn up one card, elicit or give an explanation of that concept, then role-play a conversation with a foreign colleague about the same word or phrase. Share out the cards and ask students to continue role-playing conversations as they reveal each new word or phrase.

2 Get students to write some more words or phrases on the blank cards. Students then continue role-playing conversations, focusing on as many different concepts as possible. While they are explaining concepts, encourage them to paraphrase or use pictures or mime. Get

students to practise appropriate language too, either before or during the activity (e.g. *It's a kind of ... , It's used for -ing ... , It's a word which means many things, It's a time when we ...*), perhaps using some of the exercises in *Learning to Learn* (Ellis, G. and B. Sinclair, 1989. Cambridge: Cambridge University Press) if you think your students need more preparation.

Variation 1

Ask students to write down three comments which summarise their opinion about some of the words or phrases. While students are doing this, quietly go to two or three students (who you think will play along) and pass them a message, asking them to write comments which don't reflect their opinion so that the discussion afterwards is more lively. Then put students in groups of two or three and ask them to explain and defend their opinion.

When students have been talking for some time, tell them that you asked some students to write false opinions. Get them to guess who was not being entirely honest!

Also ask students the following questions:

- *What do you think other people in other countries think?*
- *Could you live in a country where everyone believed the opposite?*

This is one time when it is good to be controversial! Your aim is to raise students' awareness of their own culture so that they are better able to discuss these topics with foreign colleagues, who may have a very different perspective.

Variation 2

Test students on words or phrases which are typically associated with British, American, Canadian, Australian or New Zealand culture. Some words you could use:

> jelly   the tube   punk   integrity   Bank Holiday
> short back and sides   waffle   The Beatles   state
> stars and stripes   freedom   democracy   parliament

© Cambridge University Press

Students pick a card and guess or say what the word or phrase means. Other students in the group correct or add comments, as necessary. Encourage students to use a dictionary (such as the *Longman Dictionary of English Language and Culture*, 1992. Harlow: Longman) to check the meaning of each word or phrase and its associations; also encourage students to draw a mindmap for each word or phrase, showing not only the meaning but also as much associated information as possible. If individual students draw mindmaps for specific words or phrases on OHTs feedback and discussion is easier and OHTs can easily be photocopied for other students.

After an initial 20-minute focus activity, the cards you prepare for words or phrases connected with English-speaking cultures can later be used as a filler between other activities (e.g. by students who finish other activities early). Other cards with new concepts can also be fed into your pile of cards to add interest and/or in preparation for reading or listening exercises in which these concepts are mentioned.

☐ QUEUED DISCUSSION

After a little preparation, students discuss subjects which might be discussed informally in a cafeteria queue or elsewhere in the workplace.

Language any
Level upper-intermediate–advanced
Time 30 minutes

Preparation

Prepare a sheet of cues which could provide students with subjects for conversation in a cafeteria queue. Also prepare cards with the same cues for use later in the activity. (Write one cue on each card.) Some examples of cues you could use are as follows:

General conversations

It's very crowded.

Prices have gone up as from today.

Some new parking rules have been introduced.

The company has just introduced a no-smoking rule.

The company's annual Dinner & Dance is this Saturday.

Personal conversations

One of you has just come back from a business trip.

One of you is working on the new ZX2000 – the company's special new product!

One of you is just about to transfer to the London office.

One of you is just about to transfer to the New York office.

One of you has just won the Sales Person of the Year award.

One of you has just been promoted.

One of you is just about to retire!

Procedure

1 Tell students that they are going to practise chatting, imagining they are in the queue at the cafeteria. Before asking them what they might typically discuss, ask them whether they consider this kind of conversation important. Remind them, if necessary, of the golden opportunities for networking and impressing bosses in impromptu cafeteria conversations!

2 Ask students to read the list of general and personal cues you have prepared and to consider what they would say. Say: *Imagine these situations. What could you say to a colleague to start a conversation on this subject?* Elicit some possible questions or comments students could use and encourage them to note down any language which they do not usually use. Then, having asked students to stand in a line (as if queuing up in a cafeteria), give out the cue cards you have prepared. Encourage students to keep chatting for as long as possible for each cue card, changing the subject if necessary but in as natural a way as possible.

3 After students have been chatting for two or three minutes, ask them to pass their cards along and to have another mini-conversation using the next cue card they receive. Continue this process until all students have practised using every cue card. Stop to give students feedback on language use – in particular on pronunciation (especially intonation), appropriacy of language and on the smoothness of any subject changes – whenever you feel this is necessary.

4 Take in all the cue cards. Ask students to change places in the queue, and improvise a conversation without the cue cards.

For other procedures which you can use to help your students practise language for this area, see the Index entry for 'colleagues, talking to'.

5.7 Reporting to foreign managers

All students working in a multinational corporation will need to gain a clearer understanding of their relationships with their foreign colleagues or boss in terms of the company's corporate culture. For students who report directly to a foreign manager – who, although English-speaking, could be any nationality – awareness-raising and language practice will be particularly important in terms of both career development and day-to-day survival. Students may well be surprised by the way in which English is commonly used with superiors and may have a very different concept from their bosses as to what constitutes 'helpful' behaviour, simply because these things are culturally defined.

The procedures outlined below will give you some ideas for practising appropriate language.

☐ WARM-UP UPDATE

Using present continuous statements, students tell each other about their current work. This is a good follow-up activity to Unit 11 of *Early Business Contacts*. Brieger, N. and J. Comfort. 1989. Hemel Hempstead: Prentice Hall.

Language present continuous questions and statements
Level any
Time 5 minutes

Procedure

Write various words or phrases up on the board which you think students may need if they are to describe their current projects. For example:

plan	formulate	look into	develop	work on
	do research		think about	

Throw a soft ball to one of the students and ask him or her *What are you working on at the moment?* Encourage the student to respond, using one of the words or phrases on the board. If the student uses the wrong tense, correct this immediately, drawing a time-line to explain, if necessary. (It's a temporary activity – they won't be working on the same thing for ever!) Finally, get students to continue throwing the ball around in the same way, changing the initial question to *How about you? What are you working on at the moment?*

Variation

If you feel uncomfortable about using balls ask students to work in pairs (with constantly changing partners) or small groups. Alternatively, ask students to stand in one or more circles and ask and answer questions in a chain. Each person asks the person standing on their right in turn.

☐ HELPFUL HARRY

Students practise sounding helpful when foreign managers make requests.

Language exponents for agreeing to requests
Level elementary–upper-intermediate
Time 15 minutes

Procedure

Ask students to imagine requests that foreign managers might make. Then get them to write out these requests (e.g. *Could you stay on a bit later tonight?*) on slips of paper. When each student has written out at least three or four requests, mix them all up in the centre of the table (or on the floor). Giving out more blank slips of paper, ask students to pick requests and write out suitable responses. Input language or review possibilities, if necessary. Some possible exponents students could use are as follows:

Yes, of course. I'll do it straight away/now/after this/straight after lunch/straight after I've sent this fax.
By all means.
Sure, no problem.
Certainly, I'll do it right away.
Well, all right. I'll have to make a few arrangements, but I think that should be possible.
I'm sorry, (reason)
I'm sorry but I'm afraid (reason)
Would it be OK if I did it tomorrow?
Well, I'm working on the ... at the moment. What's more of a priority?

© Cambridge University Press

Monitor carefully as students write responses to the original requests, encouraging them to think about appropriacy for different situations. When all the original requests have responses prepared for them, mix up all the pieces of paper. Then, get students to match up the requests with possible responses. Review the 'answers' as a group, discussing reasons and other possibilities and writing other possible responses on new slips of paper. After practising the pronunciation (especially sentence stress and intonation), get students to practise mini-conversations in pairs, making reference to the slips of paper. Finally, get students to role-play mini-conversations with foreign managers in pairs, milling around as if walking around at work and calling out to subordinates!

☐ LATECOMER BEHAVIOUR

Students become sensitised to appropriate behaviour when late. Excuses and reasons are considered, then appropriate ones for English are role-played with suitable body language.

Language apologies and excuses
Level elementary and above
Time 10 minutes

Preparation

Write several exponents for apologies and excuses on index cards or strips of paper. The apologies should be separate from the excuses and a wide range of both should be used. Be sure to include some totally inappropriate excuses. Some apologies and excuses:

Acceptable apologies	Acceptable excuses
Sorry!	I got held up.
Sorry I'm late.	The phone rang just as I was leaving the office.
I'm sorry I'm late.	I got held up in traffic.
Terribly sorry I'm late.	The train was late.
I do apologise.	I got stuck in a meeting.
My apologies.	I had to sort something out.
I hope I haven't kept you waiting too long.	I had some urgent business to attend to.
Unacceptable apologies	**Unacceptable excuses**
(nothing)	It's raining.
I'm awfully sorry I'm late.	I was busy.
Dreadfully sorry.	I had some more important work to do.
I apologise.	I wasn't feeling well.
My sincere apologies.	I was feeling tired.
I humbly apologise.	I overslept.
I deeply regret being late.	I missed my train.

Note that you may disagree about what constitutes an acceptable (or unacceptable) apology or excuse. Change your lists as you consider appropriate to suit your students' work situation. In other words, take into account the cultures within which students will be working as you make changes to these lists, as well as your own opinion!

Procedure

1 Ask students to decide which apologies and which excuses are acceptable for use in an English-speaking international business context. Encourage them to focus on when and why certain expressions would be used. If they are having trouble sorting out the cards tell them how many there are of each type. Next, tell students what you think, explaining why some seemingly acceptable apologies or excuses are not appropriate in English. (This may be because certain information which is understood in the students' culture or context may not be widely understood. *It's raining* in Lisbon, for example, means the traffic was heavy because everyone uses their

private cars – not buses and trams – on rainy days. With other excuses the style may not be appropriate and/or a formulaic expression may be more widely used.)

2 Get students to practise using the apologies and excuses in role-played pairwork. Insist on good use of body language and pronunciation, especially intonation.

☐ COMPETITOR FOCUS

Students do a listening exercise which focuses their attention on competitors and gives them a springboard for further oral work. They then make statements about their own competitors, which leads into a discussion. The activity can be adapted to various levels and can lead into meetings practice.

Language any
Level elementary–advanced
Time 1 hour

Preparation

Get a set of Cuisenaire rods (for information and stockists see pp. 105–106) or prepare sets of coloured strips of paper of different lengths. Next, find a tape about competitors, such as the one provided in Unit 19 of *Early Business Contacts* (Brieger, N. and J. Comfort. 1989. Hemel Hempstead: Prentice Hall); the tapescript for this listening is provided on pp. 180–181 as an example of a suitable conversation. This type of listening exercise is an excellent springboard for oral practice.

Procedure

1 Get students to listen to the recording once or twice.
2 After asking gist questions, tell the students that they need to make a diagram of the information in the tape using the rods. Tell them to choose one colour for each competitor and assign different rods to represent market share (one, two or three rods of the same colour can represent different sizes of market share), prices (low = one rod, high = many rods of the same colour), age of company and number of products. Get students to work in two or more groups if you have a large class.
3 Help students to check their 'answers' by listening again and again and consulting the tapescript, if necessary.
4 Ask students to make comparative and superlative sentences, pointing at the rods as they do so. Insist on perfect grammatical accuracy! Note that this is important if students are going to be able to convey information about competitors accurately.

179

5 Next, get students to ask each other questions and to answer them (as if they are talking about their competitors), all the time using the rod diagram on the table as their source of information.

6 When students are confidently and accurately using comparative and superlative statements about these fictitious companies get them to construct a similar diagram which represents their own company's competitors, again using the rods. (In in-company classes this can be done as a class; on public Business English courses students can work in pairs, focusing on each of their companies in turn and using diagrams on paper as a reference point.) Encourage students to ask each other *When ... ? or Why ... ?* questions as they are doing this.

7 Finally, get students to role-play conversations with foreign managers about their competitors. Stop students and get them to do some controlled practice of 1st and 2nd conditionals (e.g. using *Early Business Contacts*, Unit 18), if necessary, before asking them to role-play conversations again. The conditionals should, of course, help students to consider possible courses of action with their bosses. If students consistently fail to use comparatives, superlatives and conditionals correctly in these contexts, try recording their conversations or using COMMUNITY LANGUAGE LEARNING (p. 104).

8 Later follow-up practice can be a larger, more formal meeting with an agenda, in which competitors and possible courses of action are discussed.

An appropriate tapescript for COMPETITOR FOCUS

Let's look at the competition. Now, our main competitor – Benton – entered the market in 1982 – ten years later than us. But since then they have grown more rapidly and are now the biggest in terms of market share. Why? Mainly because of their product development. Their products are better, sold at lower prices and presented more attractively. At the moment their main weakness is that they have the lowest profitability.

Now our second major competitor is Zecron. They entered the market at the same time as us. They have a lower market share than us and their products are sold at slightly higher prices. However, their annual return shows greater profitability and much heavier investment in plant and machinery over the last two years. So they are in a good position to overtake us soon.

The last competitor is Mansell. They have been in the market slightly longer than us and Zecron. They have a much smaller market share but their products are sold at the top end of the market at much higher prices. As a result, they achieve the best profitability of the four companies with much lower turnover.

So, what can we say about our own position? Well, our products are medium-priced but less attractive than Benton's. We're getting a problem with reliability. Certainly Benton's range has a reputation for being much more reliable. Our market share is higher than Zecron and Mansell but they are more profitable than us. So, we must become more competitive during the next two years if we are to hold on to our market share and increase profitability.

Answers to this task:

	Age in market 1 = oldest	Market share 1 = largest	Product price 1 = cheapest	Profitability 1 = most profitable
Brotherton	2	2	2	3
Benton	4	1	1	4
Zecron	2	3	3	2
Mansell	1	4	4	1

(From Unit 19 of *Early Business Contacts*. Brieger, N. and J. Comfort. 1989. Hemel Hempstead: Prentice Hall)

☐ CHECKING UP

In order to review past simple questions and appropriate responses, students practise a rather stilted dialogue which can provide a springboard for more natural versions.

Language past simple questions and natural responses
Level elementary–upper-intermediate
Time 20 minutes

Preparation

Write a possible dialogue (consisting of questions and answers) between a foreign supervisor and your students. As well as a good copy of the dialogue (which you could photocopy onto an OHT), extract and mix up words in the questions for students to sort out. If you put these on strips of paper, possible answers on other strips and provide some blank strips, students can reassemble the conversation, as suggested below. (Alternatively, you could make a worksheet in which students have the space to write out the unscrambled questions.) A possible conversation (with mixed-up questions on the right) might be as follows:

Questions to unscramble	Complete conversation
that did type letter you _____?	Did you type that letter? Yes, I typed it this morning.
to it send did who you _____?	Who did you send it to? I sent it to Mr Chan.
it you when send did _____?	When did you send it? I sent it at lunchtime.
address it department to did which you _____?	Which department did you address it to? I addressed it to Engineering.
you it how did send _____?	How did you send it? I arranged a courier.
dispatch deliver department didn't the it why _____?	Why didn't the dispatch department deliver it?
	Because they're shortstaffed.
it what cost did _____?	What did it cost? It cost $35.00.
receipt the where's _____?	Where's the receipt? Oh, dear!

© Cambridge University Press

Procedure

Ask students to unscramble questions from the dialogue. If you are using strips of paper (as suggested above) ask students to copy the correct questions onto the blank strips of paper. Elicit possible answers, then get students to match your suggested answers with the questions. After students have put the strips in the order of a possible conversation, get them to practise the conversation in pairs. When students are producing responses to the questions quickly and confidently, get them to add extra words or comments (e.g. *Well, I'm afraid …*) and to shorten answers, where appropriate. To follow up, get students to script similar dialogues which they might possibly have with their own foreign managers, either now or in the future.

☐ ADDING INFO

Students give managers extra information or opinions when asked for comments.

Language controlled by the teacher
Level intermediate
Time 15 minutes

Procedure

1 On strips of paper, get students to write some statements about their customers' preferences. For example, students manufacturing make-up with a high sun-protection factor (SPF) could write: *Consumers want a foundation which has a high SPF.*
2 Get pairs of students to consider other students' slips of paper and produce another 'ending' for each statement; they should make a private note of their 'alternative' endings. For example, the above statement could be changed to: *Customers want a foundation which is long-lasting.*
3 Then, get students to return all slips to the centre of the table and role-play an exchange, such as the following:

A: *Do you think consumers want a foundation which has a high SPF?*
B: *Yes, but I think they also want a foundation to be long-lasting.*

4 Extend one of the exchanges into a complete dialogue, eliciting as much as possible.
5 Finally, ask students to improvise similar conversations with a partner, using statements of their choice.

☐ GIVING INFO

Students give managers information or opinions when asked for comments.

Language free – only the format of the conversation is controlled
Level intermediate–advanced
Time 30 minutes

Procedure

Remind students of the importance of providing managers with information on problems. Tell them how frustrated foreign managers sometimes feel when they get little response from their foreign staff. Then, using the following diagram as a guide get students to build, then practise conversations using the same pattern.

problem?	e.g. I hear there's problem with the x ...
yes	Yes, I'm afraid there is.
what exactly?	What's the problem exactly?
information	Well, the plastic end-piece keeps breaking.
why?	What do you think is causing that?
maybe A or B	Well, it could the plastic, or maybe it's the design.
your opinion?	What do you think it is?
perhaps B + suggested action	I think it's the design. Shall I contact Jo in PD?

☐ REQUESTS TO THE BOSS

This procedure helps to raise students' awareness of different exponents for making requests and also of how requests are frequently made (successfully!) in English.

Language exponents for making requests, plus related language
Level intermediate and above
Time 20 minutes

Procedure

1 Tell students to imagine they want to do one or two of the following:

- postpone a meeting
- leave work early
- have an extension for a project because work hasn't been finished on time
- have a day off (for personal reasons)
- get a letter of recommendation

2 After students have selected one or two situations, ask them to role-play making requests to their boss in pairs. After they have practised, have pairs perform in front of the rest of the class.
3 Elicit or give feedback on the approaches students used to make the request and the exponents (for making requests) which they used. If students only used one or two exponents elicit or give them others. Some exponents you might encourage students to use are as follows:

> Could you ...
> Would you mind if I ...
> I'd really appreciate it if ...
> I wonder if you could possibly ...
> Any chance you could ...

Get students to decide which exponent would be appropriate for which situation.

4 Next, having introduced the idea that one doesn't simply walk up to one's boss and make a request, give students a diagram, as below, which can act as a pattern for making a request:

> APOLOGY FOR INTERRUPTING
> BACKGROUND/REASON FOR THE REQUEST
> **REQUEST**
> REASSURANCE

5 After practising the pronunciation of the new language introduced (i.e. the exponents for requests) – making sure that students note and produce the characteristic fall-rise pattern – get students to role-play each of their situations in pairs, using the exponents and the pattern suggested above. The best performances can be acted out in front of the class.

For other procedures which you can use to help your students practise language for this area, see the Index entry for 'managers, reporting to'.

5.8 Presentations and Q&A sessions

Presentations can take many forms. They can be in one's own company, at a client's, at a conference, at home or abroad; they can be for one person or many people. They are often part of a meeting or constitute the beginning of a meeting. Since students at all levels may find them frightening – perhaps because they can have such an impact on a person's career – this is an important area of language to practise. Q&A (question and answer) sessions can be even more nerve-racking, even for the most advanced students, because they cannot be planned and practised in quite the same way as the presentations which trigger them; they need to be an integral part of presentations practice if students are to feel well-prepared and confident.

Before focusing on language for this area, you will need to help students to understand what makes a presentation good. To do this you could invite students' comments, then get the class to consider the notes below. You will then need to help students to refine their non-linguistic skills, as well their linguistic skills; body language, planning and the effective use of visual aids are all as important as language. You will also need to help students to avoid being a 'bad audience' through inattention or poor, or offensive, body language because attending presentations might provide excellent opportunities for making contacts or building rapport.

When practising specific language for presentations, divide the class up into groups as often as possible so that boredom levels are not too high! After individuals have practised giving presentations to small groups, they can then give a final presentation to the whole class.

Some notes for students on presentations

BUSINESS ENGLISH THINK SPOT

If you want your presentation to be a success ...

- Consider your audience carefully. How much do they already know and how much do you need to tell them?

- Consider your aim in giving the presentation. Discard any material which doesn't directly help you to achieve this aim. If something is not directly relevant, it is likely to distract your audience and dilute your message.

- Make your message easy to understand by organising your material carefully and using visual aids at appropriate moments.

- Check you know how to use any equipment which you plan to use.

- Be confident! Don't make excuses for your English or your ignorance. Say what you can and in the Q&A session be honest. Encourage constructive discussion.

© Cambridge University Press

☐ INTRODUCTORY PRESENTATION

Students give an initial short presentation to a few other students so as to get a feel for giving presentations and also to give you the opportunity to see their strengths and weaknesses.

Language work-related vocabulary
Level intermediate–advanced
Time 15 minutes

Procedure

1 Divide the class into groups of four. Alternatively ask students to put themselves in groups if you feel they really lack confidence, so need to be with 'friends'! Tell students that they are going to give a presentation to the other members of their group. They should imagine that they are speaking to some new recruits at their company.
2 Give students about five minutes to prepare a short, 2-minute presentation. Allow them to choose from the following titles:

- A general introduction to their company
- An introduction to the organisational structure of their company
- A new product or service being offered by the company
- An overview of the promotion prospects within the company
- A summary of training opportunities within the company

3 Ask students to deliver their presentations in turn. Remind them to be attentive and supportive while they are listening to other students' presentations. Tell them that they should feel free to ask questions or give some encouraging feedback after listening to each 2-minute presentation.
4 Finish off by giving some positive feedback and elicit some areas to work on. Also encourage students to record and listen to their presentation at home as a possible follow-up.

☐ DISAPPEARING INTRODUCTIONS

Using a model, which is gradually reduced to a mere matrix, students practise an introduction to a presentation, focusing on pronunciation features (e.g. sentence stress).

Language formal introduction to a presentation
Level intermediate
Time 15 minutes

Preparation

Select an introduction to a presentation which seems suitable and write it on the board. (Many introductions can be found in listening tapescripts at the end of Business English coursebooks; one example is provided on p. 193.) Record the text on tape, reading it out at a natural speed, or use the original version from the coursebook.

Procedure

1 Get students to listen to the recorded introduction, while following the words on the board. Ask gist and detail questions so as to ensure there are no comprehension problems.
2 Get students to decide which words or syllables are stressed in each sentence. Then get students to practise reading out the whole introduction in pairs.
3 Erase some key phrases in the text on the board (e.g. *I'll start by looking at ...* and *Next I'll move on to ...*) and ask students to take it in turns to 'read out' the text, filling in the gaps from memory. Continue until nothing is left on the board but symbols or notes indicating the structure of the introduction. Perhaps mark key 'content' words (e.g. the subject of the presentation, the first and second points, etc.) by boxes in a different colour.
4 Ask students to 'read out' the introduction again, this time substituting their own content. Encourage students to make the introduction as relevant to their work and as realistic as possible. At all stages of practice make sure that students stress key words (previously marked) so as to bring the message out clearly.
5 Ask students to consider (then practise) alternative ways of introducing the same presentation, using anecdotes, visual aids or demonstrations, for example.

☐ PROJECT PROJECTION

Students practise projecting their voice by speaking to a partner across the room.

Language any
Level intermediate and above
Time 10 minutes

Procedure

1 Ask students to stand in two lines facing each other along opposite walls of the classroom. Tell them that the person they can see across the room opposite them is their partner. Next, tell students that they are going to tell their partner something across the room – and they

cannot move! The only way that they can make sure their partner hears what is being said is to talk more loudly. Insist that students remain pinned to the walls at the side of the classroom throughout the activity!

2 Ask students to talk about one of the following, perhaps using different themes in different lessons:

- Three pieces of advice I would give my present or future children about the world of work
- Three pieces of advice I would give a new employee, working under me
- The three things I think are most important for a successful career
- The most important thing I've learnt since starting work
- Three of my aims in life

3 Before students start speaking – or just after! – ask them to stop and think about their breathing for a few seconds. Get them to place their hand on their abdomen and feel their breath making their abdomen rise and fall. If it is their chest which is rising and falling, they are not breathing correctly! Ask them to say *Good morning!*, *Good afternoon!* or *Good evening!*, as appropriate, across the room to their partner before starting the exercise proper.

4 When students have changed partners several times, invite students to share any good bits of advice they have heard with the rest of the class.

☐ FRUITY INTRODUCTIONS

Students practise language for introductions to presentations, using types of fruit as a lead-in.

Language phrases for introductions, such as *I'll start by, Then I'll look at*
Level lower–upper-intermediate
Time 30 minutes

Procedure

1 After a warmer activity to focus students' attention (such as SIMPLE SERIES on p. 82), ask students to think of types of fruit. Students can work in one big circle if you have a small class or alternatively in groups. First each student should say one fruit (e.g. *banana*), then he or she should say the names of three fruits (e.g. *banana, mango and pineapple*). After each turn another student (picked at random) should repeat the same list so as to check that he or she has heard and understood all the fruits in the list.

2   Next, ask students to imagine that they are giving a presentation about fruit. Instead of simply listing three fruits, they should insert their list into a mini-introduction, which you could elicit. One possible introduction is as follows:

> Good afternoon, everyone. Thank you for coming.
> This afternoon I'm going to take at look at fruit in Sri Lanka.
> I'll start by talking about bananas.
> Then I'll look at mangoes.
> I'll finish by considering pineapples.

Get students to practise their fruity lead-ins in pairs.

3   Next, ask them to take a pen and paper. First they should write down a possible topic for a presentation – anything will do! – then, they should write a list of three things which could be discussed in the presentation. For example, if the subject is transport the three things could be buses, trains and aeroplanes. Students should then incorporate these three things into an introduction as before, with the fruits, and another student should repeat each student's main points (i.e. the list of three items) after each mini-introduction. (Note that getting students to list other students' items is tantamount to asking them to listen out for main points, which is a useful listening exercise to supplement the speaking practice.)

4   Next, ask students to use long phrases (e.g. *The Kobe Dentetsu Line* – a railway line) instead of single words in their list of three things, so that the exercise is more of a challenge and more similar to what might be said in a real-life introduction to a presentation. Help students to compose phrases which would be appropriate in a business setting. While students are practising their introductions, focus individuals' attention on pronunciation and on the impression they might make in a real-life business setting. See 4.5 and 4.6 – especially FOREIGN PERSONALITY CHECKING (p. 115) – for ideas on how to do this.

5   Finally, ask students to spend a few minutes talking about the subjects they have mentioned in their introductions. Ask them to imagine that they are continuing their presentations beyond the introduction. It is, after all, better that they do this in English in class rather than in their L1 over coffee later on!

☐ CHANGE CHARTING

Students review and practise key vocabulary for describing change in business situations.

Language vocabulary for describing change
Level intermediate and above
Time 20–30 minutes

Preparation

Draw approximately 16 L-shapes on the board, to represent x and y axes of imaginary graphs. In each L-shape draw a very simple graph to represent vocabulary for describing change. Some of the vocabulary you might like to illustrate might include: *rose, fell, slumped, reached a peak at, levelled off, fluctuated wildly, dramatically increased, decreased slightly.* Your board work can be very simple, as the following four L-shapes to illustrate the last four phrases illustrate:

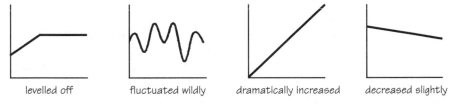

| levelled off | fluctuated wildly | dramatically increased | decreased slightly |

Don't write the vocabulary under each graph but have a phrase in mind as you draw each one!

Procedure

1 Without any preparation, ask students to write words or phrases under the 'graphs' you have drawn on the board. Help them with vocabulary if it becomes clear that nobody can label certain graphs.
2 Explain any words or phrases which most of the students seem to be unfamiliar with, giving students time to make notes.
3 Erase everything on the board before giving a dictation of 10 'graphs'. In other words, for each of the ten items make a short sentence about a corporate situation and ask students to draw a simple graph to represent the situation. If possible, make your sentences relate to the students' companies and their own situations. For example, if you say *Turnover increased dramatically last year* students simply need to draw the third graph in the example above.
4 After checking students' answers (by getting students to draw the 10 graphs on the board), ask students to make a list of 10 more graphs.
5 Next ask students to 'dictate' their graphs to a partner, while sitting

back-to-back. Help students to explain their graphs by providing relevant language, while you are monitoring.

6   After students have checked their graphs review any extra vocabulary which has come up.

7   Finally, either in class or for homework, ask students to prepare a short section of a presentation in which they describe recent changes in their industry, company or department. (Note that this might provide background information to proposals students make in the same presentation.) Encourage students to write out the section and add any visual aids which they would use in a real-life presentation so that you can check they are using the language accurately and appropriately. Remind students that it is important to use this language correctly when attempting to communicate information about changes because major decisions may be made by colleagues or bosses based on this same information. Later in the course provide students with the opportunity to give a complete presentation which includes a corrected version of their work.

□ PRESENTING PROBLEMS

Students write a quick plan for an imaginary presentation on problems at work and then improvise a short version of the actual presentation. Since the focus is on students' own problems this activity could be a springboard to some interesting discussion! The feedback students receive from each other could also be useful when planning a real presentation on the same subject.

Language phrases for presentations
Level lower-intermediate–upper-intermediate
Time 40 minutes

Procedure

1   Tell students that they are going to give a short presentation about problems in their workplace. Encourage them to consider who they would be giving this presentation to (e.g. their boss or their colleagues), and what their aim might be (e.g. to persuade their boss or their colleagues to make some changes).

2   Ask students to write out a short plan for the introduction to their presentation, based on the following matrix:

1 Introduction
2 Description of focus area
3 Problems
4 Recommendations/Suggestions

Improvise a couple of introductions based on this matrix so that it is very clear to students what kind of plan you are asking them to produce. Alternatively, use the following example, which you could put on an OHT or write up on the board:

---

1 Good afternoon, everyone.
2 I'm going to start by giving you an overview of the Supersound in-company programme.
3 Then I'll look at some of the problems, both from the perspective of Supersound and from the perspective of the instructors working on the programme.
4 I'll finish by considering some possible solutions to these problems, focusing in particular on cost per trainee, test results and the self-access centre.

---

3 When students have prepared their plans, ask them to practise saying their introductions to a partner. Encourage students to use the phrases given in the example introduction above and correct students whenever they make mistakes, however small. Mistakes will, after all, affect the impression students make in real life when giving presentations and these presentations may be important for the students' careers or for their companies' success.
4 Get students to improvise mini-presentations based on their introductions in small groups. Encourage students who are listening to ask questions at the end of each presentation and to offer constructive suggestions. Also while you are monitoring, encourage supportive discussion so that individuals will have an interesting and rewarding experience of presenting, which may be especially important for students who are nervous!

☐ PHONEMIC PRESENTATIONS

This is another fun activity which will help to focus students' attention on pronunciation so that their presentations are clearer and easier to understand. Using phonemics has the bonus that students will later eventually also be able to decode phonemics in the dictionary in order to check the pronunciation of specific words. See p. 81 for a key to phonemic symbols.

Language words selected by the teacher
Level lower-intermediate–advanced
Time 20 minutes

Preparation

Make an ongoing list of words which students are mispronouncing. Focus particularly on words or phrases which are important for students in their work. Ensure that there are some words which are relevant to each student. Write these words up on the board in phonemics before the lesson starts. Use slashes to mark the beginning and end of each word so that it is clear that you are not misspelling words students know!

Procedure

1   As students come into class hand them a pen or chalk and get them to write the word or phrase above each set of phonemics. Make sure that all students participate. (Note that it is not necessary to have pre-taught the phonemic script for this to be possible.) Help students to decode the words which they find the most difficult.
2   Next, get students to decide which syllable is stressed for each word by asking them how many syllables each word has and whether the stress is on the first, second or third syllable, etc. Use small boxes to mark the stress on each word.
3   Drill all the words so as to ensure they are pronounced correctly.
4   Ask students to choose three words from the board to put into a mini-presentation. Allow five minutes' planning time.
5   Finally, ask students to give their presentations in small groups. Encourage other members of each group to ask questions.

Variation

Get students to match words written on cards with the equivalent phonemic transcriptions, which are also written on cards. This can be done on the floor or on tables as students come into class.

□ FREE IMPROMPTUS

This activity gives students an opportunity to practise key expressions which have been previously introduced or to develop fluency and confidence. It's usually fun because students can be unexpectedly good!

Language determined by the students
Level intermediate–advanced
Time 20 minutes–1 hour

Procedure

1   Tell students that they are going to give two short presentations each. Brainstorm possible subjects with the students and write these on the board.

2 Next, tell students to choose two subjects each and allow 5–7 minutes for preparation. Allow students to 'choose' another subject they are expert in if they prefer. The list of subjects on the board is simply intended to help those students who have no ideas or inspiration initially! (Each mini-presentation should last only about three minutes.) Provide vocabulary or help with planning as you monitor. Encourage students to prepare basic visual aids so that students take their presentations more seriously. (Encourage students to use whatever equipment is available.)

3 Having put students into pairs or small groups, taking account of equipment requirements, get students to give their presentations to each other. Ask students who are listening to prepare at least three questions for each presenter.

4 Ask students to change partners or groups and deliver their presentations a second time.

5 Finally, get students to choose one presentation which should be made to the whole class.

Variation 1

Get students to prepare and deliver only the introduction of a presentation or, alternatively, only the conclusion.

Variation 2

After students have done their initial planning, get them to consult each other for ideas on improving the content. Make sure that they then pair up with students they haven't previously consulted before giving their presentations.

☐ CONCLUSION-BUILDING

Students practise language which might be useful when concluding a presentation after an informal, interactive lead-in. Balls are used so as to encourage free-flowing ideas when preparing the often difficult final section of a presentation.

Language phrases for ending presentations
Level lower-intermediate–upper-intermediate
Time 40 minutes

Preparation

Write the following phrases and questions on the hidden side of a double-sided board, on a flipchart or on large white cards:

> One problem that we often/sometimes/occasionally/constantly experience is that ...
> Another problem is that ...
> A third problem is that ...
> What do you think could be done to improve the situation?
> How do you think you could improve your approach to ... ?
> Is there any way problems with ... could be minimised?

Find several light balls, one for each pair of students if possible.

Procedure

At each stage of this activity, except the last, when conclusions are practised, students speak, throwing a ball to another student, and then get the ball thrown back with a question about whatever they have said, before throwing the ball on to another student (in silence). If students sit at the outer edges of the classroom, as far away from each other as possible, balls can be thrown around properly and voices projected with confidence! At each stage it is a good idea to start with one ball going round in a clockwise direction, then to add other balls so that several are circulating at once, and finally to allow students to throw balls in any direction in order to allow free communication. Eventually, and at every stage, students can be working in pairs if you have enough balls for one per pair of students. Your role as the teacher is to help students by providing vocabulary or correcting mistakes.

1 Start some small-talk by throwing balls to students and asking questions or making comments (e.g. *Hi, how are you?*). Wait for students to respond and throw the ball back to you or on to another student, asking a question or making a comment as they do so.

2 Ask students to say any word or phrase when they first throw a ball. Get students who are returning balls to ask a question about the word or phrase they have just heard. As soon as they have got an answer (and a returned ball) students should continue the process by throwing the ball on to another student in silence.

3 Next, ask students to say any word or phrase which comes to mind to do with work or their company. Students who are returning balls should ask about this word or phrase, as above. When the student who initially said the word or phrase answers he or she should use a sentence if possible, before passing the ball on in silence. In other words, he or she should give a long response.

4 Revealing the phrases which you have previously written up on the board or on large cards placed in the centre of the floor, ask

students to make a statement about a problem they experience at work. Get students to use both the sentence beginnings and the questions, while continuing as before (throwing balls back and forth). Emphasise that the phrases and questions would be appropriate for a conclusion or for a Q&A session after a presentation.

5 Ask students to 'throw' lists of problems to other students. As at every other stage, the person who is listening fires questions back, but only when they have heard the whole list! Again insist that students use the phrases which you have written on the board or cards.

6 Stop students throwing balls and get them to practise saying the following sentence: *Having described the main procedures in the department, I'd now like to mention a couple of problems we experience and suggest some possible solutions.* Use backchaining (see Glossary) to drill this effectively.

7 Finally, get students to use this sentence and their previous statements about problems in imaginary conclusions to presentations. If you have a language lab get students to record their conclusions and to listen to themselves and other students on tape.

8 In a follow-up lesson, give students the option of giving the entire presentation which might include this 'conclusion', either to the whole class or in small groups.

☐ QUESTION ZAPPING

Students have fun answering questions (as in a Q&A session) and are rated on five key areas of performance. The activity is sufficiently guided for weaker students to be able to develop confidence but also sufficiently free for others to take risks and experiment.

Language exponents for answering questions in a Q&A session
Level upper-intermediate–advanced
Time 40 minutes

Procedure

1 Brainstorm problems with students for particular areas of work or for departments or activities (e.g. launching a new product). Make notes on the board or divide the class into groups and get one person in each group to record individuals' contributions.

2 Tell students to select three or four related problems, then give them time to prepare 'solutions' for these problems. When they have done this, students need to write one or two questions to go with their own problems and solutions. They need to write these on strips of paper and put them in the centre of the room.

3 Elicit, then write, key phrases for introducing solutions on the board.

197

For example:

> One way of dealing with this would be to ...
> In order to improve our ...
> Another way of cutting costs would be to ...
> This would result in greater ...

Organise pronunciation practice of these exponents, at first as a class (marking sentence stress, etc.), then with pairs facing each other and projecting their voices across the room.

4 Get students – one at a time – to pick up slips of paper and put questions to the line of students sitting opposite, who can now be considered a team. The person who has prepared solutions can obviously answer but so can anyone else who can think fast enough. Each team scores points for effective answers on the following basis:

- 1 point for answering the question, i.e. not avoiding it
- 1 point for clarity, i.e. if the answer is clear and easy to understand
- 1 point for good use of exponents, i.e. appropriate use of language
- 1 point for accuracy, i.e. both grammar and details
- 1 point for good pronunciation, i.e. both confident and clear.

Note that this scoring system gives a possible total of 5 points for each turn. Help with scoring, where necessary!

5 Follow up by asking students to work in small groups without scoring. This time, instead of working in teams, individual students must 'zap' their own questions!

Variation 1

The same practice can obviously be done without scoring if you prefer, although this will mean there is less 'zap' to the Q&A practice!

Variation 2

If a language lab with pairing facility is available, this practice can be much more intense for individuals. Follow the procedure described above with students working in pairs, then ask individual students to evaluate their own performance after listening to the recording. Add your own tips and comments when you listen in.

☐ DEFINITIONS PRACTICE

Students practise defining words which they might get asked about in a presentation. The exercise gives students strategies for defining difficult terms.

Language any
Level intermediate–advanced
Time 15 minutes

Procedure

1 Put students into groups according to their department, speciality or industry, making groups of students as homogeneous as possible. Tell each group to list about 20 (English) words related to their speciality, which outsiders or non-experts might not understand.

2 Ask students to exchange their lists with other groups (e.g. Group A might get Group B's list of words, Group B might get Group A's list of words, Group C might get Group D's list of words and Group D might get Group C's list of words).

3 Elicit and/or suggest strategies for dealing with questions about words in presentations and language associated with each of these. Some strategies and language you might like to introduce and practise with students are as follows:

- classifying, e.g. *It's a kind of xxx*
- giving a use, e.g. *It's used for xxx*
- giving an example of a category, e.g. *A xxx is an example of a xxx*
- likening it to something else, e.g. *It's a bit like a xxx but it's ...*
- drawing a diagram, e.g. *It looks like this*
- giving an example of a situation, e.g. *This is something which happens when ...*
- asking the questioner for more information, e.g. *Are you talking about x or y?*

4 Ask students to find a partner in a group who prepared the list of words they have so that they are talking to someone who knows the answers! Then encourage students to ask *What's a xxx?*, *What exactly do you mean by xxx?*, *Can you clarify what xxx is?* and to say, *I'm sorry I don't know,* or *I believe it's a ...,* if they are not sure about a particular term! Also encourage students to give an action-related answer whenever possible, as they might in a real-life presentation, e.g *Can I get back to you on that?*

☐ MANAGER QUESTIONING

This is a good activity for in-company students who work in companies where there are foreign middle managers. Students practise asking questions which they are likely to really want to have answered! It is a truly communicative activity which can be the springboard for much else.

Language questions
Level upper-intermediate and above
Time 40 minutes

Preparation

1 Chat to a key foreign manager, then ask if he or she would be willing to come into a class. Explain that you want to give the students practice in asking questions and that the visitor will, of course, be free to refuse to answer certain questions if they like!
2 Explain what you have arranged to the class and get students to prepare questions to ask this manager. Get them to categorise the questions under headings, then put the categories in a logical order. They can then write out a mini-agenda for the visiting manager.

Procedure

Having copied and distributed the agenda beforehand, bring the manager into the lesson at the prearranged time. Ask one student to 'chair' the meeting. Round up at the end with some diplomatic comments and thanks to the manager! Feel free to interrupt the meeting at any time if you feel that the manager is being intimidated by the students or if you feel too much time is being spent on one area. After the meeting, students could write up minutes of the meeting or a report for their manager (a pretend one!) on the issues discussed. Alternatively, select one or two issues and lead into memo-writing to take action or arrange follow-up meetings.

☐ SKETCH-BASED Q&A

Students use a simple diagram to introduce a product or service. Their partner then asks them questions, imagining that they have heard a much more complex presentation.

Language student-controlled questions and answers
Level intermediate and above
Time 10 minutes

Procedure

1 Tell students that they are going to give a very short presentation about a product or service and then answer a client's questions. Demonstrate how they are going to do this by drawing a diagram on the board which represents a product or service, giving a 30-second presentation immediately afterwards and inviting questions from students so that they can get more information.
2 Ask students to decide on a product or service first of all, then give them one minute to draw a very simple diagram of this.
3 Having asked them to find a partner, tell students that they must briefly introduce their product or service to their partner. As soon as they have finished, their partner must ask questions as if they were a potential client asking questions after a much longer presentation.
4 As a useful follow-up, ask students to write up a text describing their partner's product or service underneath the original sketch. When the texts have been written, get students to pass them back to their partner for checking (of both details and grammar). Finally, having put students in groups of four, ask students to imagine they are at a meeting to approve or reject purchase requests. They must agree which one of the four products or services presented by the group they are going to spend money on.

For other procedures which you can use to help your students practise language for this area, see the Index entry for 'presentations and Q&A sessions'.

5.9 Meetings

Successful participation in meetings in English is often necessary for advancement within a company, especially if it's a multinational, so practice of this language area is essential, even if difficult for many students.

Students may, naturally, find participation much more difficult than comprehension of conversations, especially if some participants are native-speakers of English; very little silence is left for hesitant contributors. Turntaking patterns and rules for etiquette may be quite different in the students' home culture so these will naturally need to be the focus of attention when you are practising relevant language. In addition, people in real-life meetings do not often use language in ways that students might expect. They make suggestions in surprising ways (e.g. using conditionals instead of *Let's*) and use many subtle ways of influencing others. They also use indirect ways of agreeing and disagreeing, which are very dissimilar to the phrases presented to students in many coursebooks (e.g. *You're absolutely right but ...* when disagreeing). Students will therefore need language so as to be able to exert influence themselves, and strategies for coping when they encounter difficulties.

Before tackling this area, note that meetings can be held for very different reasons in different cultures (cf. Japan, where meetings often only ratify decisions previously made, with the US and the UK, where meetings are seen as a forum for the airing of ideas). If your students are unfamiliar with the type of meeting common in English-speaking countries, give them the notes on p. 203. In order to prepare yourself and your students further also attend meetings, observing both native and non-native speakers' use of language, and study dialogues from scripted meetings as much as possible. (Note that transcripts of meetings appear in some coursebooks.) Also, find out about the type of international meetings students need to attend and about the problems they experience. If it is not possible to attend a meeting formally it should certainly be possible to glean a lot of useful information about students' work, in-company politics and attitudes, simply by asking students about issues that they have brought up previously. For example, if a student has prepared a presentation on a particular problem area, ask about the outcome. In addition, ask students questions such as the following:

- *What do you think your managers complain about?*
- *Do they hold meetings to discuss these problem situations?*
- *Do your managers ever ask you to discuss solutions to problems in meetings?*
- *Are meetings in your department formal or informal? Are they large or small?*
- *What kind of meetings have you had to attend recently? What was discussed?*
- *What kind of meetings do you expect to be attending soon?*
- *How easy is it for you to participate?*

In order to make role-played meetings in class more realistic:

- Prepare students thoroughly in advance, possibly eliciting or giving them information about why meetings are held in English and what they are like. You can use the notes for students given in the box on the opposite page as part of an information sheet or questionnaire.
- Get students to prepare an agenda for every meeting role-played in class.
- Insist on the normal preliminaries (i.e. brief socialising before meetings and opening comments by the chair person) and include other related activities (such as telephone calls, e-mails, faxes,

minutes, memos or reports) around class role-plays as often as possible so as to set meetings in a seemingly realistic context and give valuable extra practice of key areas. Some of these related activities can, of course, be suggested as homework tasks.

- Get students to bring in real product samples and real statistical data (on OHTs, if possible) to back up their contributions in meetings.
- Get students to refer to real-life faxes, e-mails, memos and reports when they speak.
- Get students to refer to managers or colleagues before or after class to get information.
- Invite an international manager to join the class when role-playing meetings.

Some notes for students about meetings held in English

BUSINESS ENGLISH THINK SPOT

Why are meetings held ...
... and how should one behave?

- Meetings are mostly held to discuss things, but can also be held so as to make announcements, share information or confirm decisions.
- Punctuality is considered important in many cultures (especially Britain and America) but different nationalities have very different ideas on what 'late' is!
- Leaving a meeting for a while halfway through or before the end is considered rude in Britain and America, unless it's an absolute emergency.
- Meetings will vary from being very formal to very informal – depending on the corporate culture, the size and purpose of the meeting and the participants.
- There is usually an agenda. In English-speaking meetings you are expected to discuss only things which are directly relevant to this agenda.
- You will probably get an opportunity to discuss other things in AOB (Any Other Business) at the end of the meeting but you may not get much time.
- Basically, anyone can talk at almost any point in the meeting – but the chair person is the boss. However, you may be invited to talk or sense that there is a 'right time' to come in with your own views.
- It's OK to disagree or mention any supporting information which you feel is relevant. You don't need to worry too much about pleasing people. Managers will usually want to hear your ideas or comments.
- You may feel you need to interrupt or 'fight' to speak. This is perfectly normal! You may also feel you get more out of meetings if you find the courage to ask for clarification whenever you don't understand!

© Cambridge University Press

☐ THE QUESTION GAME

Students formulate then practise questions which they might need when attending meetings with people they don't know (e.g. at a conference or at head office). As well as helping students to get to know each other, this procedure should also help you to gauge your students' level and should make you aware of any problems your students are having relating to grammar, vocabulary or pronunciation.

Language determined by the students
Level any, except absolute beginner
Time 40 minutes

Procedure

1 Explain to students that they are going to ask each other questions, imagining they are making conversation at a conference welcome party. Elicit and write question words and phrases on the board (e.g. *What, Who, How long*). Then get students to write one question for each word and phrase. Remind them that they must prepare questions which are suitable for first meetings at a conference. They should write two sets of questions, each set on a separate piece of paper. The first set should be questions which they think are appropriate to ask generally. The second set should be questions which they would like other people to ask them.

2 Monitor carefully while students are preparing questions and correct as much as possible (grammar, use of vocabulary, etc.). This is important because students will then practise 'correct' questions in the next stage. Encourage students to avoid over-personal questions.

3 Get students to mill around, asking each other the general questions they have prepared and following up with other questions which seem appropriate on the spur of the moment. Insist that students use 'interested' intonation patterns. Stop them for some choral drilling, if necessary.

4 Give students some initial feedback and encouragement. Then ask students to pass their lists of questions to a partner. Students then have other role-played chats which incorporate the prepared questions. Remind students that they still need to imagine they are meeting strangers at a conference.

5 As a possible follow-up, ask students to role-play introducing new contacts to old colleagues. They should include some information from their initial chats in each introduction.

Variation

Ask students to think of questions which it would be appropriate to ask colleagues before meetings. Typical questions they might practise could be as follows:

> How are things going, Mr Tan?
> Have you finished preparing for the party yet, Ms Hayashi?
> What do you think our bonus will be like this month?!

Then get students to role-play an informal pre-meeting conversation, using these questions.

☐ DEEP-END RECORDED MEETINGS

Having identified a realistic purpose for a meeting for a particular group of students, students role-play and record the meeting. Since there is no preliminary preparation or practice of key language, students should truly feel like they have been thrown into the deep end of a swimming pool! The recording of the meeting provides a starting point for detailed language work and will clearly focus complacent students' attention on problem areas.

Language any
Level lower-intermediate and above
Time 1 hour+

Procedure

1 Find out from students (or their bosses) what type of meetings they are or will be attending. Get students to fine-tune the purpose of the meeting, imagining and agreeing any necessary background information. They should then write out an agenda for the meeting and/or any preliminary memos informing people of the need for a meeting.

2 Allowing no practice or double-takes, record students role-playing the meeting, using a mike in the middle of the table. Either use a multi-dimensional mike (e.g. a PZM flat mike) or a normal hand-held mike; with hesitant or low-level students it's a good idea to use a remote control mike which can be turned on and off by each person who makes a comment. It will be easier to analyse language if there are few pauses between utterances.

3 When going over the recording, focus students' attention on the following areas, where applicable:

- turntaking patterns – would they be OK in an English-speaking context?
- inappropriate use of vocabulary
- inappropriate use of functional exponents
- inappropriate style of language (too formal or informal, or an inappropriate mix)

- strange intonation when speaking (e.g. giving the impression of arrogance or lack of interest)
- wrong use of word or sentence stress resulting in poorly emphasised points
- mispronunciation of certain sounds, which may cause incomprehensibility
- non-verbal behaviour which is likely to cause offence in an international setting (e.g. blowing one's nose – which is offensive to many Asians, sniffing, sighing, sleeping)
- inappropriate responses (e.g. to questions when socialising before a meeting)

Take care to give students feedback sensitively. See 4.5 for suggestions.

4 If possible, as a follow-up, type up a corrected or improved transcript of the meeting before the next class. Get students to identify differences between this 'improved' version and the original recording in pairs or groups. Then ask students to read out the improved version or to role-play the original meeting again. (Note that it is a good idea to leave students to assign names to comments in the transcript because it's difficult for you to identify students' voices when transcribing and also because it gives students a task for their first reading of the transcript.)

5 Later, you can use this transcript again if you cut it up for students to sequence or gap key phrases. Students will appreciate the opportunity to focus on detailed use of language.

☐ STRATEGY DEVELOPMENT

Students practise useful phrases which help them to cope in meetings. They are encouraged to use the phrases in a game-like situation so they are not in danger of losing face.

Language *Could we go over that again, please?*, *How would that work in practice?*, etc.
Level intermediate and above
Time 20 minutes

Preparation

Select a list of phrases which you think would help your students when participating in meetings. Type out the list with plenty of space between each item. Consider presenting phrases such as the following:

> Sorry, I didn't catch the question …
> Could we go over that again, please?
> How would that work in practice?
> Can you explain how that would work?
> I don't really understand what the advantages of your idea would be.
> Sorry, I don't follow.
> I'd like some more time to think about it.
> I've got nothing to add.
> I can see time's running out, so perhaps we could summarise the ideas we've generated so far?
> How about if we all write down our thoughts before the next meeting and distribute them so we can consider them carefully?

Enlarge the text, photocopy it (one copy for each student) and cut the sheets up into strips. In this way, you can prepare a set of comments for all your students. Photocopy one list onto an OHT (if possible) for your initial input phase.

Procedure

Elicit or present the phrases you have listed, using your OHT or writing the key phrases on the board. After drilling each individual phrase, get students to role-play a meeting as a class, having given each student a set of strips. (Ask students to do this in small groups if you have more than eight students in the class.) While they are participating, the students' aim is to 'get rid of' as many of their strips of paper as possible; every time they use a phrase, they put the strip of paper into the middle of the table. (They are free to use phrases more than once.) The 'winner' is the student who is left with the fewest strips of paper at the end.

Variation

If you prefer, instead of preparing strips of paper give students copies of the list of phrases you've prepared and ask them to tick off each phrase as they use it. The student with the most ticks – in the most places – is the winner at the end of the discussion.

☐ MANAGEMENT CONUNDRUMS

Students are asked to solve problems of greater or lesser importance which a manager might have to tackle. This is a good procedure for helping students to develop fluency and confidence.

Language any – the focus is on fluency development, not accuracy
Level intermediate and above
Time 20 minutes

Preparation

Find some management problems. Useful sources are management books, management magazines, coursebooks or real life! Consider using cartoons which convey the problem situations, as well as short texts. Alternatively, elicit problems from students by getting them to think of problems and write them out in small groups. Problems from one group are then passed onto other groups for 'solutions'. Some example problems:

> While some people in the office want and need to smoke, others complain it's unhealthy. How can you keep everyone happy?

> Everyone seems to go to the cafeteria for lunch at around the same time so the queues and the crowding are terrible. What kind of system or solutions might improve the situation?

> A few people in your department seem to spend too much time chatting. You yourself, as manager, are working under terrible pressure and know that everybody in your team is needed if deadlines are to be kept. What can you do?

> One of your staff is persistently late. Every day he has a good excuse. What do you do?

© Cambridge University Press

Procedure

1 Pass some management problems to students on slips of paper, or explain or elicit them, as suggested above. Tell students that they have ten minutes to decide on a solution with a partner.
2 Ask students to change partners and discuss the solutions they have come up with.

3 Next, get students to write memos or role-play telephone conversations in preparation for a meeting.
4 Finally, get students to role-play a meeting to decide on the best solution for one or more of the problems.

☐ CONDITIONAL PROBABILITIES

By completing a statement about a possible strategy, students practise first or second conditionals (which might be useful in meeting discussions). They then move on to discuss the details of each strategy proposed.

Language first or second conditionals
Level lower–upper-intermediate
Time 15 minutes

Procedure

1 Write a provocative *If*-half of a conditional sentence on the board. Some examples you could try:

If we reduce the price of our products ...
If we all received a 20% cut in salary ...
If half our company's employees were fired ...
If all enquiries were dealt with by computer ...
If we gave free samples of all our products ...

© Cambridge University Press

Alternatively, ask students what their strategy might be if sales of their products fell or if a new competitor came onto the market, then elicit an *If*-half of a conditional sentence from students. Elicit one or two endings for the conditional sentence. Then get students in pairs to brainstorm other possible consequences and to write out other second halves of the sentence.

An example of one *If*-half of a conditional sentence and some possible second halves:

If we reduce the price of our Super-Line range ...
... we'll have to save on the cost of raw materials and packaging.
... we'll attract a lot of new customers.
... we'll be able to compete with Super-X Inc.
... our profits will go down.
... we'll have to extend our product range.
... our turnover will double.

209

> ... our manufacturing processes will have to become more efficient.
> ... we'll have to reduce the quality of our products.
> ... sales to teenagers will probably increase.
> ... we'll have to improve our logistics system.

2 While students are working, elicit or feed in three or four more sentence beginnings (which would constitute alternative strategies) and encourage pairs of students to think of consequences. When numerous endings have been generated in pairs get students to exchange them in simulated meetings. As each student suggests a strategy, others must suggest consequences, each time explaining why. Encourage students to add comments which indicate whether they think a particular strategy is a good idea or not by adding extra expressions, such as *That's a great idea, If we did that, ...* or *Well, I don't know, I think ...*

3 If you find that students make a lot of mistakes when using conditionals or if, even after this kind of practice, they fail to use them altogether, record these simulated meetings, so that problems can later be pointed out and rectified.

□ PRODUCT DEVELOPMENT

After pairwork to consider ideas for new products, students role-play meetings in which their ideas are discussed. This motivating procedure gets students practising being persuasive.

Language any
Level upper-intermediate and above
Time 40 minutes–1 hour

Procedure

1 Tell students that they are going to develop a new product because their company needs to diversify if it is to survive. Ask students to work in pairs and to brainstorm ideas for new products (e.g. tobacco that doesn't smell bad, disposable frying pans, liquid floor-fill which sets to be spongy, as a replacement for carpets).

2 After students have generated a few ideas ask pairs to decide on the best idea and consider the product's selling points. Then ask them to join up with another pair of students and decide which pair's product is the best. Continue the process of joining up pairs or groups until the class is divided into two groups, each of which has decided on a product to develop. (Note that one half of the class

should know nothing about the other half's product if the two halves of the class have been kept separate.)

3 Next, ask each half of the class to prepare a presentation to 'sell' their favoured product to the rest of the class. Each group's presentation should include various OHTs (if possible); one OHT should be a picture of the product (probably a hand-drawn annotated diagram), another should be an advert to be used in magazines and a third OHT should be a list of benefits the company would enjoy if it should choose this product to diversify its product range. Students in each of the two groups will also need to decide on the target market for their product, the unit price and the market share they will be aiming for, taking local and international competitors into account.

4 Before inviting students to deliver their group presentations, ask group members to decide which company position they are going to role-play in the Q&A session and meeting which follow the presentations (e.g. Finance Director or Sales Manager). Encourage students to adopt a range of different roles so that the ensuing discussion is more interesting.

5 Ask students in each of the two groups to give their presentations in turn to the whole class. Encourage students who are listening to ask questions after each product has been presented so as to get as much information as possible, to clarify any points which are unclear and to challenge the other group's ideas.

6 Finally, tell studetns to take position round a large table, if possible, to discuss and decide which product would be suitable for product development. (While they are discussing this question individual students will, of course, be in the roles they have decided on beforehand.) Before the meeting begins, explain to students that they will need to have decided on a suitable course of action by the end of the meeting so that one of the products can be developed and marketed successfully. Naturally, any tasks which need to be done as part of this will need to be allocated to individuals. While the meeting is taking place, focus mainly on listening to students' use of language but also encourage quiet individuals to participate if you think it is language difficulties which are holding them back. Also encourage students to be competitive by asking a few difficult questions of your own or by making a few strategic comments! If you need a role, it is probably most appropriate to take the role of the company President or Managing Director, who might well be virtually silent in this kind of situation in real life.

7 When decisions have been reached, give students some feedback, as usual, following the guidelines laid out in 4.5.

☐ STRIP DISCUSSION

Students discuss a controversial subject, using exponents for agreeing, disagreeing, interrupting, etc. They prepare their opinions in advance (writing these on strips of paper) so that they can focus fully on language during the discussion itself. This is a good procedure for classes where student participation is uneven.

Language exponents for agreeing, disagreeing, clarifying, etc.
Level intermediate
Time 30 minutes

Preparation

Cut up at least ten strips of paper for each student. On other strips of paper, copy out some of the controversial statements listed below. Note that only one statement should appear on each strip of paper. Also copy one statement onto an OHT, if possible.

> Companies have a responsibility to society and should be forced to help those in need.

> Governments should run services which are essential to society.

> All national borders should be destroyed because they only create barriers to trading and international understanding.

> Children no longer need to be taught maths or handwriting in school because computers can do what we used to have to do ourselves. Companies can provide any relevant computer training.

> Fathers should be given more paternity leave so that they can help with new babies.

> Smoking should be made illegal in all work places.

> The retirement age should be lowered so as to cut down unemployment.

Procedure

1 Introduce one of the provocative statements to the class, either by writing it on the board or by flashing it up on an OHT. Encourage any initial comments and any spontaneous discussion between students before telling the students that they are going to practise some more language for discussions by considering several controversial topics.

2 Divide the class into three groups (or more, if you have a very large class) and give each group another statement, written out on a strip of paper, as well as a pile of blank strips. Stop students from discussing the statement and instead insist that they write out some comments on the subject on the blank strips of paper. Make sure that each individual student prepares at least seven strips of paper.

3 Elicit or introduce some exponents for making points, supporting points, agreeing, disagreeing, interrupting, clarifying, etc. (You may need to use your course materials at this stage.) Organise any practice activities you feel might help students to use these exponents effectively in the next stage.

4 Tell students they are going to use the exponents in a simulated discussion by combining them with the comments they previously wrote out on strips of paper. Every time they want to 'say' one of the comments they have written out they must find a suitable opportunity in the discussion and put the appropriate slip in the centre of the table as they speak. Each student must get rid of all his or her strips of paper by the end of the discussion. Tell students they can change the subject as often as they like, as long as they manage to make their comments seem natural and relevant to the conversation in progress.

5 Regroup students for follow-up discussions (by changing student groups from AAA, BBB, CCC to ABC, ABC, ABC, for example) – one or more times, depending on how individual students' scores are improving! Get individual students to keep track of how many strips of paper they manage to get rid of in each round, then tot up totals at the end.

6 Next, ask all students to come back together to discuss the controversial statements as a class. In this class discussion stage students can be allowed to talk without using their strips of paper!

7 Your feedback should, obviously, focus on how appropriately students used the exponents that you practised earlier on in the session, as well as on any other language points which arise.

For other procedures which you can use to help your students to practise language for this area see the Index entry for 'meetings'.

5.10 Negotiating

Even if they are not involved in major negotiations for contracts, most students will need to conduct small-scale negotiations (to arrange or change meetings, to get rooms reserved, to persuade foreign colleagues to change procedures or systems, etc.). Find out about the type of negotiating your students are – or will be – expected to do before embarking on practice activities. Don't base practice on your own preconceptions! When embarking on practice activities, remember that the most successful negotiations involve a sharing of problems and a final agreement which is satisfactory and beneficial to both parties. Also, note that students will have to be very much aware of cultural differences if they are to be successful negotiators. When dealing with certain nationalities, students may find they have to do a lot of 'chatting' before or during serious negotiating sessions because personal relationships between people who do business are considered especially important in some cultures (e.g. Japan). In any cross-cultural situation, the ability of students to build rapport with their negotiating partners will be of paramount importance; this means that initial chatting, effective listening and the ability to stress areas of common ground (i.e. points of agreement) are especially important.

Students will also need to understand that negotiators in many cultures may not be able to make decisions, as their counterparts often do in the UK and the US, because power and decision-making structures may be completely different in the students' home or corporate culture. If sent to a negotiation as a junior negotiator on the other hand, students may find themselves facing senior staff on 'the other side'.

If you are to help students to survive in their early negotiations, you will need to provide them with language which gives students control (e.g. *Perhaps we should look at a few alternative approaches*) and puts individuals back in control when things become unclear (e.g. *Can we go over that again?*). Encourage students to consider other ways of exerting influence than those they have learnt so far. (This should provide endless 'food for thought' for you, as well as for your students.) Also encourage students to check what has been agreed at every stage of a negotiation and to recap what action is to be taken as often as they feel is necessary. After all, the consequences of misunderstanding could be enormous! In other words, give students the language they need to do this effectively, and practise it in the ways suggested in this section. Specific language has been provided for each procedure so that you can help your students to build the relationships they need in order to conduct business amicably and effectively at an international level.

☐ PRE-NEGOTIATION PONDER

Students consider what makes a good negotiator before embarking on practice of language relevant to negotiating.

Language any
Level intermediate and above
Time 15–20 minutes

Preparation

Collect several photographs of business people involved in negotiations and either mount them on card or photocopy them onto OHTs. (Note that photographs gleaned from adverts or business magazines may often be appropriate since negotiations might take place in all kinds of settings, for all kinds of reasons.) Also photocopy the sheet provided on p. 216 for students' use or compile and photocopy a similar list of your own suggestions which relate more closely to your students' situation.

Procedure

1 After telling students you are going to be considering what makes a good negotiator, flash up the photographs you have prepared on your OHP or lay photographs on the tables in front of students. Elicit as many comments about the negotiations as you can, asking *Imagine being in this situation. Who are the people? What do you think they're talking about? Who's going to get the better deal?!*, for example.
2 Ask students to draw up a short list of 'dos' and 'don'ts' for negotiating, either working in pairs or small groups.
3 Discuss everyone's ideas, writing these on the board or on an OHT.
4 Next, distribute the photocopies of additional ideas. Ask students to decide with a partner whether they agree or disagree with each piece of advice. After getting comments from the whole class, ask students what their answer is to Question 2: *Do cultural differences affect negotiating style?*
5 Ask students to imagine they have been asked to write a memo, e-mail or report to inform and prepare some colleagues who have less experience than they have of the international negotiating world! Get them to plan the text together in class (again, in pairs or groups) and write it up for homework.

A worksheet for PRE-NEGOTIATION PONDER

BUSINESS ENGLISH THINK SPOT

Q1: What makes a good negotiator?

A good negotiator …

… loves negotiating.

… has a view of the big picture.

… thinks about the other side's perspective and problems.

… remembers what has been negotiated and agreed before.

… has integrity, i.e. can be relied upon.

… doesn't need to be liked.

… can tolerate ambiguity and conflict.

… is prepared to ask questions about anything.

… knows what he or she wants and expresses this clearly.

… keeps quiet about what he or she is not prepared to do.

… keeps quiet about his or her minimum terms.

… understands the possibilities of a deal in great detail.

… pays attention to even the smallest problem.

… finds out the reason for special requests.

… negotiates on more than price.

… is good at working out the fine details of cost.

… uses information about creditworthiness to good effect.

… works to gain goodwill as well as profit.

… is prepared to discuss hypothetical situations.

… has the courage to discuss what seems impossible.

… is patient and persistent.

… accepts and is constructive about conditions made.

… is not afraid to ask for a firm commitment.

… follows up on all promises made.

Q2: Do cultural differences affect negotiating style?

Yes! But why? … and how? …

(Based on McCormack, Mark H. 1995. *McCormack on Negotiating*. London:
Arrow Books Ltd.)

☐ ESTABLISHING GROUND RULES

Students work in groups and decide on an appropriate procedure for a task. Since establishing ground rules is so important at the beginning of negotiations this procedure prepares students for real-life situations.

Language any + exponents for making suggestions
Level lower-intermediate and above
Time 30 minutes

Procedure

1 Give students a task which is quite difficult to perform, such as one of the following:

> Find out how many people in your company use English on a day-to-day basis.
> Review the types of self-study options available to you in and outside your company.
> Find out about the number and type of e-mails written in your company.

2 Divide the class into groups of four, five or six students. Without giving any introduction or rationale, ask students to tackle the task in their group. If students ask when or how they are to complete the task tell them that it's up to them and that you will be giving them some class time to do it.
3 After a few minutes, stop the students and tell them that they will not really have to complete the task. Explain that instead, you want to focus on establishing procedures and ground rules in negotiations. Ask each group how they decided to tackle the task, making notes on the board as you listen.
4 Elicit and discuss the language students actually used to reach their decision. Some possible language you might present and practise is as follows:

> So ... how are we going to go about it?
> First of all, I think we should establish the overall procedure.
> Our main objective is to ...
> How about if we look at ... first?
> What if we ... (did ...) first of all?
> I think we should start by ...
> We could then move on to ...

I think it's important that we ... before discussing ...
Is that OK with you?
Does that seem acceptable to you?

(Adapted from O'Connor, P., A. Pilbeam and F. Scott-Barrett. 1992.
Negotiating. Harlow: Longman.)

5 Give students another task to consider in their groups. This time, as well as deciding on a procedure for tackling the task, students must also use the phrases you have elicited and practised as a class.
6 Ask students to discuss a third task if you feel they need more practice using appropriate language but get students to change round first so that they are working with other people.

☐ TRIO REFLECTIONS

This procedure helps students to develop their reflective listening skills. By reflecting back to each other what they think they've heard, students find out just how effectively they have been listening! Students who have been speaking also find out how clearly they have expressed themselves.

Language any
Level lower-intermediate and above
Time 30 minutes

Procedure

1 Explain to students that they are going to do a special exercise to develop their listening skills. Put students into groups of three, taking care as far as possible to group students who don't usually work together or who have little in common. This will make the task a little more difficult and will allow more scope for misunderstandings later on!
2 Give each student a subject which is related either to learning, negotiating or to the student's line of work. For example:

- My first experiences of using English in the workplace
- My first experience of negotiating
- My fears about negotiating an important contract
- Possible future products for our company
- The future of (students' product or service, e.g. banking) in the 21st century

3 Label students A, B and C. In the first phase of this activity, Student A is the speaker, Student B the 'reflector' and Student C the 'corrector'. Student A must first of all talk about the subject for five minutes; Students B and C simply listen during this phase and do not speak. At the end of the five minutes, Student B should 'reflect' back to Student A what he or she has said; stress that Students A and C must say nothing at this point, but can take notes if desired. Student C must then 'correct' any errors that Student B has made when 'reflecting' – with no interruptions from Student A! Finally, Student A can correct (or affirm) what Students B and C have said.

4 Organise feedback as a class on the number and type of 'errors' that were made. Remind students that any errors might be due to lack of clarity on the speaker's part as well as to poor listening on the part of the 'reflector' and the 'corrector'.

5 Ask students to change roles and continue, using different topics or the same topic.

6 After further feedback and discussion ask students how misunderstandings can be avoided in real-life negotiations. Stress the importance of interrupting to check or clarify points whenever there is a feeling of uncertainty. Elicit and/or give students appropriate language for this (e.g. *How do you mean exactly?*), organising pronunciation practice as necessary.

7 Follow up with role-played mini-negotiation tasks in which students use the language you have just presented. (After considering the task, students can choose their own roles.) Encourage students to interrupt again and again by emphasising, once again, the necessity for this before students begin their role-plays and also by indicating to them (non-verbally) any ambiguity you yourself perceive when you are monitoring. Get students to check whether or not there were misunderstandings at the end of each mini-negotiation.

Two possible negotiation tasks might be as follows:

> Imagine your non-software company is setting up a joint venture to produce software. Negotiate how you are going to do this (e.g. which personnel are going to transfer where), how much your company will pay for each software package produced, how the software is going to be marketed and who is going to finance this.

> Imagine you sell men's clothing. You want to buy some jackets and trousers from a foreign company. Negotiate prices, discounts and delivery terms. Also agree on how the clothing is going to be advertised and who is going to finance this.

☐ CLARIFYING QUESTIONS

This procedure is an extension of TRIO REFLECTIONS (p. 218). Students get an opportunity to practise questions which help them to clarify precise meaning.

Language any
Level lower-intermediate and above
Time 20 minutes

Preparation

Write out a list of several cues, all of which should be spoken comments that include some vagueness or ambiguity. They should all be comments which a negotiator might plausibly make at some point in a negotiation. Some possible cues to use:

> We're going to expand soon and set up a new company.
> I'm going to sort it out soon.
> I'll check on that.
> I'm not sure we agree with what you're proposing.
> We'll have to look at the details again.
> There are a few things I need to check up on.
> There could be some practical problems there.

Procedure

1 Tell students that they are going to practise clarifying comments made in an imaginary negotiation. Focusing on the first cue comment in your list to do this, e.g. *We're going to expand soon and set up a new company*, elicit possible questions that could be asked. For example:

> How do you mean exactly?
> What kind of company are you going to set up?
> When do you propose to do that?
> What products or services will you offer?
> What sort of market research have you already done?
> Will it be a subsidiary of your present company?
> Who's going to finance this new venture?

Also elicit and/or give students some other useful phrases to practise using in this type of situation.

For example:

> If I understand you correctly, you're saying ...
> You mean ... ?
> When you say ... do you mean ... ?
> Not necessarily.
> That's not quite what I meant.
> Yes, that's right.
> Exactly!

(Adapted from O'Connor, P., A. Pilbeam, and F. Scott-Barrett. 1992. *Negotiating*. Harlow: Longman.)

2 Using the next cue comment in the list, ask students to get as much information from you as possible. Set a time limit and award students points for each appropriate question asked, if you like.
3 Ask students to continue with the other cues, working in pairs or smalll groups.
4 When you give feedback focus students' attention on intonation and appropriacy of language use, as well as on other errors they may have made. Remind them of the importance of not causing offence when using this kind of language!

Variation

To make this activity more demanding and stimulating for students, as well as more useful in the whole class stage, allow students to score a possible total of three points for each question: one point if the question is grammatically accurate, one point if it is expressed appropriately, and one point for appropriate pronunciation. After awarding points, only answer questions which are accurate!

☐ TRICKY TREATMENT

Students practise dealing with difficult challenges from imaginary negotiating counterparts.

Language any
Level lower-intermediate and above
Time 30 minutes

Procedure

1 Get students to think up a list of five possible statements which they might have to make in a negotiation and which might provoke a negative reaction from 'the other side'. Some examples:

> The price will increase at the end of this year.
> We can only offer discount on orders over 5,000.
> We only offer those terms to our regular customers.
> Our high prices are justified by the high level of service we offer, compared to our competitors.
> This really is the best product you can buy at this price.
> This new product will do everything you need it to do.
> We need more information on your stock levels if we are to agree to do business with you.

2 Elicit and/or teach students how to challenge negotiating partners politely! Some phrases students could use are as follows:

> Does that mean that ... ?
> When you say ... do you mean ... ?
> Do you ever make exceptions?
> Would you consider ... ?
> Would it be acceptable to you if we ... ?
> Have you considered ... ?
> Could we perhaps make an arrangement whereby you ... and we ... ?
> Why is that exactly?

3 Ask for a volunteer. This student must sit at the front of the class, make his or her statement and then deal with the barrage of unpleasant questions from you or other students! Insist that all questions in the 'barrage' are phrased politely.

4 When one or two students have sat in the 'hot seat', get the class to continue in small groups. (Groups of four, five or six are most effective.) Within each group at least two students can deal with questions; other students will practise asking questions. Make sure students change roles periodically.

5 In your feedback stage, discuss with students any alternative strategies or language they might use so as to achieve better outcomes.

☐ PERSUASION FOCUS

In a group task in which joint decisions need to be made, students have the opportunity to practise their skills of persuasion.

Language any + exponents for persuading
Level intermediate and above
Time 20 minutes

Procedure

1 Give students a task which involves discussing items for a list. Two example tasks are as follows:

> Imagine you all work for the same company. Personnel have decided that work is slack and that reviews of individuals' performance need to be made once a year. The results of each annual review may mean an adjustment in salary (up or down) and in some cases people may be fired. With this in mind, draw up a list of ten things which are fundamental to being a good employee, which you would be prepared to be judged on. If you fail to agree on a list of qualities the Human Resources Manager will select ten qualities on your behalf.

> Imagine you work for a company which has many offices abroad. You have been asked to help select personnel who are to be transferred to these various offices. They want your help because many people who have been sent abroad have either had problems (which have affected their work) or have come home too soon. Draw up a list of ten qualities which are important for a person who transfers to a foreign office. Think of qualities which might be important for four- or five-year postings abroad.

2 Firstly, working in silence, individual students make their own list of ten items. This will ensure that students should have time to consider possibilities and it will also maximise the chances of everyone contributing to the group discussion which follows.

3 Next, elicit the kind of language students are likely to need in order to persuade other students that their opinion is right! In order to get students to consider language with an appropriate level of formality, remind them that they may be negotiating with people from another department or company in a real life negotiation.

   Some phrases which students might use are as follows:

> It seems to me there are a number of ways we could …
> I suggest we list the options first, and then examine them in more detail one by one.
> Should we brainstorm the options before we discuss anything in detail?
> I'd like to start by suggesting …
> How about … ?

> Do we need to include ... ?
> Although that's certainly important, I think it's more
> important that ...
> Do you think that's as important as ... ?
> So which of those two would you prioritise?
> I have my doubts about that.
> I think that's an essential point.
> What would the implications be?

(Adapted from O'Connor, P., A. Pilbeam and F. Scott-Barrett. 1992.
Negotiating. Harlow: Longman.)

4 Get students to practise the pronunciation for the expressions, focusing especially on sentence stress.
5 Next, divide the class into groups and remind students that they will need to agree on a procedure before starting their discussion proper. Also remind them that they will need to conclude what they have agreed at the end of their discussion.
6 Regroup students for follow-up discussions. For example AAAA, BBBB, CCCC, DDDD becomes ABCD, ABCD, ABCD, ABCD.
7 When everyone has come to a conclusion, give students feedback on their use of language, paying particular attention to the style of language they used, pronunciation features and non-verbal features (e.g. gestures, eye contact, timing of comments, interruptions), especially those which would be conspicuous or offensive in an international negotiation.
8 Give students another similar task if you feel they would benefit from some other practice. If you have the facilities available, you might also ask groups to record their discussions so that they can listen to them and critique them afterwards.

□ SIMULATED NEGOTIATION

Students role-play a negotiation, scoring points according to the advantages they negotiate.

Language any
Level intermediate and above
Time 1 hour+

Preparation

Photocopy the role-play cards provided on pp. 225–226, or devise a similar role-played negotiation with a point-scoring system. Also find photographs of Hong Kong and New York if at all possible so that students can picture themselves in the situation!

Student A: Sales Director, Island Silks

Island Silks, a medium-sized clothing company based in Hong Kong, operates in a highly competitive environment and is in danger of losing market share to Thai silk manufacturers. As Sales Director, you are delighted, therefore, to have the chance of a contract with Trendsetters Inc., a major American clothing retail chain, based in New York. Trendsetters is interested in buying 5,000 silk scarves from your new 'Miriam Designer Collection' at a unit price of $US50, including the cost of insurance and shipping to the US.

You have some temporary cash-flow problems at the moment. It is November 1, and you really need a deal which will bring in some money quickly. You know that Trendsetters will require the scarves as soon as possible as the company is approaching its peak selling period (the six weeks before Christmas). Despite your cash flow problems, however, you would prefer not to deliver before early December, as you are behind schedule with your orders and must give priority to existing customers. Also, you know Trendsetters will expect a wide range of colours and patterns and although your factory can cope with this, it will cost more and mean employing more staff.

Your objective is to negotiate a satisfactory deal for your company. Use the following points system as a guide to your priorities.

Decisions	Points	Decisions	Points
Delivery date		*Terms of payment*	
Nov. 15	1	By irrevocable letter of credit:	
Nov. 30	2	90 days presentation	1
Dec. 7	3	60 days presentation	2
		30 days presentation	3
Different patterns		at sight	5
20	1		
15	2	*Discount*	
10	3	4%	0
		3%	1
Colours		2%	2
12	1	1%	3
10	3	0%	5
6	4		

Student B: Chief Buyer, Trendsetters Inc.

Trendsetters Inc. is a major American clothing retail chain, based in New York. You were very impressed with the silk scarves in Island Silks' new 'Miriam Designer Collection' on show at last month's Hong Kong Clothing Fair. You have been quoted a unit price of $US50, including the cost of insurance and shipping, and are keen to place an order for 5,000 scarves from the collection.

It is now November 1 and you need the goods quickly as you are approaching your peak selling period – the six weeks before Christmas. The scarves should sell well if they hit the shelves at the right time and mid-November would be ideal. Your customers like bright colours and intricate patterns and expect to be able to choose from a wide range of designs.

Your objective is to negotiate a satisfactory deal, making as few concessions as possible – the retail clothing market in the US is highly competitive. Use the following points system as a guide to your priorities.

Decisions	Points	Decisions	Points
Delivery date		*Terms of payment*	
Nov. 15	3	By irrevocable letter of credit:	
Nov. 30	2	90 days presentation	5
Dec. 7	1	60 days presentation	3
		30 days presentation	2
Different patterns		at sight	1
20	3		
15	2	*Discount*	
10	1	4%	5
		3%	3
Colours		2%	2
12	4	1%	1
10	3	0%	0
6	1		

(Based on Cotton, D. and S. Robbins. 1993. *Business Class*. London: Nelson. p. 71 and p. 145.)

Procedure

1 After some initial language practice, using other procedures in this section, get students to role-play the negotiation in pairs and tot up points afterwards. As well as needing first and second conditionals (which you can get students to practise in preparation for this simulation) you might also elicit and/or give students the following language:

> I'm afraid we couldn't possibly accept that.
> We couldn't accept that but we'd be prepared to ...
> If you increase that to ... I think we'd have a deal.
> We would be prepared to accept ... if you guaranteed us ...
> We couldn't ... unless ...
> If you are prepared to ... we may be able to ...
> I think we could go along with that.
> That would certainly be acceptable.

(Adapted from O'Connor P., A. Pilbeam and F. Scott-Barrett. 1992.
Negotiating. Harlow: Longman.)

See p. 242 for a sample follow-up fax.

□ ROLED SUMMARIES

In this activity students get the opportunity to develop their summarising skills. After listening to an extended conversation on tape or video, students decide what the main points are, then summarise them to other groups as if they were one of the speakers in the conversation.

Language any
Level lower-intermediate and above
Time 30 minutes

Procedure

1 Play students a recording of part of a negotiation. Ask gist and detail comprehension questions to check students fully understand the situation.
2 In pairs or groups of three, as appropriate, get students to imagine that they are the characters on the tape or video and to role-play the same discussion.
3 Ask students what language they might use to summarise the points made in the negotiation. Elicit and/or teach the following:

Perhaps I could just recap your main points.
Perhaps I could just summarise our conclusions/agreements/
decisions so far.
So you've agreed to ...
So you'll be responsible for ...
The question of ... remains to be clarified.
I'd just like to go over ...
As I understand it, ...
As I recall, you said ...
So you'll ...
By our next meeting you'll have ...
We'll discuss ... at our next meeting on ...
Have I covered everything?
Is there anything else you'd like to add?

(Adapted from O'Connor P., A. Pilbeam and F. Scott-Barrett. 1992
Negotiating. Harlow: Longman.)

4 Ask students to continue role-playing the negotiation but this time
   adding summaries at key points. Play the video or tape again if
   students want to be reminded about any points in the discussion.
5 As well as giving feedback on their performance in this practice
   exercise, insist that students continue to use similar language in class
   on an ongoing basis so as to summarise key points.

☐ REASSURING PROMISES

Students practise making promises about follow-up action which has
already been suggested in a previous discussion. This is similar to what
students will have to do in real life at the end of a negotiation.

Language any + exponents for making promises
Level lower-intermediate and above
Time 20 minutes

Procedure

1 Organise a negotiation role-play (e.g. SIMULATED NEGOTIATION on
   p. 224) but get students to work in groups of three.
2 Before students start role-playing the negotiation discuss with
   students language they might need to make promises to reassure the
   other side. Elicit and/or teach language such as the following:

I'll check up on a few details, then get back to you by the end of next week.
As we've agreed, we'll take care of … . We'll also …
So we've agreed we'll …
So that means we need to …
I'll confirm the details in writing as soon as I get authorisation.
I'll check the … with … and get back to you by the end of next week.
We'll confirm the details in full by fax as soon as we get back.

(Adapted from O'Connor, P., A. Pilbeam and F. Scott-Barrett. 1992. *Negotiating*. Harlow: Longman.)

3 After any necessary practice activities, ask students to start the negotiation. While Students A and B negotiate, Student C should take notes on anything agreed or promised. If at all possible, record each negotiating pair's conversation. (Note that this can easily be done in a language laboratory with a pairing facility.)

4 After the negotiation, ask Student C in each threesome to review what has been agreed or promised by recapping or cross-questioning the negotiators. Student C's questions should be as simple as possible and simply aim to focus on the precise follow-up action the negotiators plan to take. If the conversation Student C was listening to has been recorded points of disagreement can easily be checked, referring to you, the teacher, if any language is unclear.

5 When giving feedback to students, focus students' attention on any occasions where they may have given a false impression or where they communicated certainty or a promise of action when none was intended. Stress to students the importance of accurate use of language in negotiations. Check whether they are familiar with the concept of a 'gentlemen's agreement' – which involves honouring any verbal promises made! Also discuss the legal situation in the countries in which students will be negotiating, if you or they know anything about this. Finally, ask students if they agree or disagree with the following statement.

Relationships in international business need to be based on honesty and clarity if companies are to survive and flourish.

Copying this quotation onto an OHT and flashing it up in front of the class is a good way of starting the discussion. Companies which have periodically enjoyed enormous success, such as Procter & Gamble or Marks & Spencer, who seem to base their business approach on this theory, might perhaps provide an interesting focus for discussion, and texts from business books about their approach to doing business could provide a useful and stimulating follow-up.

For other procedures which you can use to help your students practise language for this area, see the Index entry for 'negotiating'.

5.11 Note-taking

Note-taking involves practising the difficult skill of writing while listening and/or speaking. It is an important skill for most students working in the field of international business because they are bound to need to take notes at meetings or presentations conducted in English, in the future if not immediately. Since notes taken will not be read by anyone else their purpose is to be functional, not beautiful, but it is probably easiest if students take notes in the language of the meeting, i.e. English, or if they use an 'international' note-taking system which will not necessitate ongoing translation.

In order to provide useful guidance and practice for students find out first how notes are usually written up in the students' companies because this may affect the style of note-taking and the level of detail you recommend. Minutes of meetings and visit reports, for example, can vary tremendously from company to company. If students cannot bring in sample copies of relevant paperwork or have little information about their future work situation, stick to general guidelines.

☐ TEXT REBUILDING

Working in groups of an ever-decreasing size, students reconstitute texts from their notes. This is a good confidence-building exercise which grades the task of taking notes effectively. If performed badly, this activity also makes clear the need for more focus on note-taking!

Language determined by the teacher
Level intermediate and above
Time 10–15 minutes

Preparation
Find about six texts on subjects which you think will interest your students and which students will not have too much difficulty understanding. Two examples of texts which could be used with advanced students are as follows:

Peters and Waterman were hardly the first people (and hardly the last, either) to draw attention to the limitations of the rationalist model of management. As we have already noted, there is a long tradition of bashing scientific management, stretching back to the human-relations school of management theorists who devoted themselves to demonstrating that man is a social animal, not just a rational calculating machine. In *The Human Side of Enterprise*, published in 1960, Douglas McGregor argued that management theory had paid too much attention to 'Theory X', which holds that workers are lazy and need to be driven by financial incentives, and not enough to 'Theory Y', which holds that, on the contrary, workers are creative and need to be given responsibility. The business press was not indifferent to the softer side of business thinking either: *Business Week* even ran a cover story on corporate culture in the late summer of 1980.

(From Micklethwait, J. and A. Wooldridge. 1996. *The Witch Doctors*. London: Heinemann pp. 101–102.)

It is true that self-disclosure is risky, but so are all strategies for improving relationships. Research indicates that positive disclosures are associated with highly cohesive and successful groups. In task-oriented groups within classrooms and organisations, disclosure can help maintain relationships. Disclosure in task-oriented groups requires some skill. People sitting around in business clothes making decisions do not reveal personal information about themselves very readily. But the presentation of at least slightly disclosive information about yourself presents you as agreeable and non-threatening. It humanises you to the extent that disclosure makes you appear open, warm, and friendly. Other people will usually respond in kind. Self-disclosure is a very useful way to improve the interpersonal attractiveness among group members.

(From Ellis, D. G. and B. Aubrey Fisher. 1994. *Small Group Decision Making*. Singapore: McGraw-Hill. p. 32.)

Procedure

1 Tell students that they are going to practise their note-taking skills through a series of exercises. Put students into groups of six.
2 Read aloud your first text, having asked students to take notes as you listen.
3 As soon as students have finished listening – once only! – allow them to compare their notes with other students in their group. Tell students their aim is now to rewrite the text they have heard. (Only

read the text a second time if students are very weak or are in shock after the first reading!)

4 When students have finished writing, show them a copy of the text so that they can compare their version with the original. Encourage them to look out for any differences of content and point out any differences that students miss.

5 Gradually decrease the size of groups (to five, four, three, two) and repeat stages 1–4 with other texts (either in the same lesson or in later lessons). Finally, ask students to work alone – because they will usually be working alone in real life. (For one-to-one students the task can be graded by varying the speed with which you read out texts: start slow and gradually use a more and more natural speed.)

6 Take in the final texts if you want to focus individual students' attention on the type of errors they are making. Mark their errors in red pen, indicating mistakes of content with a large C, circled. Then give students an overview of the types of mistakes being made by the group as a whole.

Variation

Reverse the grouping process, i.e. start with individuals thinking privately after the reading, then pair students, then put pairs with other pairs and finally get groups of six to produce a text. This should help diffident and/or weak students to experience greater success on an ongoing basis and they may be able to learn more from stronger students in the class.

□ PHRASED JIGSAW NOTES

Students 'take notes' using phrases or single words written on small pieces of paper. The focus is not on speed of writing but on listening for key points, then extrapolating the rest of the text.

Language any
Level intermediate and above
Time 20 minutes – 1 hour

Preparation

Select a recording of a presentation. Write several key words and phrases from the tapescript on a sheet of paper. Decide how many sets of 'jigsaw notes' your class will need if students are to work in pairs or threes, then photocopy your sheet of key words and phrases the appropriate number of times (i.e. five times if you want to make five sets). Next, cut up each sheet so that you have one word or phrase on each piece of paper, taking care to keep the sets of 'jigsaw notes' separate by using envelopes to store each set. Note that writing or mounting each set of 'jigsaw notes' on a different colour card will help both you and your students to keep the sets intact and laminating all the cards will mean your sets can be used again and again.

Procedure

1 Give out the sets of words and phrases, explaining to students that they are key words and phrases from a presentation that they are going to hear. Explain to students that their focus in this note-taking practice is listening for key points, not writing as fast as they can! Give students time to look through their words and phrases before you start playing the tape. Tell students they should put the words and phrases in order as they listen.

2 After students have listened once, ask them to compare their 'notes' with those made by other groups. (There will be no problem with legibility!) Then ask them to 'reconstitute' the whole text, orally in pairs or small groups. Play the recording again (several times, if necessary), but remind students that they only get a chance to hear things once in real life.

3 Finally, discuss any problems as a class and reconstitute the presentation together, writing it up on the board if students have found it particularly difficult.

Variation 1

While students are reconstituting the text, allow them to ask you questions, just as they might do during the Q&A session after a presentation. Answer any questions they ask. If you pre-teach appropriate exponents you can also insist that questions are asked correctly or using an appropriate style of language.

Variation 2

Having divided the class into pairs, hand out various tapescripts of presentations to different pairs. Then ask students to prepare key words and phrases on pieces of paper. (This will save you preparation time and will encourage students to focus on key points.) Working in groups of four (after each pair has teamed up with another pair) students then need to read out their tapescripts so as to give other students an opportunity to 'take notes' using the pieces of paper. Encourage students to ask each other questions and offer help, remembering that students' poor pronunciation or mistakes when reading may make the 'presentations' more difficult to follow. Explain to students that this is a useful exercise because non-native speakers working in the international workplace often have to listen to non-native speaker English.

☐ NOTING NOTES

Students share abbreviations for notes and develop new symbols for use in emergencies! The non-language-based shorthand encouraged through this procedure is particularly useful because it means that students will not have to translate back and forth as they participate in meetings. Not translating means that students should find note-taking easier.

Language any
Level upper-intermediate and above
Time 15 minutes

Procedure

1 Write a few symbols on the board and ask students to guess what they stand for. Some symbols you might use are as follows:

%	per cent/percentage
∴	therefore
=	this means/this meant
≠	does/did not mean/not equal to
#	number

© Cambridge University Press

2 Get students to write on the board any other symbols they know. Then get them to develop extra symbols in pairs – after brainstorming words which frequently crop up in presentations they hear, students should simply develop an appropriate symbol. Move students around so that they work with different partners and the symbols are shared amongst the class.
3 Type up students' note-taking symbols later and distribute copies so that everyone has a convenient reference sheet.

Some possible extra symbols

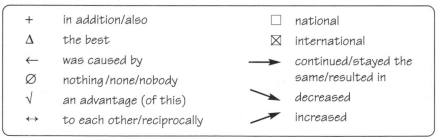

+	in addition/also	☐	national	
Δ	the best	☒	international	
←	was caused by	⟶	continued/stayed the same/resulted in	
Ø	nothing/none/nobody			
√	an advantage (of this)	↘	decreased	
↔	to each other/reciprocally	↗	increased	

© Cambridge University Press

4 As a follow-up, get students to write short texts (about their company or the world) using words for which they have developed symbols. While they then read out their text, other students take notes. After reconstituting the text, writers compare their version with the original.

□ NOTED MEETINGS

Students make notes when listening to recordings of meetings, then write either minutes or follow-up memos.

Language any
Level upper-intermediate and above
Time 40 minutes

Preparation

Find a recording of a meeting (in a coursebook) which you think will be of interest to your students.

Procedure

1 Ask students what type of writing they need to do after attending meetings. (Note that they are likely to need to write either minutes, memos or e-mails.) Tell them that they are going to practise taking notes in preparation for this kind of writing. Encourage them to consider what the purpose of the minutes or the follow-up memos would be, and who might read them and why.
2 Play students recordings of meetings and get them to take notes for either minutes, follow-up memos or e-mails. Give students 10–15 minutes to write up minutes, memos or e-mails (on OHTs, if possible) after listening once only.
3 Get students to compare their minutes, memos or e-mails.
4 Play the recording of the meeting again and give feedback on students' writing, as appropriate. Focus students' attention on the following areas:

   • accuracy of content – i.e. did they listen carefully enough?
   • grammatical errors which could cause confusion
   • cohesion of the text overall – i.e. does it fit together and make sense?
   • consistency of grammar when bullet points are used
   • stylistic consistency

5 Give students the option of improving their initial version for homework.

To help your students practise language for this area also see DIAGRAM DEVELOPMENT (p. 267).

5.12 E-mail, faxes and memos

E-mail

E-mail is used increasingly in international business to replace letters, faxes, memos and even telephone calls, partly because it is convenient and inexpensive and partly because e-mail is so easy to use within a networked system. The style of writing can vary as much as for letters or faxes (depending on relationships of correspondents and the purpose for writing) but is usually much more informal than in other types of written communication. Headings are usually put in automatically by the computer so are little cause for concern! Some sample messages are provided on the following pages for information.

Some notes for students on e-mail

BUSINESS ENGLISH THINK SPOT

Why use e-mail? How to use it?

E-mail is fast, reliable and easy to use ... once you know how!
However ...

- Think carefully about who you are writing to and what they might be thinking. Impressions are important because you probably want agreement and action!

- Think carefully about your purpose for writing before you start and organise your ideas, just as you would when writing a letter.

- Adapt your style of writing according to who you are writing to.

- Beware of humour. Although writing an e-mail might feel like chatting over the telephone, a written joke is very different from its spoken equivalent.

- Consider who else might read your message. Since parts of your message can easily be copied and conveyed to other people using e-mail, check that you would be happy for other people to read what you have written before sending off your message.

- If you are sending something important, follow up with a fax and/or a letter because some people may not read their e-mail regularly!

- Keep track of e-mail in the same way as you would any other form of written correspondence, printing out and filing copies if this seems useful.

© Cambridge University Press

A sample e-mail

---

jennifer.cummings

From:	peter.nelson
Sent:	Monday, December 7, 2000 7.37 PM
To:	jennifer.cummings
Cc:	john.andrews; sue.marks; zoe.fielding; anjula.freelands; 'pat.morgan@intcomm.lanka.net'
Subject:	Intellidraw

Sue says quite a few people are not using Intellidraw. Apparently, most people are unfamiliar with how it works. The training video which came with the software has gone missing. Sue suggested we order another one.

We will need to cancel the training seminar for this software until we have better training materials – the video in particular. Can we leave the date open until I get a reply from the software company?

I suggest we get people to use MacDraw until Intellidraw is familiar to all!

Peter Nelson
Software Management Officer

© Cambridge University Press

☐ E-MAIL EXPLORATION

Students search for an e-mail message which is hidden in seeming gobbledygook!

Language any
Level elementary and above
Time 5 minutes

Procedure

Show students a copy of the e-mail on p. 238. After asking them how they would feel if they got this kind of e-mail – so as to help less confident users of English to feel they are not alone when intimidated – ask the students to find the message. Getting students who are not yet using e-mail to locate the message should reassure them that they will be able to cope, even if messages seem complicated at first sight!

A 'hidden' e-mail message

Author: Phil James <pjames@commuserv.org.sg> at Internet
Date: 17/12/10 11.17
Priority: Normal
TO: camella.bond at intcomm
TO: "'camella.bond@intcomm.lanka.net'" at Internet
Subject: New contracts
_ _ _ _ _ _ _ _ _ _ _ _ _ _ _ _ _ Message Contents _ _ _ _ _ _ _ _ _ _ _ _ _ _ _

Received: by ccmail
Received: from sri by lanka.net (UUPC/extended 1.11) with UUCP;
               Thur, 17 Dec 1998 11:17:07 GMT
Received: from stern.pacific.net.sg by sri.lanka.net with esmtp
               (Smail 3.1.28.1 #8) id m0yRtmf - 0009T7C; Thur, 17 Dec 98 07.17 GMT
Received: from mail-server.intcomm.org.sg ([707.33.707.2))
               by stern.pacific.net.sg with ESMTP
               id JFF00320 for <camella.bond@intcomm.lanka.net>; Thur, 17 Dec 1998
               09:08:3
4 +0800 (SGT)
Received: by MAIL-SERVER with Internet Mail Service (5.0.1457.47)
               id <JY9Y3G47>; Thur, 17 Dec 1998 09:12:00 +0800
Message-ID: <71C7BD7E1791D22290500030977S1449082C40@MAIL-SERVER>
From: Phil James <pjames@commuserv.org.sg>
X-ccAdmin: jennifer@sri
To: "'camella.bond@intcomm.lanka.net'"
               <camella.bond@intcomm.lanka.net>
Subject: New contracts
Date: Thur, 17 Dec 1998 09:12:00 +0800
X-Priority: 3
MIME-Version: 1.0
X-Mailer: Internet Mail Service (5.0.1458.49)
Content-Type: multipart/mixed;
               boundary="---- =_NextPart_000_-1BD6DCE.B54524E0"

This message is in MIME format. Since your mail reader does not understand this format, some
or all of this message may not be legible.

------ =_Next Part_000_01BD6DCE.B54524E0
Content-Type: text/plain

Camella
A couple of documents you might be interested in (123 and Wordperfect).
Phil
PS I'll send you a note about personnel in the next day or two.

------ =_NextPart_000_01BD6DCE.B54524E0
Content-Type: application/octet-stream;
 name="Res21498.wk4"
Content-Transfer-Encoding: base64
Content-Disposition: attachment;
 filename= "res21498.wk4"
Content-Description: Res21498

AAAaAAIQBAAAAAAANAAABQEAHgABCgAAAAAAAAAHwAIAAAAAS8AADQA
HwAIAAABAS8IAC4AHwAIAAACAS8KACAHwAIAAAAEAS8IAC4AHwAIAAAAFAS8KA
C4AAwAGAAAEAAAABAAQAHAABAQEAAAAJFEUEBABXNQ4AAQAAAMrymRZ3LF
oABQAQAAAA7z4mAAAAAJgAAAAAAAAAGAAUAAADhSgkHABAAAADhSgALAQcC
BgMDBAgFByEAAQAAAAaAAIQBAAAAAAANAAABQEAHgABCgAA

Some extracts from e-mail

Dear Mr Sena,

I have read with interest your contributions on the IMTA web page and have tried to contact you at the number given but have since discovered that you have now set up your own company and therefore have found a way to contact you directly.

I am undertaking a study for the Australian National Space Centre looking at market opportunities for Australian manufacturers in the GPS market and would therefore be interested in talking to you about your views on the in-car navigation market potential. Below I have put my views, followed by a few questions, which I would be grateful if you could consider.

It seems to me, from my research, that Australia has rather missed the boat on the GPS hardware area. As far as I can tell, almost all GPS cards, or chip sets are manufactured by American companies. However, ...

Thank you in advance for any answers you may have been able to provide.

With best regards,

Fran Lodge

Here is the report, as promised. Let me know your thoughts – you will see I have given my recommendations for possible solutions. If you want me to go ahead and make the changes I will, of course, be happy to do so.

Will be away as of tomorrow until January 3, after which I can be contacted at this e-mail until Jan 11.

Regards
Chris

Chris – Thanks for the report and the two e-mails. I appreciate the effort. Happy New Year.

First, let me say that I hope you are feeling better from your trip. I have heard some pretty awful accounts of tummy bugs from Africa and India. Please keep yourself healthy.

As to the summary report you sent and the previous e-mail, I've cut/pasted below a couple of comments and questions … you may want to respond with ALL CAPS inside my comments …

1) I haven't forwarded to ExtraZot/Pete Oldham yet because I wanted to clear everything with you first before sending them something. Let's continue to discuss the issues in your meeting report and this e-mail before getting them involved. …

Nelson – Spoke to Forsching last Monday and we agreed that we could re-write the Exec Summary and Chapter 7 of the Final Report to provide them with a little extra flexibility to implement our recommendations. We'll also remove Section 4 (Implementation Plan) and will make it a standalone document 'as is' for their internal use.

Do you think you could schedule a couple of days this coming week to perform this work? Speak to you soon. Please feel free to call me at the office or on my mobile.
Best regards
AEG

Thanks for the response, Andy. Jean is coming into GHQ Geneva next week (I think) to work a couple of days on the report and make the changes as noted below. After they are made, we will forward you the report for review/editing.

Best regards,
PJM

PS – Family is progressing, thanks for asking … Nina is due to deliver in about four weeks (around September 7). We know it's a little girl and we are quite excited about the whole thing. Will let you know how things go.

Faxes

Faxes are a well-established means of communication in modern business. They are likely to continue to be used widely because of their speed, convenience and flexibility. Apart from the time it takes to actually prepare the message, they are as fast as a telephone call to send and – because of their speed – are relatively cheap. They are more convenient than e-mail (though more expensive) because any sheet of paper (if A4 size) can be put through a fax machine, and they can be used by companies with no computers or Internet connections. They are also flexible inasmuch as they are capable of sending both text and graphics (in any format). No special hardware or software is required to prepare a document which includes graphs, photographs or diagrams; these simply need to be photocopied onto a sheet of A4 paper.

The format used for faxes varies widely but will mainly be dictated by a company's preference or the software used to generate the faxes. There are certain practical considerations which affect some aspects of the layout, e.g. the need to know how many pages are being sent and the need to specify senders' and receivers' telephone numbers in case of failed transmission. An acceptable format is given in the 'typical fax' on p. 242.

The style of text in faxes is similar to that used in letters but can sometimes be much more informal. This informality comes from the speed – and consequent feeling of informality – of the technology. As already mentioned (in 5.3) the formulaic expressions (e.g. *Many thanks for your ... of ...*) which are so common in letters are also used in faxes, so it is essential that students become familiar with these. (See 5.3 for some more examples of formulaic expressions and some suggested procedures for helping students learn them.)

Also draw students' attention to the following points if they are unfamiliar with faxes:

- Addresses are not always written out in full in the same way in faxes as in letters.
- Each page of a fax will be clearly numbered (e.g. page 2 of 7 or 2/7).
- Faxes sent through a normal fax machine will include a full signature, not just initials.
- Faxes sent through a modem will not include signatures because of the difficulty of 'getting them into' the computer!
- Handwritten faxes may also be acceptable in some lines of business or in certain situations because faxes are primarily used to transmit written messages quickly.
- Impressions are made when sending faxes, as with any other type of business communication so care about details may be equally important when sending faxes!

A typical fax

FAX MESSAGE

To: June K Tan
       Sales Director
       Island Silks
       7 Tai Wan San Tsuen
       Lamma Island
       Hong Kong

Tel: (852) 933 1373
Fax: (852) 933 1374

TrendsetterS Inc.

160a New Texas Avenue, New York, USA
Tel: 78923444 Fax: 78923445

Page 1 of 1

July 17, 2007

Miriam Designer Collection Silk Scarves

First of all, I would like to thank you for your hospitality during my stay in Hong Kong. I am pleased to confirm our order for 9,000 Miriam Designer Collection Silk Scarves. The details, as agreed in our discussion last week, are as follows:

Unit price	: US$50, inclusive of insurance and shipping
Delivery date	: November 28, 2007
No. of different patterns	: 15 (your 'Cool Cat' selection)
No. of colours	: 10 (beige, peach, yellow, cream, white, rose, burgundy, russet, stone and azure)
Terms of payment	: 30 days presentation (irrevocable letter of credit)
Discount	: 3%

We look forward to doing more business with you in the future.

Best regards,

JAMIE DONALDSON
Chief Buyer

☐ FAX PHILOSOPHISING

Students consider the differences between faxes, letters and old-fashioned telexes so that they have a better understanding of why the conventions and style are as they are in faxes.

Language any
Level intermediate and above
Time 10 minutes

Procedure

1 Write the words *fax*, *letter* and *telex* on the board or show photos of each on OHTs. Ask students to consider the differences, first in pairs and then as a class. Elicit or point out that:

- The price of a fax is dependent mostly on the number of A4 pages sent but that any amount of information can be transmitted on any one sheet of A4. Make sure that students are aware of how this differs from the cost of sending a telex, where every character (i.e. letter, space or number) costs money, so that abbreviations became common.
- Since the 'transmission' of faxes is much faster than letters, the language in faxes is often (but not always) more informal.

2 Show students the sample fax on p. 242 and invite comments about the layout. Make sure that they are aware of the other points about faxes mentioned on p. 241, especially the need to include telephone numbers and number of pages on faxes in case of failed transmission.

Memos

Old-fashioned paper memos, although still used in some companies, have been phased out by many companies in favour of faster and more convenient e-mail. However, written messages are still frequently sent around within companies so 'message-writing practice', which can be thought of as messages sent on paper or e-mail, still needs to be done by most Business English students. Even students who think of e-mail messages as nothing more than written out comments or spoken messages might do well to consider how the quality of internal communications can and does affect relationships and promotion prospects of individuals, not to mention the efficiency of a company's day-to-day business. Poorly written internal messages can result in a great deal of lost time, confusion or bad feeling. The procedures in this section will help your students to improve the effectiveness of their writing.

The format, style and organisation of memos can vary enormously, mainly because of the influence of corporate culture but also because memos can be used to communicate with one or many people, who may be of similar or very different status. On public Business English courses perhaps ask students to use a particular format, style and organisation in class practice, adapting this as much as possible to students' needs; encourage them to find out what is required or preferred by their company too, if they are already working. When you are teaching in-company find out as much as possible about the format, style and organisation of memos written within that particular company and ask students to adopt these; also make students aware of anything which seems unusual just in case students ever move to a different company!

See p. 247 and p. 254 for typical memos.

A *worksheet for* MEMO NOTES

BUSINESS ENGLISH THINK SPOT

What is a memo?

A memo – or 'memorandum', to give it its proper name – is a form of written business communication. Memos are passed internally, i.e. within a company. They never go out to clients. For this reason, they differ from other forms of written business communication which are sent to clients or other parties not directly employed by the same company. However, although less formal than some correspondence to clients, memos are serious documents which are almost always carefully filed. They're not like telephone messages or quick notes to colleagues about lunch plans or tennis matches!

Every company may have its own in-house rules for writing memos and the format may vary slightly but, generally speaking, the following are some basic rules:

a   Memos always have a subject heading and this must be written clearly.

b   They are only about one subject.

c   They need to be clear and concise.

d   They should not be longer than one page.

e   Names are kept brief (e.g. P Jones, rather Mr P Jones – even Peter is possible!). In some companies, positions (e.g. Sales Manager) are used instead of names.

f   No addresses are used (although sometimes departments may be included).

g   They do not have full greetings or closings.

h   A company will often insist that employees use a certain style of language. For example, however inelegant it may sound, some multinationals insist that all memos begin 'This memo recommends the purchase of …' or 'This memo summarises the conclusions of the recent meeting held between staff in Logistics on 3.4.08.'

i   They are usually just initialled by the sender – not signed in full.

TASK 1   **Can you think of some practical reasons for these basic rules?**

TASK 2   **Put the following parts of a memo in the correct order:**

    a   the body of the memo

    b   the name(s) of anybody else who will receive a copy of the memo

    c   the conclusion or recommendations

    d   the date

    e   a deadline

    f   the name of the person sending the memo

    g   the initials of the sender

    h   a request for cooperation

    i   the name of the person to whom the memo is sent

    j   a brief introduction to the memo, either giving background information or the main point of the memo

    k   the subject heading

© Cambridge University Press

☐ MEMO NOTES

Students consider the conventions used for memos before using them in an experimental memo.

Language any
Level intermediate and above
Time 15 minutes

Procedure

1 Give students a copy of the worksheet on pp. 244–245; ask them to consider their answers in pairs before feeding back as a class. Encourage students to guess answers, giving reasons, before you supply the answers. (They are provided on p. 246.)
2 Ask students to write a memo about one of the following topics:

   • The facilities provided for lunchtime in the students' company
   • The inadequate air conditioning provided in the offices or factory
   • The provision and use of company cars

Answers for the worksheet on pp. 244–245

TASK 1   **Some practical reasons for the basic rules:**

a   Memos always have a subject heading so that people can immediately see what they're about. People may postpone reading a memo if the subject seems unimportant.

b   They are only ever about one subject so that they are easy to file.

c   They need to be clear and concise because people are busy. If they're not clear the message won't get through and no action will be taken.

d   They should not be longer than one page because people are busy.

e   Names are kept brief because they're internal documents.

f   No addresses are included because everyone can easily find out where individual employees work. (There will always be an internal list giving this information.)

g   They do not have full greetings or closings because they're internal documents.

h   This is probably so as to make memos more comprehensible!

i   They are usually just initialled by the sender – not signed in full – so as to save time.

TASK 2   **A possible correct order:**

i   the name of the person to whom the memo is sent

b   the name(s) of anybody else who will receive a copy of the memo

f   the name of the person sending the memo

d   the date

k   the subject heading

j   a brief introduction to the memo, either giving background information or the main point of the memo

a   the body of the memo

c   the conclusion or recommendations

h   a request for cooperation

e   a deadline

g   the initials of the sender

© Cambridge University Press

A memo containing a request

MEMORANDUM

To: Andrew Knows

From: Claire Compton

Date: February 2, 2015

Subject: Forthcoming trip to New Zealand

As you may know, Ms Wellington will be going to the University of Waikato for a conference next month. At the conference she will be meeting various people who are interested in setting up a joint venture with us.

I understand you have some information on New Zealand in your files from a recent market research project. Naturally, the more background information Ms Wellington has on the country, the more informed her discussions will be at the conference. She is particularly interested in knowing about the following:

- the current political situation
- the market for software in the educational field
- prospective competitors for educational software
- main advertising channels in the NZ market

Could you please pass this information to me by the end of next week, i.e. February 6? Ms Wellington will then have time to study the information before her departure and obtain any additional information, as necessary.

Many thanks in advance.

© Cambridge University Press

Message-writing practice

The rest of the procedures in this section can be used to help students to develop their writing of any kind of message – whether e-mail, fax or memo. Many of them will even be helpful for students who need to practise letter-writing.

While you are working through these procedures, encourage students to bring e-mails, faxes and memos into class for correction or editing. When looking over them, make comments about organisation of information, notable omissions and inappropriate use of language (while taking into account the notes on giving feedback in 4.5). In other words, don't only consider surface details, consider the letter or fax as an attempt to communicate and to achieve an objective. This will help students to understand where they need to improve in order to become more successful communicators. Inspiration gained from these mini-consultation sessions – which will mostly last less than five minutes! – will give you ideas for future lessons and give you more understanding of your students' work.

Get more model e-mails, faxes and memos from coursebooks, dictionaries, students' colleagues (if your students are already working), or from your students' in-trays ... with their permission, of course!

☐ PRIORITISING PAIRS

Students prioritise correspondence and decide what action needs to be taken, before comparing notes with their classmates. This is a good way of exposing students to models of correspondence!

Language any
Level upper-intermediate and above
Time 15 minutes

Preparation

Make copies of several different model e-mails, faxes and memos, and include some other types of correspondence (e.g. notes, letters, junk mail, invitations) to add interest. Prepare enough sets for your students to be able to work in small groups.

Procedure

Give each group of students a set of correspondence. Tell them to prioritise the correspondence and decide on action needed. This will involve categorising correspondence as 'urgent', 'important' or 'pending' and making a list of action necessary, with dates. When students have finished, change round the groups (i.e. instead of AAAAA/BBBBB, have pairs of AB/AB/AB/AB) and get students to compare how they have prioritised the correspondence. Insist that they explain the reasons behind their decisions. Give students the option of writing some of the follow-up correspondence for homework.

☐ MESSAGE PUZZLES

Students reassemble messages which have been 'dismantled'. This procedure is good for focusing attention on planning and typical language of messages; it can be a useful warmer or revision slot after more focused work.

Language any
Level intermediate and above
Time 15 minutes

Preparation

Collect several messages – e-mails, faxes or memos, or a few of each – which are good models of messages appropriate for the students' context. Cut each message into sections; the top sections – i.e. To/From/Date/Subject line in the case of a memo – can be one whole section, while paragraphs form other sections. Mix up the sections from all the messages. Prepare several sets of these sections for different groups of students to work with.

Procedure

Place sets of sections on the table or on the floor before students come into class. Ask students to reassemble the messages. Tell them how many messages there are altogether! If some groups are much stronger than others ask individual students to move from one group to another periodically, or for groups of students to move from one table to another.

Variation 1

Add some false paragraphs to the sets, i.e. paragraphs which would be superfluous to the messages. This is an especially good tactic if the 'extra' paragraphs are relevant to the messages but unnecessary or repetitive. Students must choose the best paragraphs, discarding any they feel are unnecessary or repetitive, explaining their reasoning.

Variation 2

Ask students to look for frequently used expressions and typical plans for specific message types, e.g. messages containing requests.

☐ JUMBLED PHRASES

After putting the words of common expressions used in messages in the correct order, students put the expressions into messages, taking care to use them appropriately. This procedure is especially useful with groups of students who are using very old-fashioned or otherwise inappropriate language.

Language selected by the teacher
Level intermediate and above
Time 30 minutes–1 hour

Preparation

Prepare a worksheet with several jumbled phrases which you want to encourage students to use when they write e-mails, faxes or memos. Alternatively, photocopy the jumbled phrases provided below.

Some possible jumbled phrases, with answers

1. for note the Just to next quick week confirm conference the a arrangements .
2. the seems ZX20 with There problem to a be .
3. on brief a update the situation Here's current .
4. you check Could your possibly records ?
5. fax possible me to Would more be it details ?
6. soon Speak you to .
7. look I again we into suggest this .
8. you back get to soon Could as possible as me ?
9. help in At achieving your difficult need these this I time objectives .
10. regards partner my your Give to .
11. these with If immediately arrangements problem know there please any me is let .
12. you me let Could ASAP have comments your ?
13. you Call have if any me problems .
14. if there's Please help anything to me let we do know can .
15. you conference look the seeing I at to week forward next .

Answers:

1 Just a quick note to confirm the arrangements for the conference next week.

2 There seems to be a problem with the ZX20.

3 Here's a brief update on the current situation.

4 Could you possibly check your records?

5 Would it be possible to fax me more details?

6 Speak to you soon.

7 I suggest we look into this again.

8 Could you get back to me as soon as possible?

9 At this difficult time, I need your help in achieving these objectives.

10 Give my regards to your partner.

11 If there is any problem with these arrangements, please let me know immediately.

12 Could you let me have your comments ASAP*?

13 Call me if you have any problems.

14 Please let me know if there's anything we can do to help.

15 I look forward to seeing you at the conference next week.

*ASAP means 'as soon as possible'.

Procedure

1 Ask students to put the words in order and write out the correctly ordered phrases. If you have copied the jumbled phrases onto an OHT and projected this onto a whiteboard individual students can come to the board and write up answers as they think of them. This makes this stage faster! (Note: Individual students might get annoyed or frustrated if left struggling on their own too long with a task which isn't terribly time-efficient.)

2 When all the sentences have been unjumbled ask students to consider when each phrase might be used and why.

3 Ask students to write a message which includes at least three of the phrases.

4 Finally, get students to pass round their messages and reply to each other's messages using at least three more phrases. In order to do this they will simply need to keep on 'imagining' new identities for themselves!

Variation 1

Using models of e-mails, faxes or memos which are appropriate for the students, blank out typical expressions which students have already met in other model messages. Ask students to fill in the gaps.

Variation 2

Give half the class a gapped e-mail, fax or memo. All the gaps must be versions of the phrases they have already unjumbled – dates or other numbers might be different. Give the other half of the class cards with the missing information. Then ask students with the gapped text to get precise dates, etc. from the other students in the class by role-playing telephone calls. Students should then check their answers by reading out a complete version of each gapped sentence to his or her partner.

□ MESSAGE WORKSHOPS

Having been given a situation, students write a message in groups.

Language any
Level intermediate and above
Time approx. 40 minutes

Procedure

1   Describe a situation to the class, either verbally, on an OHT or on a piece of paper. You can use the following situation:

> Your boss, Ms Wellington, is going to New Zealand next month. She has asked you to get some information on New Zealand from Mr Knows in Market Research. Write a message to Mr Knows, asking for information.

2   Put students into groups and give each group a transparency and OHT pen, if an OHP is available. Tell students that after they have written their message, one person from the group will have to present it to the rest of the class, explaining why it was written in that way. Give students as much time as they need to write the memo – probably around 20 minutes.
3   To start off the individual presentations, get each group representative to read out the text of the message. Ask the representative to read out the subject line of the message first of all, e.g. *Subject: Forthcoming trip to New Zealand*, because the students will also need to consider whether this is helpful in introducing or clarifying

the purpose of the message. (*New Zealand* or *Information* would be inappropriate subject lines in this case, for example.)

4   After the representative has made comments, invite comments from the rest of the class before making comments yourself.

5   After the class, select one or two of the students' messages, type them out, improving them where necessary, and distribute them as model messages. A model version of this message – in memo format – is provided on p. 247.

☐ FOLLOW-UP MESSAGES

After a speaking or listening activity students write a follow-up message. This is a good excuse to give students useful writing practice with a clearly defined context.

Language any appropriate to messages
Level intermediate and above
Time 20 minutes

Procedure

After giving students feedback on oral work, ask students to write a follow-up message, if this would be appropriate in real life. Speaking activities which could warrant a message include:

* a conversation with a client in which an agreement was made or information requested
* a telephone conversation in which a complicated request was made, which needs to be confirmed or clarified by e-mail, fax or a memo
* a negotiation, as in Unit 7 of *Business Class* (Cotton, D. and S. Robbins. 1993. London: Nelson); see p. 242 for a sample message
* a meeting which requires follow-up action in terms of requesting support or information from another department
* confirmation of a reservation for hotel rooms or conference facilities

Variation

Ask students to write a message after doing a listening task. An example of a listening activity which could be used is in Unit 6 of *Insights to Business* (Lannon, M., G. Tullis and T. Trappe. 1993. London: Nelson). In this taped extract a Japanese woman explains what her company's seminars are about since a company is considering arranging some seminars. Students write a follow-up message which includes a recommendation. A sample message for this situation – in memo format – is provided on p. 254.

A sample memo

To: Philip Groves

From: Vincent Mills

Date: February 5, 2011

Subject: Preparation for TR10 Joint Venture Meetings in Japan

I spoke to Ms Moriwake, the Japanese business consultant, about her seminar, as you suggested. She told me she focuses on three key areas:

1 The emphasis on groups, rather than individuals, so companies are more important than positions or specialities.

2 The importance of human relationships and the need to maintain harmony. In negotiations this means people avoid conflict and prefer compromise.

3 The role of managers as generalists and facilitators of decision-making.

I feel this seminar would be of great value to our delegates. Ms Moriwake made me feel that the Japanese make decisions in a very different way from us. Understanding their different approach may help us if we are to get the contract we are hoping for on our forthcoming visit.

I can go ahead and book up places on Ms Moriwake's next seminar as soon as I have confirmation of your final decision. She says places normally need to be booked up at least three weeks in advance of each seminar, which means a deadline for us of March 14.

V.M.

☐ ONGOING PROBLEM-SOLVING WRITING WORKSHOPS

Individual students bring in messages which need a response or they describe problem situations which require a message. Students work in pairs or groups initially and then write messages as a class.

Language any
Level lower-intermediate and above
Time 30–40 minutes

Procedure

1   Get students to consider the message which needs a reply or the situation which requires a message. Ask them to prepare questions (about the situation) to put to the student who needs the message. Some example questions:

  * *How well do you know the writer of the message?*
  * *What do you need to tell him or her?*
  * *Is there anything you don't want to tell him or her?*

2   After these questions have been dealt with, get students to plan and write a first draft of the message in groups or pairs.

3   Elicit a class version of the message, improving students' language whenever necessary and writing this version on the board.

4   Ask the student who needs the message to copy it down and type it up after class. In the next class, copies of the message can either be distributed to the other students or put in a class 'message file'. For future situations, students can consult their previous collection of model messages or the class 'message file' before planning and writing messages for other situations. When several messages have been collected, students can be encouraged to deduce basic principles for message-writing and useful expressions. For ideas on how to use model messages see MODELS THROUGH READING (p. 100), GHOST RECONSTRUCTION (p. 121), CUT-UP TEXTS (p. 122) and FOCUSED GAPFILLS (p. 123).

☐ 3-D MESSAGE SCRUTINY

This is a good procedure for small classes. It helps students to focus on accuracy of language and appropriacy of style for message-writing.

Language any
Level lower-intermediate and above
Time 90 minutes

Preparation

After obtaining your students' permission to do so, type up students' messages, improving them or correcting errors and keeping the original memos for comparison in class. If the messages are badly or strangely planned reorganise the text, making as few changes as possible. Take care over conventions and use block layout. Make four copies of each message (three copies for students and one copy for yourself). These copies can then be circulated around the class, irrespective of the number of students.

Procedure

1 Explain to students that different notes need to be made on each of the three sets of messages. Perhaps write the following instructions on the board:

> **Set 1:** Using a highlighter pen, mark anything which is different from the original message. This includes changes in layout or punctuation.
> **Set 2:** Underline all the verb forms and label them in the margin.
> **Set 3:** Note in the margin the plan behind each message (e.g. Intro, request for purchase of PCs).

2 Get students to volunteer to deal with Sets 1, 2 or 3. Distribute the messages, remembering to give students dealing with Set 1 copies of the original memos. While students are working, consider switching round individuals once or twice if they seem bored or if they have finished early. Help students, where necessary.
3 Regroup students (AAA, BBB, CCC can become ABC, ABC, ABC) and ask them to share their findings, focusing on the possible reasons behind things. After some discussion, ask students to pick out any messages which they want to improve further and get them to rewrite these. Messages can either be rewritten on OHTs or on a double-sided board. Both these options allow for easy follow-up discussion.

☐ LEGO MESSAGES

This procedure is surprisingly motivating for students, perhaps because of the results that are possible. It focuses students' attention on accuracy and appropriacy of language. Students experiment with grammatical structures while remembering the context of a message.

Language any
Level lower-intermediate–upper-intermediate
Time 2 hours

Procedure

1 Before you start, explain that you are going to give the students an opportunity to experiment with verb forms and/or grammatical points. Stress that you expect them to make mistakes but that these mistakes will help them to work out how and when certain verb forms, etc. are used. Illustrate the importance of mistakes in language learning by using the persistent inventor Edison as an example – he failed to invent the light bulb hundreds of times before he succeeded!

2 Make a list on the board of verb forms and/or grammatical points which you think students are having problems with. Get everybody to choose four items from the board: two they're happy with using (and think they understand) and two they're not. Write names of individual students against the points on the board to give students a sense of responsibility and also so you can later use individuals as 'consultants' at the end of this procedure.

3 Ask students to write one or more sentences for each item, making sure that all the sentences could fit together to form one message (about the students' work).

4 Get students to make their groups of sentences into complete messages.

5 Ask students to circulate their finished messages for checking by other students. Students who are 'marking' should indicate mistakes or questionable points by putting black dots in the margin – one for each mistake or query. When papers are passed back to the original authors, individuals should correct their own message.

6 Elicit and/or discuss any problems which arose and make suggestions for follow-up self-study work.

Variation

If possible, get students to work at computers during this procedure. Two or more students can work at one computer. Move students around periodically so that final messages are jointly written. This takes the pressure off weaker students in the group and helps them to learn from other students. Using computers is helpful because 'handwriting' is

257

always anonymous and corrected mistakes invisible! Messages can also be printed out after your feedback has been acted upon.

□ DODGY DRAFTS

Students edit messages which include deliberate and carefully planted mistakes. This procedure is good for reminding them of key points or raising their awareness of their own typical errors.

Language any
Level intermediate and above
Time 10–15 minutes

Preparation

Carefully insert errors into model messages which you have written yourself or which you have extracted from the students' course materials. Include mistakes of layout, conventions, style or grammar, as appropriate for the group of students. Also focus students' attention on accuracy of information by including subtle mistakes (e.g. *on 25th*, rather than *by 25th*) if you have back-up information sheets, reports, letters, messages or faxes which students can consult. Only include a few errors so as to simulate real life.

Procedure

Tell students to edit the messages, imagining they are messages their less proficient colleagues have written. Tell them how many errors they are looking for in each 'contaminated' model.

□ DOMINO RESPONSES

Students imagine typical situations in their companies (or departments) and write messages to each other. The situations evolve as students respond to other students' messages.

Language any
Level upper-intermediate and above
Time 1 hour

Procedure

1 Divide the class into different groups, preferably according to department or speciality. Get each group to think of at least three situations which might arise in their department or in their company generally. They should describe these situations in detail on cards you supply. (Note that these cards can later be used with other classes.)

2 Next, ask students to write to somebody else in the company (i.e. class) about one of the problems.
3 Pass the messages around the room and ask other students to reply to the messages.
4 Allow the exchange of messages to continue until problems are resolved or until other types of communication become necessary, i.e. phone calls or meetings. These can also be role-played! Take notes while students are working so that you can elicit or give feedback afterwards. Provide model versions of the messages as a follow-up if you have time, and use these for further work.

☐ EARLY FINISHERS' FUN

Students who finish class activities early write 'fun' messages to other students on rough paper. The teacher acts as a low-tech e-mail circuit, telephone line or delivery boy!

Language any
Level intermediate and above
Time 5–10 minutes

Procedure

Simply ask students who have finished early to write a message to someone else in the group. Insist that they specify what type of message it is (e-mail, fax, memo, etc.) and that they include the usual greetings, etc. as they would when preparing a real message. (To be reasonable, however, let them omit any formats which would be put in automatically by their computer or which would be written on a pre-printed sheet.) Deliver the messages for students and encourage recipients of messages to reply either immediately in class or as homework.

☐ MESSAGE EVALUATION

After writing a message in class, students use an evaluation sheet to evaluate their own and other students' work.

Language any
Level intermediate and above
Time 10 minutes

Procedure

Before giving students feedback for any of the messages they write themselves in class, ask them to evaluate their own – and other students' – work using an evaluation sheet, such as the one provided on the next page.

A student evaluation worksheet

BUSINESS ENGLISH THINK SPOT

Evaluating e-mails, faxes and memos

Look at your partner's message and make notes in answer to the following questions:

1 Does it look business-like?
2 Is there anything unusual about the layout?
3 What is the message trying to achieve?
4 What do you think happened before the message was written?
5 What do you expect to happen next?
6 Are the ideas within the message organised into clear, logical paragraphs?
7 What is the plan behind the message?
8 Is the message written in an appropriate style? Is anything too formal or informal?
9 Can you suggest any improvements?
10 Does this message remind you of any problems you have when writing messages?

Pass your notes on to your partner.

Consider you partner's notes about your own message.

What improvements (if any) would you now like to make?

© Cambridge University Press

For other procedures which you can use to help your students practise language for this area, see the Index entry for 'e-mail'.

5.13 Report-writing

Reports can be anything from a long memo (i.e. a single page) to a 50-page, well-organised and formatted analysis of a particular situation. Whatever their length, reports can effect enormous change so they are extremely important to students.

When teaching report-writing the most important area to focus on is probably organisation of material, especially if students are unused to

Western forms of content organisation. Students must also take care to gear their message to their reader(s) and differentiate clearly between fact and opinion. Obviously, the consequence of suggesting something is fact, when it is merely opinion, could be far-reaching and could cause bad feeling if found out! Above all, when helping students with this important skill, be as encouraging as you can – because the task of writing a report can be rather overwhelming! – and help students to see each report in the context of their company's politics and its desire for positive change. The notes below might be the starting (or finishing!) point of a discussion on report-writing.

Some notes for students about reports

BUSINESS ENGLISH THINK SPOT

Why are reports important?
... and why are they difficult to write?

Reports are important because they often influence decisions made, so can have far-reaching effects. However, they are difficult to write because they usually involve collecting, summarising and organising large quantities of information and making recommendations which make sense. Selection of information is probably the most important part of writing a report. The reader(s), as well as the purpose behind the report, must be remembered at all times and irrelevant or unnecessary detail omitted.

Typically, reports include the following sections: Introduction, Findings (body), Conclusion, Recommendations ... although these headings may not be used. If very long, the body will be subdivided into many sections and paragraphs or sections will be numbered carefully for ease of reference.

In addition to long, analytical reports (which may be written annually or in order to analyse problem situations) there are other types of report, e.g. visit reports (written by sales people about visits made to clients), personnel reports (which will help Human Resources Managers to keep track of employees' performance and attitudes) and weekly or monthly reports (which will provide an update on work done for supervisors and other senior staff).

The language you use in any report should be clear and succinct. Never add extra phrases merely to impress and never disguise opinions as fact. The key to success when writing reports is to communicate your message clearly.

A typical internal report

REPORT ON SMOKING

INTRODUCTION

This report is a summary of a survey which was conducted:
- to investigate the extent of smoking in offices
- to investigate attitudes towards smoking, and
- to make recommendations for improvements.

It was conducted by the Staff Welfare Committee after the Human Resources Department received several complaints from staff. The recruitment of two nonsmokers also prompted this study.

In order to obtain information, a questionnaire was distributed to all staff and a percentage was interviewed at random. The people who had complained about smoking, as well as ten of the company's nonsmokers, were also interviewed. 96 people returned completed questionnaires and many of the comments made by respondents were checked or explored in the interviews conducted afterwards.

FINDINGS

Overall

At the moment, only two departments (out of 23 in the company as a whole) have policies as regards smoking during work time. These two departments insist on non-smoking. In the company as a whole, 24% of employees are smokers. 10% of these smoke more than 20 cigarettes a day, mostly while working. Of the remaining 90% of non- or light-smokers, 40% say they are disturbed by the smell of smoke in their working area, 36% said they would prefer a non-smoking policy throughout the company and 12% of staff said they were not bothered by smoke.

Specific problem areas

1 Irritation levels

Among nonsmokers who are disturbed by smoke in their offices, irritation levels seem to be high. Several disputes over the smoking issue were reported and some staff mentioned ongoing comments directed at smokers by nonsmokers, which might indicate mild irritation, even if not fully expressed.

2 Pregnant women

There have been a few cases of pregnancy amongst our female staff over the last few years. Since a large proportion of our workforce is female, this needs to be taken into account; the risks of passive smoking to pregnant mothers (e.g. the link between this and low birth weight) are well-documented.

3 Legal vulnerability

There have been several cases of employees suing their company for damages in the case of illness (especially lung cancer) in recent years. The fact that long-term employees have been successful in establishing their company's culpability should be taken into account because we may be vulnerable to similar attacks. The publicity any court cases might bring would not team well with our image of a producer of healthy, environmentally-friendly skin-care products.

4 Nonsmokers' rights

Most of the nonsmokers interviewed felt they had a right to work in a smoke-free environment, given that the health risks of passive smoking are now well-established. Several of them reported increased problems with coughing, eye-irritation and eye strain, which could all be related to smoking. The new nonsmoking recruits were particularly articulate on this point and were surprised we had no clear policy on smoking, especially since it has even become illegal in public places in some parts of the world (e.g. Singapore and New Zealand).

5 Ventilation

Smoke is often recycled in the aircon system, which might be exacerbating some of the health problems or aesthetic aspects of the situation (since the smokiness never fully disappears). Windows are rarely opened because of both the aircon (which fails to function properly with open windows) and traffic noise from nearby streets.

CONCLUSION

It seems clear that our company does need a policy on smoking because a high proportion of employees are dissatisfied with the present situation. The potential for legal problems, as well as the health risks to staff (especially when pregnant or susceptible to bronchial problems), suggests the need for a more cautious position.

RECOMMENDATIONS

For the sake of our health and company image I recommend the following:
• We should ban smoking in all working areas.
• We should make one of the outside prefab buildings a smokers' common room.
• We should raise smokers' awareness of health risks by distributing information from the World Health Organisation or other sources on an ongoing basis.

Claire Reynolds   23.2.06

A typical visit report

VISIT REPORT – METRO, Singapore – 30.7.17

Present: P J Howells*   *ATY Office Supplies (S) Pte Ltd
           W Smith*
           K S Tan, Distribution Manager
           A Yeo, Sales & Marketing Manager

Decided to visit after receiving several phone calls from
Ken Tan re delivery problems and quality control.   **ACTION**

1 Ken Tan explained that stock levels of writing paper and
       pencils had recently been inconsistent due to our delivery
       problems. Agreed to inform him of any expected delays at
       least two weeks in advance or to give 10% compensation.   **PJH**

2 Several consignments for Metro have apparently been
       incomplete recently (e.g. order nos. 2486210 & 2689178)
       and Metro had considerable difficulty getting action. WS
       suggested that we had been slow in completing consignments
       because Metro had been signing our delivery notes without
       checking the contents of each consignment. PJH stressed the
       need for cooperation on their part and Ken Tan agreed to
       remind his warehouse staff to check before signing in future.

3 Marketing strategies for the new 'Love Lines' paper products
       were discussed in the light of low sales. Metro agreed to use
       our new 'Valentine' display stands as long as we would cover
       the cost and agreed to offer a special discount for four weeks
       at their own expense.   **WS/AY**

4 Alison Yeo complained that she had not been kept sufficiently
       informed about new products (e.g. our new aerogramme
       package) and suggested that delivery/stock problems with
       other products (e.g. our regular, blue airmail paper) could
       have been alleviated if more information had been given.
       Instead of apologising to customers for lack of stock, they
       would have been able to offer an alternative product. WS
       apologised and agreed to keep her up-to-date on all new
       products on his weekly visits.   **WS**

5 Agreed to make follow-up visit on 6.9.17 at 3.00 p.m.
       in addition to WS's usual weekly visits.   **PJH/WS**

PJH/sdk

☐ TRIO PROBLEM EXCHANGE

Working in groups of three, students each read texts about problems in international corporations. They then tell each other about the problems and discuss possible courses of action which might reinstate the corporation's positive public image. Finally, they prepare reports which present recommendations for courses of action.

Language selected texts by the teacher, free speaking, then report-writing
Level upper-intermediate and above
Time 20 minutes

Preparation

Find texts on, or write up, three cross-cultural problems from business magazines, management books or the media, or use those presented below. Make separate photocopies of each text, ready to give to students A, B and C, who will be working in groups of three, and possibly stick each text on a separate card.

Example texts

> One laundry detergent company certainly wishes now that it had contacted a few locals before it initiated its promotional campaign in the Middle East. All of the company's advertisements pictured soiled clothes on the left, its box of soap in the middle, and clean clothes on the right. But because in that area of the world people tend to read from the right to the left, many potential customers interpreted the message to indicate the soap actually soiled the clothes.

> A well-known American designer tried to launch a new fragrance in Latin America. The advertising message emphasized the perfume's fresh camellia scent. Naturally, sales were slow there because camellias are flowers used for funerals in most of Latin America.

> An advertisement for a men's cologne recently pictured a man and his dog in an American rural setting. The picture was well accepted in America, but was not effective when used in North Africa. The advertiser simply assumed that the American 'man's best friend' was loved everywhere when, in fact, Muslims usually consider dogs to be either signs of bad luck or symbols of uncleanliness. Neither interpretation helped sales of the cologne.

(Adapted from Ricks, D. A. 1993. *Blunders in International Business.*
Oxford: Blackwell.)

Procedure

1 Put students into groups of three and give Students A, B and C different texts to read. Encourage them to check vocabulary with you or to use monolingual dictionaries.
2 When everyone is ready, ask students to tell each other about their texts, then discuss what they think the companies should do.
3 Next, ask students in each trio to prepare ideas for a meeting to discuss one or all three of the problems. Get each trio to join another trio for a 10-minute meeting.
4 Finally, ask students to plan reports on one of the problems in their original trios. Individuals can write up the whole reports for homework. Tell students it's OK if their reports are short, as long as they are clear and well-organised!

□ PROBLEM CREATION

A possible problem situation for which a report might be needed is elicited from students. This is a good way of eliciting typical problem areas without making students feel exposed.

Language any
Level upper-intermediate and above
Time 20 minutes

Procedure

1 Tell students they are going to imagine a problem which might occur within a company. Ask students to prepare a mind map or diagram for a situation, using the following instructions:
 • *Draw three or four simple faces.*
 • *Add details, e.g. a moustache or earrings, to give each face more character.*
 • *Give each face a name and job title, imagining that the people all work for the same company.*
 • *Discuss with the person sitting next to you some typical frustrations each person might experience at work.*
 • *Draw some speech bubbles for each person and fill each speech bubble with any comments or questions which you think appropriate for each person. You don't need to write in English if you don't want to!*
 • *Again, working with your partner, discuss the attitudes of the other characters to each speech bubble.*
 • *Finally, select or refine one of the problem areas you have identified among this particular group of people, making notes under the faces to help you remember the details later on.*

Note that much of what students suggest is likely to come from their own experience – and this may even be very obvious! Don't point this out because the whole point of making the problem 'fictitious' is to give students the feeling that they are not having to expose their real-life problems. If students accuse each other, remind them (jokingly!) that the situations are fictitious, however similar to reality they may seem; even if this is not true, your light-hearted reminder should take away some of the tension among students.

2 Next, using an example situation of your own (with cartoons on the board, on OHTs or on handouts), demonstrate how a plan for a report might result from the cartoons. While you are doing this, elicit the main points about writing reports, e.g. the need to consider the reader(s), the relevance of items to be included, organisation of points, etc.

3 Get students to write out similar plans for their own reports in pairs. Whole reports or simply their introductions and conclusions can be written up in class, either in one big group or in smaller groups. If smaller groups are used students will be able to compare and evaluate each other's writing. Final reports can be written up for homework.

Variation

Use case studies from business books or video clips to establish problems and elicit the main points from students before getting them to plan a suitable outline for a report.

☐ DIAGRAM DEVELOPMENT

This procedure helps students to focus on explaining diagrams clearly – face-to-face – before doing the same thing in writing, as they might in a report. The initial presentations help to liven up a class which has been engaged in a lot of stodgy report-writing practice.

Language any
Level intermediate and above
Time 40 minutes–1 hour

Preparation

Find a diagram which you feel would be of interest to your students, which might be included in a report to illustrate a procedure or process. Alternatively, use the one given below from *Business Reports in English* (Comfort, J., R. Revell, and C. Stott. 1984. Cambridge: Cambridge University Press.) p. 36 (3.4.2).

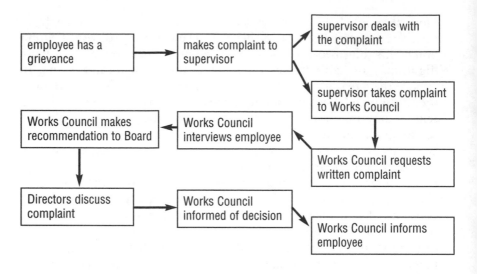

Procedure

1 Ask students to take notes while you describe the procedure or process in your diagram. Don't show the actual diagram while you are talking! Invite students to ask questions before you describe the diagram a second time.

2 Give out OHTs and pens (if you have an OHP) and ask students – working in pairs – to draw a diagram to go with your explanation. It's best if you don't give students any help while they are doing this. (If any students finish early, ask them to prepare another diagram, also on an OHT, to represent the recruitment procedure a company might follow when recruiting new staff.)

3 Next, ask one student from each pair to show and describe their diagram(s) to the rest of the class.

4 Discuss any points in the students' diagrams which are factually inaccurate or confusing and focus students' attention on the principles by which they have organised information.

5 Show students the original diagram and ask them to write a summary of the procedure or process, as they would do if they wanted to include the diagram in a report.

☐ REPORTING BIAS

By examining reports from different newspapers on the same story, students become more aware of how each newspaper (or journalist) tries to influence the reader's perception of facts.

Language newspaper articles
Level upper-intermediate and above
Time 30–40 minutes

Preparation

Buy at least three different newspapers of different types. Examples of British newspapers which you might use might be the *Independent*, the *Sun* and the *Daily Mail*. Find a story which has been covered by all three papers but with a slightly different bias each time. Make enough copies of these articles for students to work in small groups.

Procedure

1 Tell students to read and compare the three parallel articles about one story. Ask them to identify and make notes (on an OHT, if possible) on the following:

- the main facts of the story (as gleaned from all three articles);
- the facts included in each version of the story;
- any notable omissions in each of the articles;
- any extra elements included which might influence readers' opinions, e.g. adjectives or words with strong connotations, as in YOUTH ATTACKS FRAIL OLD LADY
- the ordering of elements within each article and how this affects the impression created.

2 Get students to report back to each other and discuss their notes.
3 Divide students into three groups. Ask the first group to write out a completely neutral version of the story; the second group to write a version which makes the central character(s) seem positive; the third group to write out a version which makes the central character(s) seem negative.
4 Discuss with students any implications this exercise has for report-writing. Focus their attention on the importance of presenting information as neutrally as possible, even if their report is to be persuasive, so that decisions can be based on accurate information, not on a distorted view of events. It's a good idea to focus students' attention on a particular report they are writing or could write.

Variation

Get students to consider news headlines about cutbacks, mechanisation, computerisation, mergers, etc. For each headline, students should decide how the story is presented and who is blamed (if anybody). Again, finish by discussing implications for report-writing.

□ EVALUATION REPORTS

Students prepare and write a report on the course they are on. This is a useful exercise because the subject is non-specialised but useful and all students also have access to the same information.

Language any
Level upper-intermediate and above
Time 20 minutes

Procedure

1 Tell students that they are going to write a report on their present English course. This will be an exercise in report-writing and will also provide valuable feedback to you, their teacher.
2 Elicit what might be included, taking the report's readership (you!) and its purpose into account.
3 Ask students to make notes (in pairs) on what could be included within each section. Some general areas which might be covered are as follows:

   • The aims of the course/the reason it was set up
   • The course content
   • Levels of attendance and participation
   • Attitudes of students before, during and at the end of the course
   • Problems experienced by students
   • Any omissions from the course or unnecessary inclusions in the programme
   • Recommendations for similar courses in the future.

4 Get students to report back on their ideas before discussing possible ways of ordering the separate items.
5 Review with the class any points about layout which you have not yet covered, especially the importance of good paragraphing and headings.
6 Ask students to write up reports, working in groups of three or four. After class, rather than correcting these reports in a conventional way, consider using them solely as a basis for discussion in class. If your students specifically request corrections or you feel there are some which need to be made, you will need to correct students' errors very sensitively. One way is to prepare a generalised (anonymous!) worksheet for students which covers most of the significant errors. For overall problems, elicit then review important points as a class and write sections of another report as an example. Alternatively, ask students to rewrite the report in groups on OHTs (which they can then share) or as a class on the board.

For other procedures which you can use to help your students practise language for this area, see the Index entry for 'report-writing'.

5.14 Understanding the news

Many Business English students need to understand the news in English on TV, on the radio and in newspapers so as to be able to keep up with international business developments. A large number will also have to read newspapers or periodicals in English so as to keep up with changes in their industry. Coverage by different news sources can be quite different, so students often get a much better insight into possibilities in their own markets if they can watch the BBC news or CNN (on Sky or cable TV) for example, or read periodicals published in English.

Before considering classwork for this language area, remember that not all students will have equal access to news sources. Check with students what they can get on their radios and TVs and what they can easily and cheaply obtain from local newsstands. Encourage them to find out what's available in any public or private libraries nearby, pointing out that some may subscribe to international newspapers or even provide facilities for people to listen to the radio or watch satellite TV. If it seems affordable, suggest that students buy a shortwave radio, or subscribe to some of the compilation tapes of news stories sometimes marketed by the BBC or commercial organisations.

Classwork can be quite ambitious. Even if your students are only low level they will probably be capable of digesting much more complex language than they can produce, especially if it involves understanding the jargon of their speciality, which will usually be very familiar. Since speed and careful, selective reading is of the utmost importance it is helpful for students to develop skills for skimming and scanning.

In class, try the following:

- Get students to scan contents pages for articles on areas of interest.
- Having set a time limit (e.g. three minutes), ask students to skim an article for overall gist. When time is up, ask students to summarise the text as far as possible. If students come up with few ideas, improvise some simple comprehension questions on the article which you think students will be able to answer without difficulty. After inviting questions about vocabulary and allowing students another five minutes for reading, continue with a few more detail questions. This is a realistic approach given that students will have limited time in real life and given the fact that the tasks reflect the real-life situation (i.e. reading through an article quickly, then checking a few words in the dictionary). It also involves no preparation on your part!

271

When doing any work in class, note that students from countries with less freedom of speech or less true democracy may be unused to reading a range of political comment, so you may well need to help them to evaluate bias. Do this sensitively, remembering the dangers involved – both for you and your students! – in speaking too openly or critically.

> Note: Before using any procedures involving news sources you must ensure that you have the appropriate licences to make off-air recordings and to make multiple copies of material from newspapers or journals.

□ PARALLEL RECORDING

Students listen to the news in English, then in their own language with the aim of improving their comprehension of the English version.

Language authentic news broadcasts
Level intermediate and above
Time 40 minutes

Preparation

Record the news from the radio in English (e.g. from the BBC World Service or from Radio 4). Then record the same version of the news in the students' language (from a bilingual channel) or another version of the news in the student's own language (from a local radio station). If possible, have copies of newspapers in English and the students' L1 to hand.

Procedure

1 Play students the news in English and get them to answer gist and detail questions. Get them to listen again, then reconstruct the stories they hear.
2 Play students the recording of the news in their own language. Then ask them to reconsider their reconstructed versions of the English news stories and make any changes necessary. If there are any details which students are confused about, encourage them to listen to the English version again (and again!) and to ask questions about vocabulary until they have a much more accurate and complete understanding of the English version. Guide students if there appear to be significant differences between the two versions, but otherwise stand back!

Variation

Ask students to write out a short version of some news items – perhaps relating the story to their company's situation – for an imaginary company.

☐ HEADLINE MATCHING

Students match headlines with texts. If this procedure is repeated periodically students should eventually get used to the vocabulary and syntax of headlines in newspapers and become better at skimming newspapers.

Language authentic newspaper articles
Level upper-intermediate and above
Time 10 minutes

Preparation

Select about seven short newspaper articles on different topics. Cut them out of the newspaper, cutting the headlines away from the texts. Arrange them on sheets of A4 paper, the headlines and texts no longer matched up together but numbered 1–7 and a–g, respectively.

Procedure

Get students to match the headlines with the texts. If they have difficulty doing this get everybody to focus on some key, preselected words from the headlines. Teach and check their meaning before asking students to continue.

Variation

Get students to predict stories from headlines alone. Then allow them to check their answers using matching articles from a real newspaper.

☐ NEWS DISCUSSION SNIPPETS

Students get minimal information on key stories through mini-articles, then they discuss the possible background and implications. This procedure is invaluable for helping students to develop the ability to discuss current affairs with colleagues or visitors on a casual basis so as to build relationships.

Language authentic mini-articles
Level intermediate and above
Time 10 minutes

Preparation

Cut out mini-news articles (e.g. from the *Guardian Weekly*) and mount them on a single sheet of A4 paper. Number each article.

Procedure

Distribute the photocopied sheet to students and allocate one or two articles to each student to read. After a couple of minutes ask students one by one to turn over the sheet and tell the other students about their newspaper story. After each student has summarised the story, other students can comment or ask questions. Encourage students to be as free in their interpretation of events as possible but also supply them with relevant background information if this seems appropriate.

☐ QUESTION MINI-TESTS

Students ask each other questions about newspaper articles in such a way as to enhance comprehension and promote discussion of the articles.

Language authentic articles; questions controlled by the students
Level intermediate and above
Time 20 minutes

Procedure

1 Distribute newspaper articles to students or – better! – get students to bring in their own. Each pair of students should have a different article. Allow students time to read the articles and to ask you any questions about vocabulary or the cultural or political background.
2 Next, ask students to prepare six questions which relate to their newspaper article for other students: three questions they know the answer to and three questions which they either can't answer themselves or which are discussion questions.
3 With a new partner, students then ask their questions to find out how much their partner already knows about their news story (from listening to the news on TV, etc.) and so as to make him or her interested in finding out more about the story. Students can say if an answer is correct but they must not give answers their partner does not know.
4 Finally, students exchange articles in their pairs and read. Then they discuss answers to their questions again.

Variation

Working alone, each student in turn explains his or her story to the rest of the group and then deals with questions or comments, keeping the article face-down as much as possible!

□ BACKGROUND PRINTING

Students assess the message and the bias behind parallel newspaper articles.

Language authentic newspaper articles
Level advanced
Time 30 minutes

Preparation

Buy copies of contrasting newspapers (e.g. the *Guardian* and the *Sun* in the UK, or the *Herald Tribune* and the *National Inquirer* in the US). Select two or three stories covered by both newspapers and cut them out. Prepare a question sheet to guide students if you think this necessary for your particular class.

Procedure

After asking a few brief questions about each newspaper, distribute your questionnaire (if you are using one) or ask students to decide what the writer's opinions are for each story. Allow students to use their dictionaries to help them understand the bias of each article.

□ FLOOR WORD JIGSAW DICTATION

This procedure forces students to focus on small words and helps them to work out where word divisions are within words. It is very 'physical' and team-oriented so is a fun start to a lesson. Although quite a bit of preparation is involved, this procedure can be used with classes at many levels and cards can be reused if the headlines are very generalised and cards are laminated.

Language news headlines from the radio or TV
Level intermediate and above
Time 40 minutes

Preparation

Record the headlines from the news (e.g. from the BBC World Service, CNN or Radio 4). Type them out word for word, then enlarge the text so that individual words are big enough for a group of students to see when kneeling around them on the floor (approx. 18 point size). Cut the text up so that each word is separate, putting the individual words into an envelope for safe-keeping. Make several sets for your class so that each pair or group of three or four has a set. Make copies of some newspaper articles on the same subjects if you want to do follow-up work on the particular news stories covered in the headlines.

Procedure

Organise students into groups or pairs and give each group or pair one set of words. Tell students they must put the words in the order they hear on tape. Explain that this is a type of dictation. Allow students time to organise their cards on the floor (or a table) however they please before you start playing the tape. Repeat the tape as often as necessary. The first couple of times play it through without interruption, then play it again in snippets, according to the instructions of the students. Rotate students so stronger students can help those having difficulty. Ask gist and detail comprehension questions when students have finished and help them to understand – by explaining the word linking – why they found some parts particularly difficult to sort out.

Follow up with a discussion of the issues in the news and then focus on related news articles for reading practice.

Variation

Proceed as above but include some pieces of paper with no words. Substitute these for some words in the headlines, which you want to focus students' attention on. When students have put the words in order, including blank papers for words not included, they need to write the correct words on the pieces of paper. Don't worry about spoiling your sets of papers – the same papers can be used with other groups later on if you simply substitute these papers for new blanks.

6 Solving or avoiding problems

6.1 Absenteeism and lateness

Absenteeism and lateness can disrupt courses to the point where they are totally ineffective. Lesson plans need to be adjusted or abandoned, progress slows down because of the need for extra review slots (when students turn up), group dynamics become strained or unpredictable, regularly attending punctual students become demotivated and the absentees and latecomers themselves lose an important proportion of their training programme. It is, therefore, vitally important to develop strategies or systems which are consistent, fair and effective.

Formal systems

Although having a system for discouraging, or 'outlawing' excessive absenteeism or lateness in a sense undermines the student's right to operate as a free individual, it is useful for several reasons:

- Until adults realise the importance and usefulness of English training they are sometimes inclined to de-prioritise it in their lives. This will set up a self-fulfilling prophecy: if they downplay its importance – and don't attend consistently – English can never have a significant effect on their lives simply because progress will be almost impossible.
- Promises made to companies cannot be fulfilled unless staff actually attend classes.
- Students cannot be motivated and subsequently empowered (i.e. made more autonomous) unless they are actually present in class.

Negotiate with in-house or in-company coordinators and agree on rules and procedures which are acceptable within your set-up and/or teaching setting. An informal system in which students telephone or fax the teacher (or receptionist, or coordinator) at least 24 hours before class is rarely effective, so you are advised to set up something more formal. A formal system for monitoring attendance on in-company courses could function as follows:

1 An Approved Absences form (see p. 278) is provided for each student at the beginning of each course and the form only has enough spaces for the number of absences which are permissible on that particular course.

2 A student who needs to be absent fills out one space each time he or she needs to be absent.
3 The form is signed by the student's manager, who 'approves' the absence.
4 The form is faxed or passed to the teacher at least 24 hours before the class begins if at all possible, or after the absence if the absence is unplanned.

If the student needs to be absent for more time than is allowed for on the form, the student is no longer allowed to attend. This last 'drop' part of the system must, obviously, be clearly explained to students in advance! Reminding students of how disruptive irregular attendance is for regular attenders will usually be enough to make people understand.

A *form for maintaining an attendance policy*

BUSINESS ENGLISH APPROVED ABSENCES

Name: .... Company: ....

Position: .... Department: ....

Contact numbers: ....

Course: .... Teacher: ....

NOTE: If you exceed the number of absences allowed for below, you will no longer be able to attend the course. You will need to join again at a later date when you have a lighter work schedule and can make a full commitment to the course.

Date	REASON FOR ABSENCE	Manager's Signature	Teacher's Signature

Total number of absences: **% of course attended:**

(Based on a form developed by Andrew Vaughan at Sumikin-Intercom Inc., Osaka, Japan)

As far as lateness is concerned, at the beginning of each course as part of your course introduction (see pp. 43–44), tell students what kind of behaviour is acceptable. Explain clearly why punctuality needs to be taken seriously. You might point out to students the percentage of the course they would miss if they were 10 or 15 minutes late for each class and also the disruption latecomers constitute for other students.

Students will usually understand the reasons for good attendance and punctuality if you explain that learning English cannot be done by magic. Students will need to attend the course if they are to benefit from it!

Informal approaches

In addition to using a formalised system, it is important not to let either absences or lateness pass unnoticed in class. When students come in late, or after an absence, do the following:

- Make a good-natured joke about it, e.g. *Good evening!* instead of *Good morning*.
- Ask other students to update the latecomer or absentee. Note that this is good practice for regular attendees and reflects what they might need to do spontaneously in a real-life meeting conducted in English. It also helps to draw the latecomer in with minimum fuss, while helpfully reviewing instructions or the rationale for the rest of the class. Repeat this procedure as often as necessary, even in one single class, explaining to students the advantages of the extra practice!
- Note the number of minutes a student is late on the register. This makes everyone aware that lateness will not go unnoticed and acts as a disincentive to students who are anxious about information going back to their company, which will probably be financing the course.
- Hand out copies of any worksheets or handouts missed. For your own convenience write absentees' names on these in advance whenever you find you have extra copies.
- Refer latecomers or absentees to work completed by other students in their absence. This serves to highlight the valuable language work they've missed and indirectly affirms what other students have done.
- In the presence of the latecomers or absentees remind all students about the course objectives and explain how that particular lesson fits into the overall programme. This will help to keep everyone aware of how the course fits together and will update latecomers and absentees on decisions they have missed. These reminders and reviews will be especially important for latecomers and absentees who might otherwise perceive the course as disjointed and unfocussed, which could, in turn, affect their motivation.

6.2 Low motivation

When courses are planned well and teacher–student relationships are appropriate for the Business English situation motivation is usually high. Low motivation might result when:

- You are not respected as a professional.
- Students feel you are manipulating them or, on the other hand, you are insufficiently decisive.
- Students' needs are not being fulfilled.
- Students feel you are wasting their time.
- Materials are inappropriate in terms of needs, level or personal preferences.
- There's a bad atmosphere in class and students do not work well together.
- Attendance is poor.

Low motivation – for any of the above reasons – usually leads to (or aggravates) poor attendance in the end and this may well result in difficult teaching, poor results and a cancelled programme, not to mention a general feeling of demoralisation for teachers. Something must be done! Various suggestions are presented below.

Present yourself professionally
Re-evaluate your personal appearance. Dirty shoes, T-shirts and carrier bags can make a bad impression on well-dressed Business English students! Check what is considered appropriate in the local or corporate culture through careful observation and informal chats with key personnel. Make sure all your handouts and OHTs are carefully produced and copied, with no shaded edges or errors. Pre-cue tapes and pre-test equipment so as to avoid embarrassing mid-lesson glitches. Think about PR!

Have a system for dealing with absence and lateness
Attendance may be poor either because students are studying when they are too busy or because they have other priorities. You need to deal with this either by persuading students to leave the programme and postpone studying until they have more time or by getting them to realise (through your attendance policy) that they will need to reprioritise English in their lives. See 6.1 for guidelines on setting up an attendance policy.

Relate to the students
See your students as individuals who have valuable life experience to offer and opinions that matter. Draw on students' opinions and experience before working on any new performance area by asking them what they know before you give information. Also, make sure you don't merely 'manipulate' your students with a series of seemingly

impressive teaching procedures. Even if it takes a little extra time, check that everybody understands the rationale behind any teaching procedures you use by asking your students why they think you are using them. If you are surprised by the responses you get, simply explain the rationale. Finally, try to understand your students' motivation for learning English, not only by asking about their precise job needs but also by asking them how they feel about learning English and by finding out how they manage to fit this extra study into their busy lives.

While attempting to 'tune into' your students in these ways, continue to feel confident about making decisions for the class. You will probably know more about language learning than your students and have a clearer perspective of how much progress is being made. You need to take a lead because it is, after all, you who is ultimately responsible for the success or failure of the course.

Check that you're fulfilling students' real-life occupational needs
Find out from course organisers why the course was set up in the first place. If you discover that no needs analysis was conducted at the beginning of the course conduct one mid-course! See 4.7 for guidelines on how to do this. With students whose needs were initially clearly established, confirm repeatedly that the initial needs analysis still applies. This may be necessary since students' work situations can change mid-course, skills are sometimes acquired or improved on the job and progress is often unpredictable and difficult to track – both faster and slower than expected at times. The following procedures will help you to establish or confirm the needs analysis: OBJECTIVES REVIEW (p. 94); PRIORITISING OBJECTIVES (p. 63), supplemented by ALTERNATIVES (p. 65); DEEP-ENDING (p. 78); STARTER PIX (p. 79); MODEL-MENTORING (p. 101); MODEL-MENTORED DIALOGUES (p. 103); EXPERIENCE EXCHANGE (p. 73) and ANECDOTE ACCESS (p. 75).

Another important way of ensuring that you fulfil students' real-life occupational needs is to encourage them to accomplish on-the-job work in class. If they do this you can be sure that the work you are doing in class is relevant and valuable to them. Students will appreciate being able to work on important memos, e-mails, reports or presentations in class. In the case of students who have longer-term objectives elicit probable scenarios and role-play what they will probably experience in the future. Well-planned role-plays will help you to make students realise that you are fulfilling their future occupational needs. The procedures listed above will also help you to do this.

Show students you are making good use of their time
There are various ways of doing this.

- Make sure that everything done in class time is 100% relevant to students' needs, either short-term linguistic or occupational. To make students aware that this is the case, relate classroom procedures to performance skills, e.g. MANAGER QUESTIONING (p. 200) helps to prepare students to participate in a Q&A session after a presentation. Exclude any classroom practice which doesn't contribute to improved performance of a performance area unless there is a very good reason for doing it (e.g. to improve students' pronunciation when speaking in any situation), but be aware that students may well perceive generalised practice activities as time wasters! If you are using a procedure as a lead-in so as to motivate or involve students more, stay alert to students' reactions. If students don't respond well, be prepared to change tack quickly because these 'fun' activities can actually have a demotivating effect if used inappropriately or insensitively.

- Show students you are making good use of their time by asking them to do role-played conversations after any controlled (and slightly contrived) language practice. This will help students to see the relevance of practice to their real-life situation.
- Make sure that everything you do in class is time-efficient by simply considering whether the time spent on each activity justifies the results. If it doesn't, your students are likely to notice. Experiment with more time-efficient procedures. Note, though, that some problems (e.g. difficulty listening to natural speech) might be so important that a seemingly time-inefficient procedure such as FLOOR WORD JIGSAW DICTATION (p. 275) might be justified for students who need to crack this problem.
- Help students to track their own progress. You can do this by regularly evaluating students' performance in terms of task achievement, appropriacy of language use, coherence, pronunciation and grammatical accuracy. Whenever you do this, as far as possible, warn students in advance and explain your criteria for assessment. See 7.2 for some guidelines on setting up assessed language practice.

In the rare but possible situation where students feel their English is good enough but you or your students' superiors disagree try the following procedures for raising students' awareness of their own language use: DEEP-ENDING (p. 78); FOREIGN PERSONALITY CHECKING (p. 115); SITUATIONAL SCRUTINY (p. 119). Use the guidelines given in 4.5 when giving students feedback and corrections.

Think about and vary the materials and methods you use
If your course materials are inappropriate for students' occupational, personal or linguistic needs arrange for them to be changed even if this involves considerable inconvenience and expense. The pay-off will be

enormous! Also, supplement or adapt any course materials you are using with the procedures explained in Sections 4 and 5 (especially 4.3–4.7 and 5.2–5.14). Consider carefully how all the procedures you use fit together to make individual lessons and a whole course, consulting the notes in 4.1 and 4.2.

Establish good group dynamics in class
Early on in a course it is well worth spending time building rapport between students simply because this will help them to work together effectively and, therefore, make good progress. The following procedures, which can be used with most types of Business English class, might be particularly useful for building rapport between students: EXPERIENCE EXCHANGE (p. 73); WORDBOARD SPRINGBOARD (p. 74); ANECDOTE ACCESS (p. 75); FLOOR CARDS (p. 79); SIMPLE SERIES (p. 82); GUIDED SPEAKING (p. 85); BALL-BRAINING (p. 91); COMMUNITY LANGUAGE LEARNING (p. 104); CUT-UP TEXTS (p. 122); INTRODUCTIONS (p. 158); MINI-CHAT MILLING (p. 161); HUMAN CHATS (p. 166); MONDAY MORNING CHATS (p. 168); WARM-UP UPDATE (p. 176); PROJECT PROJECTION (p. 188); THE QUESTION GAME (p. 204); STRIP DISCUSSION (p. 212); TRIO REFLECTIONS (p. 218); TEXT REBUILDING (p. 230); DOMINO RESPONSES (p. 258); QUESTION MINI-TESTS (p. 274).

At any time during a course it is important to encourage good group dynamics by helping students to work together and by giving sensitive and appropriate feedback. You can help students to 'share' their strengths by asking stronger students to work with weaker students and by asking them to perform or comment when appropriate. As for feedback, make sure it is balanced and honest. In other words, give credit and praise whenever it is due so as to help students to feel comfortable about 'performing' in a potentially threatening group situation and avoid praising students when performance is unsatisfactory, given your teaching objectives and the students' general level. Tolerating or praising poor performance in a misguided attempt to save individuals embarrassment may mean that students end up silently mocking each other. This will, obviously, do nothing to improve group dynamics so is to be avoided at all costs. See 4.5 for further advice on feedback and correction.

Check the Index for other references to motivation
Motivation is affected by so many factors that it is mentioned constantly in this book! Explore causes for problems until you make a breakthrough.

6.3 Mixed status classes

A mixed status class is a class which includes both high and low status students, e.g. managers and secretaries in one class. Some teachers consider this a problem because lower status students may feel inhibited by the presence of their bosses and high status students may be worried about losing face when making mistakes in class.

Having a mixed status class needn't be a problem, though, if you are aware of the potential difficulties and you acknowledge status differences between students. Trying to overlook them is pointless because your students are bound to be well aware of them. It is better to simply use the opportunities that the status mix gives you and develop strategies for dealing with the embarrassment which students might initially feel.

Deal with any inhibitions that lower status students might have when studying in the presence of managers and make sure that managers don't dominate by using the following strategies:

- Elicit more responses from lower status students and be especially supportive towards them. The higher status students will assert themselves whenever they want to! Also, ask lower status students to demonstrate how specific words are pronounced whenever you feel fairly sure they know how to pronounce them correctly. Using lower status students' language skills in these ways will give them an acceptable role in class.
- When setting up role-plays, the first time allocate roles contrary to normal expectations and give the highest status students the most ridiculous roles. For example, when practising telephone skills make top managers act the receptionist and secretary and ask the Managing Director to make the sound of the telephone! (This works especially well when you have taken the role of the 'telephone' yourself first.) As usual – taking note of the style of language recommended in 1.3 and 3.4 – ask students politely, as if leading a departmental meeting. A dead-pan expression is helpful! Managers are usually keen to play along, recognising your attempts to lighten the atmosphere.

As soon as the ice has broken, allocate roles according to students' real-life work situations. Elicit comments or contributions more freely, encouraging even weaker higher status students to contribute. In other words, reintroduce egalitarianism into the classroom when inhibitions have been dealt with!

In the course overall, so as to make status differences work in your favour, embrace the following approaches.

Establish systems for accommodating different students' practical needs
Since higher status students probably need to be absent more often than their subordinates (because of the need to attend meetings or go off on business trips) and since students of different status are likely to have different needs, you will probably need special systems if you are going to truly accommodate all the students in your class. Firstly, in order to ensure that classes continue to run smoothly when absentees appear, you will need to keep a 'class file' which is kept up-to-date with records of work done and handouts. A regularly attending clerical officer could be in charge of maintaining this. (Alternatively, you could stay in touch with managers by fax or e-mail.) Secondly, you may need to ask different groups of students to use different self-study books for homework. For example, managers who need to improve their reading skills could use *In Print* (Revell, R. and S. Sweeney. 1993. Cambridge: Cambridge University Press) while secretarial staff work through *Secretarial Contacts* (Brieger, N. and A. Cornish. 1989. Hemel Hempstead: Prentice Hall).

Get comments from all parts of the hierarchy
This is especially important when you are asking students about problems they experience with language. The very different perspectives you get from different students will increase everyone's awareness and make classes more interesting.

Encourage discussion between different status students
To start discussion off initially, separate managers from lower level staff when preparing pairwork activities, asking each group to discuss something they are likely to know about. (Managers will be Group A, lower level staff Group B.) Then mix the two groups (making AB, AB, AB pairs) so that individuals can learn from each other or gain greater insight into typical problems. For example, when introducing memo-writing ask two separate status groups to discuss the problems of memo-writing separately before comparing notes.

Make tasks open-ended
Limit your instructions so as to allow individuals to tailor tasks (in class and for homework) to their precise needs. For example, simply ask students to write a memo including a request that they would need to write as part of their job.

Above all, when teaching mixed status classes focus on creating a supportive, humorous working atmosphere in which all students can feel comfortable about making mistakes and discussing their experiences.

6.4 Mixed level classes

Since some students get ongoing experience of English in the workplace and/or have a great deal of real-life work experience levels seem to vary even more dramatically in the Business English classroom than on more general English courses.

Instead of considering this a disadvantage, try to use the wide range of skills (language-related or life-related) to your advantage. For example, students who understand why good memo-writing is desirable – in terms of company politics or getting things done – can contribute as much as, if not more than, students whose English grammar is good in terms of high school performance!

Try the following strategies for drawing on all students' knowledge and experience:

- Get students with extensive work experience to explain real-life language problems to other students. For example, get them to describe the situation in which an e-mail needs to be written. This will ensure that writing practice is appropriate to at least some of the students' real-life situations and should motivate other students. It will also help everyone in the class to understand the context and applicability of language practised in class.
- Ask students who have 'survived' using English on-the-job to suggest language which might be appropriate for a particular situation, or which might typically be heard. It is possible they might have picked up some of the many formulaic expressions used in business (e.g. *Further to our discussion this afternoon, we confirm ...*). However, since 'survival' suggests that students might have been using broken, incorrect or inappropriate English, don't hesitate to correct experienced students' suggestions!
- Get students with mixed strengths working in groups, then get students to change groups; students in a group can simply move round to the next table or, alternatively, they can all be remixed with the instruction, *OK, move to another group!* This not only allows all students in a class to share their skills, it also ensures that weaker students will learn without 'loss of face' because it will not be immediately obvious whose work is being improved by whom. The technique works equally well whether done at tables around paper (or OHTs), at boards or at computer screens.
- Get students to edit each other's faxes, e-mails, reports, etc. Work can be anonymously stuck up on walls or distributed and redistributed so

many times that authorship is forgotten. If necessary, it can be retyped with personal or confidential details removed. Before suggesting this approach, remind students of the importance of making mistakes and of learning from each other; reassure them that their work will be distributed and rewritten so many times that they will no longer be able to be held responsible for it. Nevertheless, ask for permission before doing any redistributing of papers (or OHTs, etc.).

- Use a wide range of criteria when evaluating students' performance so that all students can excel in certain areas and score respectable marks. Even beyond the criteria you have selected, find something valuable in everyone's performance when you are giving feedback. This will reinforce in students' minds the idea that there is value in everything they do and will encourage individual students to remain open to even the weakest students in the group.
- Capitalise on individual students' strengths. Someone whose grammatical accuracy is poor may have excellent pronunciation, so can be used to model language for other students. Other students who are highly inaccurate may have extensive knowledge of their field, or alternatively, may have a good awareness of appropriate business style. When technical or business terms come up get the knowledgeable students to explain to the rest of the class – don't even attempt to explain yourself! When one student has finished explaining, ask *Is there anything else that's important?* or *What about ... ?* if you're aware of any omissions.

Beyond this, make sure you give all students an appropriate level of challenge during class activities. Higher level students can be given challenges in custom-made tasks or by being allocated more difficult roles in role-play practice. When they have finished work originally set they can be given extra tasks which you regularly prepare, just in case! Weaker students can be encouraged via comprehension exercises which develop their receptive skills before their productive skills or be reassured via simple or mechanical tasks (e.g. adapting memos or copying work onto OHTs) which help other students to achieve objectives. Simply learning together with stronger students can help or inspire weaker students, as long as they are given the necessary support. Stronger students will gain confidence as they realise the benefits of their strengths for their day-to-day work. As long as both stronger and weaker students are stimulated by classes, their English should continue to improve.

6.5 **Unexpected students and unplanned changes**

When new students turn up without warning, when your room is changed at two minutes' notice, when your equipment refuses to work, there is only one viable solution for Business English. Cope! You can try to improve the situation – whatever it might be – by informal liaison later, but while the lesson is in progress or students are around you must continue to appear professional and unruffled. Expressing anger or frustration is not a good idea!

There are two main reasons for this. The first is that there is probably a good (enough) reason behind any suggested change; the decision for the change has probably been taken by people with more information than you – and they are unlikely to change their decision. The second is that people are liable to lose face if openly challenged in front of their clients, colleagues or subordinates and would therefore feel less charitable towards you, the Business English teacher. This is one time when it is important to remember that the student is primarily the client and must be treated as such, whether on a public course at a language school or on company premises.

Here are some practical suggestions which might help you to cope in any eventuality:

- Have two or three contingency plans (i.e. alternative courses of action) for every lesson!
- Have some lesson ideas up your sleeve which require no materials or pre-planning. See 'contingency plans' in the Index.
- Keep spare copies handy of any worksheets which you think might be usable with many types of students.
- Keep dictionaries and other reference material handy for times when nobody knows 'the answer'!
- Memorise a repertoire of amusing stories or puzzle problems so as to be able to refocus students' attention when waiting or suffering some sort of inconvenience. See QUESTION STORIES (p. 90) and PUZZLE PIX (p. 89).
- Keep extra videos and cassettes (pre-cued) containing material which you are prepared to use in a variety of ways (depending on the students).
- Carry spare board pens (or chalk), transparencies and spare batteries for cassette recorders you use regularly. Don't depend on someone supplying things at the last minute in the case of exhausted batteries or power failure.
- Carry a blank cassette around with you, as well as a plug-in mike, for impromptu recording or COMMUNITY LANGUAGE LEARNING (p. 104).
- Carry a ball with you at all times! This can be thrown around to diffuse any tension or frustration in students, who might also be

flustered by the unexpected change. Study the procedures which involve use of a ball. See 'balls, using' in the Index.

6.6 Bad feedback

If you have received bad feedback – either directly from students, via your boss or by some other indirect means – you may feel dismayed or resentful. You may feel people's expectations of you are unrealistic if you were not originally trained to teach Business English. If you have worked hard to develop a course, you may feel unappreciated or misunderstood.

Try not to feel too demoralised because it is likely you will be able to reverse the situation. Regard the feedback as helpful (especially if it comes mid-course) because it is invaluable, extra information about what students want or dislike. As long as you take constructive action in response to the feedback you will be at an advantage in the longer term.

Before you respond, consider how 'valid' the feedback is. For example, if students complain that progress is slow or that they need to do more on understanding movies in English, respond with caution! Students need to be realistic about the speed of progress that is possible and about the purpose of their classes. If they are worried about understanding movies they may have forgotten the original reasons the course was set up. Remember that you need to satisfy the people funding the course as well as your students.

In cases where students' feedback shows that they misunderstand the rationale of the course or the problems of language learning, the best course of action is probably to talk to the students informally in class. Gently remind them of the initial needs analysis, share your experience of teaching with them and give them guidance on becoming better learners.

In cases where the students' feedback shows a misunderstanding or misjudgement on your part, you must take very clear and decisive action. Apart from re-examining priorities and explaining objectives to students more clearly on a class-by-class basis, consider the following as possible follow-up action to students' comments:

- *We never do anything relevant to work* ... Review the needs analysis! See 'needs, students'' in the Index.
- *I can't really see the point of our lessons* ... Explain why you do what you do!
- *The teacher's always using strange methods* ... Explain what you're doing and why!

- *The materials are too difficult* ... Change either the materials, the methods or the tasks!
- *I can't understand the teacher* ... Slow down your teacher talk, simplify instructions!
- *We seem to waste a lot of time* ... Examine your time–results ratio for every activity!
- *The teacher doesn't understand our problems* ... Find out more about your students.

After taking action or making suggestions to students (e.g. about becoming better learners), again ask them for comments a few weeks later. Take care to phrase your comments and questions constructively so as to elicit a positive response, for example:

- *Let's review what we've done over the last two weeks.*
- *What have you practised over the last two weeks?*
- *What do you feel you've learnt?*
- *What have we achieved so far in the course overall?*
- *Which language practice has been useful for your work?*
- *What other language practice do we need to do to help your work?*
- *Why did we do x ?*
- *How are you finding the materials now?*
- *What are you doing when you find words you don't understand?*
- *Can you understand me now?!*
- *What do we need to do over the next few weeks and what can we drop?*
- *Are we still working too slowly?*
- *Are we going too fast?*
- *What do you feel your language problems are now?*
- *What are our present priorities?*

In addition to this kind of dialogue, try to get students talking with the help of some of the procedures listed below. Giving students opportunities to express themselves in a less formal or less confrontational atmosphere may help the more reticent students express themselves:

- KEYWORD INTRODUCTIONS (role-playing the beginning of a conference seminar) (p. 44)
- FIND SOMEONE WHO (adapting the cues to comments made in the feedback discussions) (p. 49)
- EXPERIENCE EXCHANGE (to give students an opportunity to restate their needs) (p. 73)
- DEEP-ENDING (to remind students of what they still need to work on) (p. 78)
- OBJECTIVES REVIEW (use periodically, since answers to questions may change) (p. 94)
- WORDBOARD SPRINGBOARD (using words related to learning) (p. 74)

- STARTER PIX (again, to allow students to clarify precisely why they need English) (p. 79)
- BALL-BRAINING (excellent for free association and the stress-free airing of thoughts) (p. 91)
- FOREIGN PERSONALITY CHECKING (for those students who are complacent about their English and their level of performance) (p. 115)
- SITUATIONAL SCRUTINY (to refocus students' attention on problem areas) (p. 119).

6.7 Lack of expertise

In the Business English classroom relevant expertise can mean familiarity with management theory, news on actual current practice, knowledge of formats used for faxes, reports, etc., preferences or practices within specific industries or corporate cultures, as well as familiarity with a wide range of specialities – such as computing or advertising, banking or telecommunications. However, although your familiarity with any of these areas will enhance your teaching, lack of expertise need not be a cause for too much concern. You are primarily a language specialist, not a teacher of a subject requiring special expertise.

On a practical level, though, gaps in your expertise may affect linguistic choices for specific situations in class so you will need to develop strategies for dealing with situations where you find you lack the necessary business expertise. Try the following:

- Get the student who has raised the subject to expand on his or her point or explain the necessary background: *How do you mean? Can you tell us a bit more about that?*
- Invite other students to do the same: *Can anyone else help? Have you heard about that?*
- Get students to find answers immediately in class, using reference materials relevant to Business English or to their particular field. Keep in touch with publishers (see pp. 333–336) and regularly attend book fairs or conferences to find out about the latest titles.
- Ask students if they can find out the relevant information before the next lesson.
- If students don't think they will be able to check something – or seem unwilling – offer to check yourself. Consult your expanding library of reference books!

In addition, do the following so as to build up your knowledge on an ongoing basis:

- Consult the introductory sections for each performance skill in Section 5 of this book.
- Build up a collection of models of faxes, e-mails, memos, reports, etc.
- Read publications such as the *Guardian Weekly* (which includes articles from the US *Herald Tribune* and the French *Le Monde*, as well as the British *Guardian*), *Time*, *Newsweek* and *Fortune*. Also listen to the news on more than one international news station (e.g. the BBC World Service and CNN) as often as possible.

Consult Section 10 for more ideas on how you can gradually increase your expertise and become a better-informed Business English teacher. Also be reassured by the fact that most Business English students already know a lot about their own speciality when they come to class, including the necessary vocabulary in English!

7 Assessing students' progress

7.1 What's important? What's possible?

It is essential to ensure that students are making progress on a course and to show this progress in quantifiable and comprehensible terms to both students and their bosses. Formal or less formal assessment procedures can be used but remember the following:

- Tests and other assessment tools must be as valid as possible if they are to be useful and fair on individuals – whose career prospects might be affected by them! See p. 14 for notes on what this means.
- Tests need to be practical to administer, taking the constraints of the context into account (e.g. absentees or factory noise).
- Tests must demonstrate a good time–results ratio (i.e. the time invested must be worthwhile for the information gained).
- Tests need to be given at an appropriate time if you intend to use them to 'fine tune' your teaching programme so as to cater more effectively to students' needs. When you have information on what students can and cannot do you will need to have time to do something about it. On extensive courses tests are best administered slightly before the end of each 10-week block – for example in Week 8 say – so as to leave time for follow-up and objective-setting. Alternatively, they can be conducted periodically (e.g. at the end of each 4-week block). On intensive courses (e.g. 30 hours a week for six weeks), tests can be given at the end of each week.
- Test results and feedback must be given sensitively because they can have a devastating effect on motivation and, indeed, on students' careers if misinterpreted by students' bosses. Consult 4.5, pp. 294–295 and 304–305 of this section, 8.1 and 8.3 for advice on how to proceed.

Approaches to assessment

Four approaches seem appropriate for the Business English context:

1 Periodic achievement tests – a new testing approach which makes assessment of speaking (as well as writing) a real possibility, provided classes are small;

2 Portfolio assessment – which involves looking at samples of students' writing;
3 End-of-course tests – the more traditional approach to assessment on courses;
4 External examinations – specially-written and recognised Business English exams.

Each type is considered in detail on the following pages.

Tasks and test items

The type of task(s) or test items you ask your students to do if choosing any of the first three types of assessment will be determined by the particular focus of your course. For example, an end-of-term test for a course on report-writing should involve writing a report! If you feel a range of task types and test items is needed to assess your students' range of skills do remember that the more realistic tasks and test items will give you the most accurate information on what students can do. Possible tasks for the first two types of assessment are suggested in 7.2 and 7.3 and a range of test items for inclusion in end-of-term tests are considered in detail in 7.4.

Marking criteria and feedback sheets

Some possible criteria and sample feedback sheets – appropriate for the different types of assessment – are suggested in 7.2, 7.3 and 7.4. If you choose to adapt these or establish new criteria and prepare new feedback sheets make sure that:

- Your criteria and the weighting of marks reflect the focus of the course.
- Your feedback will be easy for students to understand.
- The sheet will make sense, even after you have taken back test papers (for security reasons).
- Your feedback is likely to be fairly consistent for all students.
- Points awarded to students are translated into a message!
- The wording you use does not invite misinterpretation. For example, a poor rating for 'accuracy' may be misinterpreted as meaning students are inaccurate in terms of fact or detail; 'accuracy/grammar' or 'grammatical accuracy' are more helpful terms.
- The feedback sheet will provide useful information later when re-evaluating objectives.

Before using criteria, consider how changing or omitting just one criterion on a feedback sheet might dramatically affect students' final marks. You can use this to encourage students (and, therefore, motivate them) or, alternatively, to remind them of the importance of certain areas (e.g. punctuation and consistent use of conventions). Having established a policy, carefully explain the criteria you have used for awarding points so that students understand why they are being praised or penalised! Also, prepare students for disappointments before you distribute feedback sheets with low marks, reassuring them that low performance at this stage need not mean ultimate failure and reminding them that they need to act on the information provided by the feedback.

Before distributing feedback sheets to students, also remember to make copies for your own records so that later feedback you give the same students is consistent and not repetitive, and so that you have something to refer to when writing reports on the same students.

7.2 Periodic achievement tests

A very effective way of tracking students' progress – and, expressed more positively, students' achievements! – on an ongoing basis is to arrange periodic achievement tests which use carefully developed marking criteria. The procedure for conducting this type of test is explained in detail on the next two pages and sample copies of all necessary forms are provided for reference. Although the forms themselves will probably need to be adapted here and there for specific groups of students most of the work has been done for you!

These tests are popular with students and useful in class for various reasons:

- They clearly show that you are remembering the course's original objectives and are taking them seriously.
- They show students that progress is being monitored in a fair and systematic manner.
- Tests are realistic (i.e. valid, in terms of formal testing) in that students are assessed on their performance of a task which simulates real life.
- Students don't have to worry about a long end-of-course test.
- Students are tested in 'batches' after relevant class practice has been completed. Absentees, poor attenders or slow learners can easily be tested in later batches.
- Students can choose when they are assessed.
- When students perform badly, they have a second chance.
- Students get feedback (mid-course) on their achievements and/or on progress made, which provides the basis for objective-setting for subsequent lessons and homework.
- Students are able to monitor their own progress throughout a course and plan their self-study accordingly.

- Some performance areas included in the original needs analysis can be 'checked off' very early on in a course, which gives students a sense of achievement and allows more time for other areas.
- The mini-tests punctuate courses and accentuate the results-oriented nature of sessions, which will be appreciated by both students and their managers.
- They allow students to be rewarded for good performance. The occasional possibility of a 4 or a 1 for 'Achievement of task' – see the next page – means that full marks are appreciated all the more!
- They allow students to become involved in ongoing objective-setting and lesson-planning because students have a say in how much practice they get before and after tests.
- You have reliable information to refer to when writing end-of-course student reports.

Procedure for conducting periodic achievement tests

1 List all the performance areas to be covered in a course on a mark sheet and a summary sheet (see pp. 298–299).
2 Photocopy forms for students – one copy of the mark sheet and summary sheet for each student – and one copy (of each) for your own records. Give out the students' forms, explaining that you will take in the forms each time students take a mini-test. Ask students to bring the forms to class each lesson.
3 Consider the tasks you will need to test each area. Performance areas which involve speaking skills can be tested by asking students to role-play situations individually, in pairs or in groups. Those involving writing will involve writing a memo, fax, e-mail, etc.
4 Agree with students on a suitable time for each test (during class time) on an ongoing basis. Before actually testing students in class, remind the class and individuals of the agreed time. Allow individuals to postpone taking their personal test if they want more time or practice of a particular performance area, but keep track of how much still needs to be tested during the course as a whole. Allow for some leeway.
5 While students are 'performing' (i.e. being tested), assess their performance using the marking scales provided on p. 300. Copy your marks and comments onto the students' mark sheets. Copy the marks and comments onto your own copy of the mark sheet too.
6 Transfer the detailed marks (on the mark sheets) to the summary sheets, converting the scores, as per the instructions on the sheet. Note that students who have not adequately performed the task will be penalised on 'Achievement of task' as follows:

---

5 The task is completed sufficiently well for this level. Refer to your own in-house syllabus objectives for each course to establish this.

4 A student has performed at a significantly lower standard than other students (e.g. a process has been described but so briefly that it is difficult to follow).

1 A student has spoken (or written) but has not completed the task (e.g. she/he has talked about his/her job, without describing a process).

© Cambridge University Press

Note that most students should score 5. Only give 4 or 1 in cases where you feel the student needs to know that their performance was inadequate (for this course). Remember that students' marks for other areas (accuracy, etc.) will be proportionally reduced according to the mark you give here.

7 Return the mark sheets and summary sheets to the students. Encourage comments!

8 Decide, as a class, whether or not to continue working on that performance area or to consider it 'checked off'. Set objectives so as to improve performance, if necessary.

9 Repeat the testing procedure (for the same or different areas) when students feel ready.

A sample mark sheet for periodic achievement tests

BUSINESS ENGLISH PERSONAL ACHIEVEMENT RECORD

Name: .... Company: ....

Position: .... Department: ....

Contact numbers: ....

Course: .... Teacher: ....

Date		Performance area	Achievement of task	Appropriacy of language/ vocabulary	Accuracy	Fluency/style/ punctuation	Dealing with questions	Cultural factors/ planning
	1	Dealing with visitors						
	2							
	1	Telephoning						
	2							
	1	Presentations and Q&A sessions						
	2							
	1	Meetings						
	2							
	1	E-mail						
	2							
	1	Report-writing						
	2							

© Cambridge University Press

A sample summary sheet for periodic achievement tests

BUSINESS ENGLISH PERSONAL ACHIEVEMENT RECORD: Summary

Name: .... Company: ....

Position: .... Department: ....

Contact numbers: ....

Course: .... Teacher: ....

Date		Performance area	Achievement of task	Average of other marks	Other marks % (average × 4)	Final % *	Comments and suggestions
1	2	Dealing with visitors					
1	2	Telephoning					
1	2	Presentations and Q&A sessions					
1	2	Meetings					
1	2	E-mail					
1	2	Report-writing					

*The final % will be the same as the 'Other marks %' when students score 5 for 'Achievement of task'; the final % will need to be reduced to 80% of the marks when the 'Achievement of task' % is 4 (i.e. 'Other marks %' ÷ 5 × 4) – or to 20% of the 'Other marks %' when the 'Achievement of task' % is 1 (i.e. 'Other marks %' ÷ 5 × 1).

Sample marking scales for periodic achievement tests

MARKING SCALES

Appropriacy of language/vocabulary
5   Language and vocabulary are appropriate to the task.
4   Some slightly inappropriate uses of vocabulary.
3   Some slightly inappropriate uses of vocabulary and the student also seems to lack sufficient vocabulary to perform the task.
2   Several inappropriate uses of vocabulary and the student seems seriously in need of more vocabulary to perform the task.
1   Inappropriate use of vocabulary and insufficient vocabulary for the task.

Accuracy
5   Almost no grammatical errors. Grammar appropriate to the task.
4   A few grammatical errors and/or several grammatical uses which are inappropriate to the task.
3   Several grammatical errors and/or several grammatical uses which are inappropriate to the task.
2   Several grammatical errors which affect the student's ability to express him/herself.
1   Many grammatical errors which seriously inhibit the student's ability to perform the task.

Fluency/style/punctuation
5   Almost no hesitation; appropriate style; excellent pronunciation (in terms of sounds, word and sentence stress and intonation).
4   Some hesitation; mostly appropriate style; some errors of pronunciation.
3   Quite a lot of hesitation; many inappropriacies of style, but none serious; many pronunciation errors.
2   Extremely hesitant; clumsy style which makes listening/reading difficult; pronunciation errors which affect comprehensibility.
1   So hesitant that listening becomes difficult; inappropriate style which makes listening/reading difficult; almost unintelligible.

Dealing with questions
5   Excellent response which is both appropriate and clear.
4   Generally good, although a little hesitant and/or unclear.
3   Copes but rather hesitant and/or unclear and/or very short answers.
2   Barely copes, hesitant and/or has insufficient language to answer questions.
1   Cannot understand questions and/or answer them.

Cultural factors/planning
5   Excellent non-verbal language; well-planned (in Anglo-American terms); no elements which would mystify an Anglo-American listener/reader.
4   Generally good, non-verbal language; fairly coherent in Anglo-American terms; one or two elements which would mystify an Anglo-American.
3   Acceptable non-verbal language; clear if not always 'coherent' in Anglo-American terms; a few 'foreign' elements, none of which would cause serious misunderstanding.
2   Non-verbal language rather strange from an Anglo-American viewpoint; several 'foreign' elements, some of which might cause misunderstanding.
1   Strange non-verbal language from an Anglo-American viewpoint; many 'foreign' elements, many of which would cause misunderstanding or create a bad impression.

© Cambridge University Press

7.3 Portfolio assessment

If courses focus mainly on writing skills assessment can be based on a portfolio of each student's work. (A 'portfolio' is simply a folder containing a student's work.) In order to use this type of assessment you will simply need to issue each student with a folder at the beginning of the course and explain that it is their responsibility to fill it with samples of their work. You will need to specify what type of samples you need to see and how many of each type. For a course which aims to develop a broad range of business writing skills you might, for example, specify that you need to see the following:

- 10 e-mails – of any kind and length, but clipped to any previous correspondence
- 5 faxes: one a response to an enquiry, two quotations and two faxes containing requests
- 3 memos: one a memo with a request, one a response to another memo and one a mini-report requested by a manager
- 1 three-page report.

Tell students they can submit these items to you at any time for assessment. Give them feedback on each piece of work using a feedback sheet such as the one on the next page. (Staple this feedback sheet to the piece of work for ease of reference later.) Allow students to resubmit any item if they wish. The only rule is that everything must have been submitted by a certain deadline, probably one or two weeks before the course ends.

There are several advantages to using this form of assessment:

- Tasks can be done in class, for homework or in the workplace.
- More time can be available in class for writing practice if you choose to ask students to do all their portfolio work outside class time (either for homework or while at work depending on the students' situation).
- Since items for assessment can be written over a period of days, weeks or months, students can work at their own pace. The generous timeframe allows for the possibility that students will be able to include samples of writing done as part of their job.
- Students get feedback on a periodic basis. They can act on this feedback during the course by requesting extra practice in class or by doing self-study.
- Students can resubmit items for assessment if they wish, so the method is less stressful.
- Students don't need to worry about having an end-of-course test.
- Writing a portfolio of samples can accentuate the results-oriented nature of the course.

If you are worried about the possible disadvantage that students can 'cheat', don't be! This form of assessment reflects real life and encourages a responsible attitude towards English.

A sample feedback sheet for portfolio assessment

BUSINESS ENGLISH FEEDBACK

Assignment: .... Date: ....

Course: .... Student's name: ....

Task achievement	1	2	3	4	5	1 = Focus on this!
Planning/organisation	1	2	3	4	5	2 = Focus on this!
Clarity/ability to express meaning clearly	1	2	3	4	5	3 = Acceptable
Grammatical accuracy	1	2	3	4	5	4 = Good
Range/appropriacy of vocabulary	1	2	3	4	5	5 = Very good
Appropriate use of conventions	1	2	3	4		
Punctuation	1	2	3	4		

General comment:

Total mark (out of 35):

© Cambridge University Press

A completed feedback sheet for portfolio assessment

BUSINESS ENGLISH FEEDBACK

Assignment: Fax-writing   Date: July 10, 2001

Course: Intermediate Business 1   Student's name: Joao Perreres

Task achievement	1	2	3	4	⑤	1 = Focus on this!
Planning/organisation	①	2	3	4	5	2 = Focus on this!
Clarity/ability to express meaning clearly	1	2	3	④	5	3 = Acceptable
Grammatical accuracy	1	②	3	4	5	4 = Good
Range/appropriacy of vocabulary	1	2	3	④	5	5 = Very good
Appropriate use of conventions	1	2	③	4		
Punctuation	1	2	3	4	⑤	

General comment: You've written a fax which is complete and easy to understand, Joao. Consider the marks I've given you – your fax would have been much better if you'd planned it first and if you'd carefully checked for errors.

Total mark (out of 35): 24

© Cambridge University Press

7.4 **End-of-course tests**

End-of-course tests are, of course, the traditional method for assessing students' progress on courses. Well-written formal end-of-course tests have certain advantages:

- They can test students' level of performance at a given date.
- They are usually easy to administer and can sometimes even be administered by non-experts.
- They can act as a gatekeeper on courses, determining whether or not students can proceed to higher levels and/or whether or not students are awarded certificates.

Badly-written tests, on the other hand, not only waste time, they might also give wrong impressions about what students can and cannot do which could in turn unjustly influence their career prospects. Make sure any test you use is valid and does not simply test a student's ability to take tests! See p. 14 for a short definition of 'validity'.

Writing end-of-course tests

Before you start writing, consider the following points:

- Your main aim is to test what has been covered in the course.
- As well as using a written format, you can also use oral interviews or role-play. To do this, you will need to establish careful guidelines for test administration and clear criteria for assessment. The procedure suggested for periodic achievement tests (in 7.2) can also be used for end-of-term tests, the only difference being that all tasks will be conducted on the same day. See pp. 15–16 for notes on interviewing students.
- Including many different types of test items may result in a fairer test because the performance of individual students will depend less on whether or not they are good at a particular type of test item. A range of appropriate test items are described in this section.
- All marks should ideally add up to 100 (so as to give a percentage) and marks for different sections should be carefully weighted so as to reflect the importance of each language area tested and the time required to complete that part of the test.
- The test should include information on marking criteria and time allowed for each task for the students' own reference.
- The test can include some optional extra reading for those students who finish early.
- The test can include some end-of-course objective-setting – either for the next level in your Business English programme or for your students' future informal study.

- The test can also include a space for the student to write a comment to you about the test, about his or her progress, or about the course in general. This will make the testing process more interactive.

You can use a mix of subjective and objective test items. Objective test items (such as the test item on pp. 17–18) have one or more predeterminable correct answers, which are not open to discussion. Subjective test items (such as the test items on pp. 19–20) involve open-ended questions or tasks which could have many 'correct' answers. Marking objective test items is obviously easier, faster and more reliable in the sense that marks are less variable if several teachers are marking the same test. Subjective test items, although more difficult and time-consuming to mark, usually involve more realistic tasks so are perhaps more worthwhile.

Specific test items – both objective and subjective – are discussed on pp. 305–313. The order in which the items are listed is a possible order for a test, should you decide to include them all! Most of the items can be used with a range of levels and can be personalised for individual clients if kept on disk, adapted, printed out and copied whenever needed.

Note: If you don't like the idea of writing your own tests, performance scales for gauging attainment are available from LTS Training and Consulting. A progress test is also provided in *Business English Assessment* (Wilberg, P. 1994. Hove: Language Teaching Publications). Alternatively, UCLES offers a Business Language Testing Service for companies needing to assess the language skills of their staff. See p. 337 and p. 334 for addresses if you want to find out more about these.

Administering tests

When you actually give students an end-of-course test bear in mind that you will need to collect all copies of tests every time you use them if you want your tests to remain confidential. Collecting in tests is worthwhile if only because it will save you a lot of work! Also see pp. 14–15.

Giving feedback

Feedback needs to be given to students in a readily comprehensible form. Since students are not usually allowed to have copies of end-of-course tests, the only record they will have of their marks and the feedback they receive might be on a feedback sheet you provide. A suggested feedback sheet is provided on p. 314 but this will naturally need to be adapted to suit your test. Note the following about the sample feedback sheet:

- It includes a space for a personal message to the student. Numbers and ratings alone can be very demotivating! Use this space to encourage students and give them advice.
- Feedback is given on specific performance skills (e.g. speaking to clients or fax-writing). This is more useful for both students and their managers than information about language proficiency in a general sense or achievement expressed in terms of generalised accuracy or use of vocabulary, etc.

☐ MULTIPLE MATCHING

Can be used to test speaking, listening, reading or writing skills. This is a good warm-up item which will help most students to relax because it only requires a receptive knowledge of English. It is a particularly useful item for sorting out real beginners from false beginners. It also provides a good lead-in to revision of language previously studied in class and to possible follow-up oral practice when going over the test. An example which would be suitable for intermediate level students is provided below.

Match the following comments. For example, 1 + b.

1 How are you?

2 Why did you leave IBM?

3 Do you mind if I leave early today?

4 I've seen some samples of your products and I'm very impressed.

5 Why do you think sales have been so disappointing this year?

6 Sales have risen by 20% this quarter.

a I'm very glad to hear that. What did you like most?

b Fine, thanks. How about you?

c Good question. I think there are two reasons.

d Well, the management structure was changed and, as a result, my job became unnecessary.

e Do you think that's good news?

f What's wrong? Aren't you feeling well?

© Cambridge University Press

☐ MULTIPLE WORD GAPFILL

Can be used to test speaking or writing skills. This should theoretically be an easy test item but in practice students often get things wrong, which is a good learning experience for them! It is an extremely useful test item if it is used to force students to focus on formulaic expressions.

To do this include many 'almost correct' answers, after warning students in class that accuracy is important! This test item is easy to prepare using texts previously studied and is fast to mark. An example is provided below.

Complete this fax, using one word from the box in each gap.

a enclose	**e** enquire	**i** enclosed	**m** sending	**q** specifications
b wants	**f** enclosed	**j** requires	**n** enquiry	**r** send
c might	**g** hearing	**k** receive	**o** seeing	**s** will
d may	**h** would	**l** request	**p** hear	**t** specify

Brilliant Batteries

....

7 Plateia Kanigos, Athens 3, Tel: 873928, Fax: 873929

To: Jane Knight, Q & S Vehicles   **Date:** September 30, 2007
Tel: 874020
Fax: 874021

Dear Ms Knight,

Thank you very much for your **(a)** _____. We are of course very familiar with your range of vehicles and are pleased to inform you that we have a new line in batteries that fit your **(b)** _____ exactly.

The most suitable of our products for your requirements is the Brilliant 77A Plus. This product combines economy with high power output. It is available now from stock.

I **(c)** _____ a detailed quotation with prices, specifications and delivery terms. As you **(d)** _____ see from this, our prices are very competitive.

If you would like further information, please telephone or fax me on the numbers above.

I look forward to **(e)** _____ from you.

Yours sincerely,

J. Jones
Jake Jones
Sales Manager

(Adapted from Jones, L. and R. Alexander 1996. *New International Business English*. Cambridge: Cambridge University Press.)

☐ MULTIPLE SENTENCE GAPFILL

Can be used to test speaking, listening, reading or writing skills. This test item encourages students' awareness of discourse features, while also testing reading comprehension. It is particularly useful if inappropriate but seemingly possible comments have been included in the list of possible answers because this will test students' ability to select appropriate comments for particular situations. Of course, the more comments you include for students to choose from, the more you will raise the level of difficulty. It is easy to prepare this test item if you use texts which have been studied in class. In order to use it to test listening or reading skills prepare an accompanying recording of a conversation or a selection of short pieces of correspondence, e.g. notes, e-mails and messages, which contain the information students will need to correctly choose the appropriate sentence for each gap. An example, for which no additional reading material is required, is given below.

Complete this transcript from a presentation, choosing one sentence from the box for each gap. You don't need to write out the whole sentence, simply write the letter (i.e. A, B, C, D or E) in the appropriate gap.

A: I think at least two of our competitors will also launch new pain-relief drugs in the next three years.
B: On the export side everything depends on the United States Food & Drug Administration.
C: Today I want to talk about our new product, the pain-relief drug CrashOut.
D: This is obviously good news.
E: At the moment we are considering Asia as our main export market.

1 _____ In general, the sales prospects for this product are good and I'm very optimistic. I'm convinced that people will prefer CrashOut to other pain-relief drugs: the pills are smaller and they taste better. Our market researchers think that demand for pain-relief drugs will increase steadily over the next five years. 2 _____ After a difficult financial year last year it's good to have something to cheer us up!

3 _____ If they approve CrashOut, then we will be able to export to the US and to many other overseas countries. 4 _____

What about the competition, though? 5 _____ However, since production costs for CrashOut are particularly low I think we will be able to cope with the competition.

(Adapted from a text in Barnard, R. and J. Cady. 1993. *Business Venture 2*. Oxford: Oxford University Press.)

☐ CLUELESS GAPFILL

Can be used to test speaking, listening, reading or writing skills. This type of gapfill is common in coursebooks so students should be used to the principle of the exercise, even though it is more difficult than the gapfill test items previously listed, in which a selection of words, phrases or sentences is supplied. Instead of merely testing recognition of correct words, phrases or sentences – as is the case with the other gapfill exercises – this test item actually tests whether students have an active knowledge of the word, phrase or sentence needed in the gap. It can be used to test listening and reading skills if the gaps are significant omissions of information (contained in a recorded conversation or in a text) on a form, or other official or formal document. When preparing these test items make sure that only one or a very small number of answers are possible for each gap. Marking can be time-consuming and difficult. An example is provided below.

Imagine you work for Jade Towers (JT). You answer the telephone.
Complete the dialogue.

JT: Good morning. Jade Towers.

CALLER: Hello. This is Karen Cole from Smiddling. Could I speak to John
          Smith, please?

JT: _____ ?

CALLER: Oh, I'm fine thanks. How about you?

JT: _____ .

CALLER: I've just received your new brochure with the invitation to have a
          product demonstration. Can I make an appointment?

JT: _____ .

CALLER: I'm away until Friday so I'd prefer to make it at the end of this
          week, if possible.

JT: _____ ?

CALLER: That'd be fine.

JT: Great. You'll need to come to our showroom in West Bromley.

CALLER: Fine. So _____ .

JT: Yes, that's right. See you then. 'Bye.

CALLER: 'Bye.

© Cambridge University Press

☐ MULTIPLE CHOICE

Can be used to test speaking, listening, reading or writing skills. This is a difficult test item if it focuses on students' ability to differentiate between commonly confused words or phrases which they may have frequently got wrong. However, there is a strong 'guesswork' element and students only have to recognise correct forms, rather than produce them. Again on the negative side, it can confuse students who initially 'knew' the correct form but get confused by being exposed to wrong possibilities. If you do manage to write some good test items you will find them very fast to mark if you use a grid (i.e. a card with holes where the correct answers are positioned) or computers. Examples are provided below.

What's the most appropriate response?

1 How do you do?

   a) Very well, thank you.   b) How are you?
   c) Pleased to meet you.   d) I'm a civil engineer.

2 What does 'turnover' mean?

   a) a type of pie   b) a type of graph
   c) annual sales   d) annual income

© Cambridge University Press

☐ MINI-LISTENING

A mini-listening is a good test item to put between timed sections of a test because students can be told to stop writing at this point and be handed the next section afterwards. If the tapescript is read out and recorded at natural speed by a native speaker of English, the task should sort out low-level students or students who have only recently resumed studying from those with more familiarity and confidence with English. An example is provided below.

Listen to the presentation, then fill in the answers below. Two answers have been filled in for you as examples.

Type of company: *Manufacturer of Office Furniture*

Best-selling product: 1

Colours available: 2

Chair recently introduced:	Support Receptionist
Number of bank loans paid off:	3
Reason debts paid off:	4
Excellent market conditions in:	5

Listening tapescript. (Not to be shown to students.)

I'd like to tell you about our range of office furniture. Our best-selling product is the Executive Chair. It's available in three colours: blue, which is the most popular colour, black and red. We also produce a smaller Manager Chair, as well as Typing and Computing Chairs which have special back supports built in. We have recently introduced a Support Receptionist Chair, which is already selling well.

Last year was a particularly good year for us. We managed to pay off almost all our bank loans and to clear all our other debts. The main reason for all this was the decrease in the price of raw materials and the excellent market conditions in Albania last year. Next year we expect to have an even better year.

© Cambridge University Press

☐ EXTENDED LISTENING

If your students are not being regularly put through TOEIC tests (see p. 316) – as many Business English students are – and even if they are, you may feel you need to test students' listening skills more extensively. In order to prepare a tape for students, role-play a situation with a colleague so that you produce a natural-sounding dialogue. Having established the parameters for your conversation (perhaps following the procedure outlined in STARTER PIX on p. 79), try to speak as naturally as possible! Alternatively, use a listening comprehension from a coursebook which uses authentic recordings. For the questions you can use many of the above test items or you can simply write questions for the students to answer in long hand, perhaps in note form. No example is provided because this is such a common test item.

☐ EXTENDED READING

If your students' reading skills are not being regularly tested with TOEIC (see p. 316), and even if they are, you may like to test your students' reading skills more extensively. Use an authentic text, extracted from a web page, a newspaper, a business book, magazine or journal – or from the students' company magazine if you are teaching in-company! Questions can be in any of the above formats or can simply be a list of questions for which the students need to write answers in longhand, perhaps in note form. No example is provided because this is such a common test item.

☐ GUIDED WRITING

This test item provides students with a realistic and useful writing task, which is a good way of testing writing skills. Students' familiarity with conventions, their active knowledge of vocabulary and their sense of appropriacy, not to mention a whole range of discourse features, can easily be assessed with this kind of test item. It is relatively easy to write good test items which are appropriate to a wide range of students. Marking is subjective though, so a clear marking guide needs to be used; the sample feedback sheet on p. 302 suggests one possible approach. Marking is, obviously, rather time-consuming. Also, since students can tackle the task at their own level there could be a wide range of marks within any one class. An example is provided below.

A Mr John Turner from a trading association telephoned today requesting information on your company because he is responsible for promoting Sri Lankan business abroad. He is also interested in meeting to discuss possibilities for import or export, or setting up joint ventures with foreign companies. Your boss has asked you to deal with this enquiry. Write a fax to Mr Turner.

© Cambridge University Press

☐ LEARNER FEEDBACK

In this item students are encouraged to make comments and set objectives. As already noted, this makes the testing process more interactive and also meaningful in real-life terms. It is an important item to include at the end of the written part of the test because it gives learners an opportunity to reflect on their learning and it also gives the test writer or teacher feedback. Even if it is sketchily filled out by students it will still provide a basis for discussion in class after the test has been marked. An example of a possible approach is provided overleaf. Note that this item should not be used to assess students' skills. Make sure it is clear on your test that no points will be awarded for this section.

BUSINESS ENGLISH THINK SPOT

How's it going?

Consider the following questions and write notes so that your teacher can also consider your answers:

1 In which areas of language use have you improved, in your opinion?

2 Which areas of language use are still a problem?

3 Which areas of language use do you want to spend most time on now?

4 What type of classwork is most useful, in your opinion?

5 What can you personally do to increase your rate of progress?

6 Do you have any other comments or suggestions?

☐ SPOTLIT ROLE-PLAY

It is extremely important to test students' speaking skills in a realistic way and this procedure allows you to do this. As well as being enjoyable for students, the procedure provides a pleasant, noisy ending to a more formal end-of-term test and it allows you to give students very clear feedback on oral work on an individual basis. It also provides a good springboard for last-minute follow-up practice or remedial work.

Initially, this procedure may seem a little difficult to organise in terms of class organisation (although students are usually keen to cooperate and give feedback on each other's performance) or time-consuming and difficult to assess. However, it has great value and any extra effort required is offset by the excellent learning opportunities which the procedure seems to provide. Make situations sufficiently general so that all students can relate to them and allow individuals to determine their own roles so that speaking is as close to students' needs as possible.

When marking students' performance use criteria similar to those suggested for the periodic achievement tests on p. 300, then simply add up students' marks. Prepare a feedback sheet similar to the one on p. 302 and give students feedback straight after a break (when you should get a chance to photocopy your feedback sheets) because immediate feedback seems to promote learning more than delayed feedback; this is especially important when assessing speaking. Examples of tasks are provided below.

STUDENT A:
You have been asked to look after a visitor from another company. Take him or her round your offices, telling him/her a little about your company as you do so. Finally, invite him/her to sit down in your office and have a coffee to discuss things further.

STUDENT B:
You are visiting a company. You are usually based in another country and are now visiting in order to find out more about this company. Find out as much as you can about the company while you are being shown round.

You have been asked to join a small project group whose aim is to discuss practical solutions for the following problem:

The company cafeteria is always overcrowded. Service is bad and the food is awful. Several cases of food-poisoning are reported each month.

© Cambridge University Press

A sample end-of-course test feedback sheet for students

BUSINESS ENGLISH TEST FEEDBACK

Name: .... Company: ....

Position: .... Department: ....

Course: .... Overall result: ....

Test results:

Section 1: matching comments   marks out of

Section 2: dialogue completion   marks out of

Section 3: role-play   marks out of

Section 4: e-mail   marks out of

Section 5: fax-writing   marks out of

                                                  Final %

Performance skill	Level of attainment			
Speaking to clients	Poor	Average	Good	Excellent
Speaking to colleagues	Poor	Average	Good	Excellent
E-mail	Poor	Average	Good	Excellent
Writing faxes	Poor	Average	Good	Excellent

Comments:

© Cambridge University Press

7.5 External examinations

Quite a few British and American examining bodies now offer Business English exams. There are many advantages to using external exams during a Business English programme:

- Students have a clear target at the end of each course or series of courses.
- Students get a qualification which they may be able to use to get work or promotion.
- The test items are written by experienced test-writers.
- Tests are checked in advance so there should be no errors or unexpected problems.
- Marking is straightforward – you have nothing to do with it!

The main reasons exams are sometimes not used are as follows:

- There may not be an exam which is suitable for your particular purposes.
- Some exams, although well-promoted and conceived, may be disappointing in reality!
- External examinations may slow down progress because areas of language use which are less important to the students will need to be practised while those which are more important in real life (but which are not examined) may be de-prioritised.
- Some students don't want to focus on accuracy to the extent often required by examiners. These students claim that simply being able to survive in a business environment is enough. Whether or not they are right perhaps depends on their situation, standards, awareness and ambitions! Accuracy can often increase professionalism, save time and generally ease communication.

On pp. 316–317 you will find brief notes on the main exams available at the time of writing. You can easily obtain an update and sample papers for a particular exam by writing to the examining body at the address listed on pp. 336–337. Consider each exam in the context of your particular teaching situation. An exam needs to suit your students' professional needs if it is to be useful and it is helpful, but not essential, if it has some level of recognition locally.

Notes

1 Many exams are only available in certain places and at certain times so check whether or not the exam can be taken in your area and whether or not the timing is suitable.
2 The particular examinations you use should perhaps be influenced by market forces since some exams (e.g. TOEIC, LCCI exams or even

FCE) are so well-known in certain countries that a school is almost forced to use them or make reference to them when first discussing a company's needs and goals. Consult your clients on this issue!

3 Different examinations will be marked according to very different criteria so it is worth getting full information on them before making any decisions.

4 Experiment and explore options until you find solutions which satisfy the real needs of your particular teaching situation. After you have made a decision actively, sell your choices to your clients.

The following exams may be of interest to Business English students:

- **UCLES (University of Cambridge Local Examinations Syndicate)**
  The Certificate in English for International Business and Trade (CEIBT) is an excellent, realistic four-skill exam which tests students at relatively high levels. Individual papers can be taken separately and certificates are awarded for each paper passed. BEC 1, 2 and 3 (Business English for Commerce), which are well-established exams in Asia, are now available worldwide six times a year. These easier graded exams also test all four skills, using similar task types (e.g. gapfill and editing) to those used in FCE (First Certificate in English). FCE, although a general English exam, is also widely requested by companies operating in certain countries (e.g. Greece).

- **University of Oxford (UODLE)**
  The main exam they offer is the Oxford International Business English Certificate (OIBEC), which is a realistic task-based exam testing all four skills at two levels (First Level and Executive Level). They also offer a Tourism English Proficiency exam (at one level only) for students in the tourist industry. Their general English exam, the Oxford Higher, also provides many realistic tasks which may be useful for working adults.

- **Educational Testing Service**
  TOEIC, the Test of English for International Commerce, is an exam in multiple-choice format widely used by companies, especially in Asia, to track general language proficiency. It is probably so widely used because students can periodically obtain a numerical score (e.g. 520 out of 800) which gives an indication of their level of proficiency in an easily understood way. However, the Test only tests reading and listening skills, using short, decontextualised items. TOEFL (Test of English as a Foreign Language) is the general English equivalent. TSE (Test of Spoken English) and TWE (Test of Written English) test productive skills, but are not as widely used as TOEIC or TOEFL. The Educational Testing Service also offers GMAT (Graduate Management Admission Test), which measures general verbal,

mathematical and analytical writing skills and is geared to the needs of graduate schools of business and management.

- **London Chamber of Commerce (LCCI)**
  LCCI offer various exams which could be of interest to Business English students:

  1 Spoken English for Industry & Commerce (SEfIC): an oral exam which operates at four levels (Preliminary, Threshold, Intermediate and Advanced)
  2 English for Business: a communicative written exam provided at three levels
  3 English for Commerce: an academic written exam provided at three levels
  4 Practical Business English: a multiple-choice test aiming to test a person's ability to survive in an English-speaking business environment
  5 Use of English: written exams for secretaries, offered at three levels
  6 English for the Tourism Industry: exams for people working in the tourist industry

- **Language Training Services (LTS) exam**
  'The Business English Test' by B. Carroll is available from LTS. The listening and reading sections can be administered and scored by non-native non-specialist teachers.

- **International Certificate Conference**
  The Language Certificate System for English provided by this German examining body is available to candidates in Europe. As well as a general exam, there are also exams for Business, Hotel & Catering and Technical English.

- **Pitman Qualifications**
  Their English for Business Communication exam is offered at three levels (Elementary, Intermediate and Advanced) and tests listening, reading and writing. It is available on dates arranged by examination centres.

- **Trinity College, London**
  They offer a number of spoken English exams at 12 grades (Initial: 1–3, Elementary: 4–6, Intermediate: 7–9 and Advanced: 10–12) in General English. These graded tests are conducted by examiners sent from the UK and may be useful for students needing to socialise in English or develop confidence.

- **Association of Recognized English Language Schools (ARELS)**
  The Preliminary Certificate, the Higher Certificate and the Diploma are all spoken exams which are designed to complement the Oxford exams. They are conducted in a language lab or with radio equipment.

8　Being accountable

We are accountable to our students, their sponsors and our bosses so we need to provide them with information at various points or allow them access to information by letting them observe or see materials. As well as being clear, any written information we provide should also be accurate because decisions about people's careers may well be based on this information, especially if it is presented in the form of test results or reports.

8.1 Providing information

Make sure that students, sponsors and bosses know what decisions have been made about course objectives, approach and materials. If you are not in consultation with all parties while deciding on these, they need to be told afterwards. Provide key people with information in the ways described below.

Provide a course outline or copies of syllabuses
A course outline is invaluable as a general summary sheet – see p. 31 and p. 48 for examples. If any confidential documents are requested in addition (e.g. syllabuses or tests), explain that you will be happy to show and discuss them but cannot provide copies. If challenged, explain the need for confidentiality and simply say: *I'm sorry, I can't give you a copy.*

Inform all parties about changes
If changes are made to any documents or information initially given out, make sure that everyone concerned is informed as soon as possible. People have a right to know about changes before they take place because they may well affect the success of the course. It is unlikely that anybody will challenge your professionalism when you make changes which seem necessary, as long as you have remembered the course's objectives and noted any comments (about preferences, etc.) made during the initial needs analysis.

Keep channels of communication open on a day-to-day basis
Course coordinators will appreciate being kept up-to-date on your ongoing objectives. If both they and the students' managers understand

your rationale, they are more likely to make positive comments to the people who make the ultimate decisions about follow-up courses! (A quick phone call can be made if you don't come into contact with key people on a day-to-day basis.) Giving students ongoing updates is also essential because students represent our main contact with our clients. If students understand your thinking you are more likely to get their enthusiastic participation.

8.2 Being observed

Your bosses and company sponsors may periodically wish to observe you teach. Allow and indeed encourage this because people are likely to be reassured by what they see. You must also allow observation because your clients have a right to check up on what you are doing! However, for your own benefit and/or protection try to establish the following:

- All observations must be arranged in advance so you can be sure only one person will be observing at a time!
- The observer should speak to you before the observation so that you get an opportunity to explain the rationale for certain approaches beforehand.
- No interruptions may be made by the observer during the observation.
- The observer must have a longer chat with you after the class has taken place so that further points can be clarified and issues explored. Do this informally, if necessary.

You will probably also find it helpful to provide a lesson plan because this will give you the opportunity to explain your rationale and the context of specific activities on paper.

8.3 Writing reports

You may be asked to write reports on your students occasionally, or it may be a good idea for you to provide these without prompting. Take them seriously! Decisions about students' careers may be made as a result of the reports you write. Your reports may determine whether or not a student gets sent away on business trips, for example, or whether he or she gets promoted to a position with a more 'international' flavour.

Before you start writing

- Think carefully about the most appropriate format to use. Numerical scores are favoured because progress is easily tracked but numbers

319

may not provide a reliable indication of real progress, so alternatives may be preferable. Written comments may be necessary to supplement or counteract false impressions created by 'scores'.
- Remember that all information must be comprehensible! Paraphrase EFL terms or provide keys to explain confusing terms.
- Consider how you can provide information on real-life skills because managers are primarily interested in knowing the answer to the question: *Can he or she do x?*

Sample report forms are provided below for both individual and group reports. Note that no details about students' performance are provided on the report on the opposite page because its main function is to show managers whether the course was worth running in terms of attendance, i.e. money invested in training people.

A *report form for reporting on individual students' progress*

For the attention of: ....   Date: ....

Company: ....   Department: ....

BUSINESS ENGLISH END-OF-COURSE STUDENT REPORT

Student's name: ....   Teacher's name: ....

Student's position ....   Course: ....

Department: ....   Overall performance grade: ....

Attendance grade: ....   Attitude %: ....

Final test marks (%): ....   Pass/fail course: ....

Grades for performance areas covered during the course

Speaking:

Dealing with visitors	A	B	C	D
Telephoning	A	B	C	D
Presentations and Q&A sessions	A	B	C	D
Meetings	A	B	C	D

Writing:

E-mail	A	B	C	D
Report-writing	A	B	C	D

N.B. Grades relate to the standard expected at this level.
        A = excellent, B = good, C = acceptable, D = poor.

General comments:

Suggested follow-up

Signed: _____ *Teacher*   Signed: _____ *Coordinator*

A report form for a whole class of students

For the attention of: .... Date: ....

Company: .... Department: ....

BUSINESS ENGLISH END-OF-COURSE GROUP REPORT

Course: .... Teacher: ....

Materials used: ....

....

....

Summary of attendance

Student's name (LAST NAME, First name)	Department	Hours attended	Overall % attendance

Teacher's comments:

Signed: _____ *Teacher*   Signed: _____ *Coordinator*

9 Evaluating courses

9.1 What's evaluation all about? Why evaluate?

Evaluation can be concerned with:

- attitudes – how positively are our courses viewed?
- effectiveness – how well do we achieve our objectives in terms of real learning?
- appropriacy – how appropriate are our programmes to our clients' real needs?

It is important to evaluate the success and effectiveness of your courses so that you can make improvements on an ongoing basis. It is also important so as to ensure continued survival, since students and sponsors act on their own evaluation of our courses (formal or informal). When programmes are not working, they seek alternative solutions to fulfil their very real need for English, e.g. programmes offered by rival language schools, multi-media self-study or simply a subscription to *Newsweek*. However, our evaluation must be effective for true improvements in courses to be made.

9.2 How to evaluate?

The most common approach to evaluation is to collect comments or ratings using feedback forms, such as the one on pp. 323–324, which are distributed at the end of each course, and then to interpret them. (For more on this, see 9.3.) Another important approach is to sit back and reflect on what seems to constitute successful practice in your particular teaching context. (For more on this, see 9.4.) A third, often revealing, approach is to collect and analyse objective data from registration and re-registration figures, attendance figures and test or exam results.

All information – statistical or impressionistic, objective or subjective – will need to be considered in relation to the course's objectives, course format (intensive or extensive, with or without self-study component, etc.), teaching approach and materials used ... amongst other things! You will need to take care to find out whether any variable was in effect which might distort your conclusions. For example, it could be that materials were adequate but either your approach or your attitude unhelpful! You will also need to be careful not to assume that things are effects, when they might be causes. For example, student absences could either be an indication of deficiencies in a course (if classwork was irrelevant to students' work), or a cause of failure (if no absence policy was in operation). See 6.1 for more on this.

A form for getting feedback at the end of a course

BUSINESS ENGLISH END-OF-COURSE FEEDBACK

Please help us to improve our courses by filling out the following form.
Circle your answers. A = excellent, B = good, C = acceptable, D = poor.
If you'd prefer to remain anonymous, just leave the first space blank!

Name: .... Course: ....

Company: .... Site: ....

Teacher: .... Term: ....

Self-evaluation:

How would you rate your own progress and performance for this course?

Attitude: A B C D   **Performance:** A B C D   **Progress:** A B C D

In your opinion, how much progress have you made in the following areas?

	Improvement				Performance grade			
Dealing with visitors	None	Little	Some	Great	A	B	C	D
Telephoning	None	Little	Some	Great	A	B	C	D
Presentations and Q&A	None	Little	Some	Great	A	B	C	D
Meetings	None	Little	Some	Great	A	B	C	D
E-mail	None	Little	Some	Great	A	B	C	D
Report-writing	None	Little	Some	Great	A	B	C	D

Course evaluation:

How would you rate this course? (Circle answers)

Overall: A B C D   **Teaching:** A B C D   **Materials:** A B C D

In general, this course was …   1   2   3   4   5
                                       useful ——————— not useful

because _____

The teacher was …   1   2   3   4   5
                           helpful ——————— not helpful

because _____

The class activities were …   1   2   3   4   5
                                      helpful ——————— not helpful

because _____

Materials were …   1   2   3   4   5
                                                    useful ············ not useful

because _____

The most useful thing we did was _____

because _____

The least useful thing we did was _____

because _____

The homework assignments were   1   2   3   4   5
                                                    useful ············ not useful

because _____

In general, I spent …   1   2   3   4   5   6   7   8   9   10
                                       hours on homework per week

because _____

Plans for next term

What do you want to do next term?

– Go on to the next level.
– Continue at the same level.
– Stop studying English because _____

_____

– Study in a different way. I want to _____

_____

Suggestions

What kind of class activities would you like to do more of?

_____

_____

What can we do to improve our courses?

_____

_____

What other course(s) would you find useful?

_____

_____

Any other suggestions?

Please write them on a separate piece of paper and attach it to this form.

Thank you

Based on a form developed by instructors at Sumikin-Intercom Inc., Osaka, Japan

9.3 Getting feedback from students

Collecting feedback from students with a course feedback form at the end of each course is probably the easiest approach. (The sample form on pp. 323–324 will, of course, need to be adapted according to the precise content of your course. If you are designing your own form, phrase questions carefully so as to prompt useful responses.) You can back up use of feedback forms with formalised interviews or informal chats, whenever this is possible.

When considering completed feedback forms, be sure to analyse ratings and comments with care because effective evaluation involves probing the reasons behind a course's apparent strengths or weaknesses. You can clarify unexpected ratings and mysterious comments by asking students and their managers indirect questions or by seemingly innocuous chatting.

If reasons behind low course ratings or poor student performance are perpetually elusive ask your clients to cooperate in discovering the causes! The need for English is sufficiently strong in today's businesses for clients to appreciate our efforts to probe their real needs.

9.4 Reflective evaluation

While feedback and statistical data are both invaluable and must, of course, be taken into account, much of course evaluation can be done simply by reflecting on the current situation. When evaluating the success of a course, consider the following questions, relating to key areas.

Teachers

- Do students perceive you (and your colleagues) as being professional?
- Could you get any extra training so as to enhance your performance?
- Is there any expertise in-house which is not being shared?

Course programme

- Are clients' needs adequately analysed before courses?
- Are courses well-planned, either by you or your managers?
- Do your lessons reflect the planning that is done for each course?
- Are you adapting your approach on an ongoing basis, as necessary, in line with clients' needs? Is this done on a consultative basis? (See 2.6 and 4.7 for guidelines on this.)
- Is full information on course planning provided to clients so as to keep them informed?

Materials

- How do students perceive your materials?
- Are you on the mailing lists of all major publishers and/or distributors so as to be able to keep up-to-date with new materials?
- Have any materials recently been published which might enhance your programme?
- Are materials which are produced in-house well-filed and/or readily available to you?

Methods

- How do students perceive the methods you use?
- How do the students' sponsors perceive your methods?
- Are your methods time-efficient?
- Is there any new technology which you could, and should, be using?
- Are there any workshops or conferences which you could attend so as to learn about new approaches?
- Are you and your colleagues sharing your collective expertise?
- How can you and your colleagues share your collective expertise about methods more?
- What can you do to encourage creativity in your staff room?

Client relations

- Are clients regularly contacted for comments and feedback?
- Are clients kept informed of any changes which may affect them?
- Do clients have a contact person at the school who they can contact for information?
- Do you, yourself, have a contact person you can easily communicate with in the case of in-company courses?
- Do you know what to do when there are problems in class (e.g. when students from a particular organisation on in-house/public courses are regularly absent)?
- Are you in communication with all the people you need to be communicating with?

After reflecting on these areas and considering answers to the questions, you will need to look for patterns or trends and consider possible improvements or solutions for specific problems. You will then need to negotiate the politics of your particular school so as to be able to try out any new approaches! When you have found things that work, share your solutions with other teachers through course files, seminars at conferences and articles – but keep an open mind because there might be even better approaches waiting to be discovered! We have a lot of refinements to make before our teaching can be considered truly effective.

10 Moving towards a better future

In this book the need to keep changing according to clients' needs has been constantly stressed. Considering the extent of changes going on in the world today, it is not surprising that changes should also be necessary in the field of teaching because it is clear that adult students' needs are changing; their needs are becoming more pressing in the light of globalisation, diminishing resources and the increasing trend towards competitiveness. This book might perhaps act as a starting point or regeneration station for your own experimentation and practice.

10.1 What else can we do?

To continue your explorations, I suggest you consult the Recommended reading section (pp. 330–332), try out a wide range of materials (which you can obtain from the publishers listed on pp. 333–336) and also invest time – and perhaps a little money too – in other activities so that you can gain a better insight into the real issues in Business English teaching. Some specific suggestions are given below! This investment could well pay dividends in the mid or long term if it means you are able to improve your performance as a teacher and, thus, guarantee survival in the workplace. Here are some ways in which you can improve your performance in the Business English context:

- Take one or more of the courses on offer for potential or practising Business English teachers. Some possible courses you could consider are as follows: the Cert TEB (Certificate in Teaching English for Business) or the Dip TEB (Diploma in Teaching English for Business) run by the London Chamber of Commerce and Industry; the Certificate in Teaching English for Business and the Diploma in Teaching English for Business offered by UCLES; TEfIC (Specialist Certificate in the Teaching of English for Industry and Commerce) or Cert. 1:1 (Specialist Certificate in the Teaching of English One-to-One) offered by Trinity College London. See p. 337 for addresses.
- Get temp – i.e. temporary – jobs in companies whenever in Britain/America/Canada, etc., working as a clerk, typist, warehouse assistant, or whatever. (Simply contact temp agencies or other employment agencies in your area.) Teach yourself to touch-type and

become computer literate, not only so as to get these jobs but also to help you cope later on when you are run off your feet as a successful Business English teacher! Many temp agencies (e.g. Brook Street Bureau in Britain) will even provide free training if you sign up to work for them.

- Make friends with any technology or software you encounter in your day-to-day life. In other words, don't just learn how to operate it, become an expert at using it.
- Read books on management techniques and problems, e.g. Charles Handy's *Understanding Organizations* (1993. 4th edition. Hardmondsworth: Penguin) or the review of management theories: *The Witch Doctors* (Micklethwait, J. and A. Wooldridge. 1996. London: Heinemann).
- Read about economics theory and practical applications, perhaps by taking a correspondence course.
- Keep up-to-date on recent company successes and failures, as well as problems in specific industries, by reading *Time*, *Newsweek*, etc.
- Learn the language of the culture you are living in.
- Study subjects which are seemingly unrelated to business and see how your outside interests inspire you to add unusual elements to your Business English classes – always remembering that success in business has often come from strange innovations, developed by people looking in unlikely sources.
- Talk informally to people who work for companies as much as possible and get them talking about problems at work.
- Use any opportunity to make new contacts in any company you visit (e.g. by staying for 10 minutes or an hour after class, doing paperwork, planning other lessons, cuing up tapes, visiting the company cafeteria) so as to maximise opportunities for impromptu conversations.
- Create and take up invitations to visit plants, warehouses or branch offices, and visit special sales outlets (open to the general public) in your spare time.
- Talk to everybody you encounter when visiting companies, including security staff, receptionists and cleaners. You will learn all sorts of interesting things and the contact you have with these people can only help you when you are teaching on in-company courses, even if you are only 'the English teacher'.

In other words, become a better, more informed, more interested person so that you become more and more in touch with your students' lifestyles and real needs. Being aware of how companies operate and what is going on in the business world will put you in touch with some of your students' concerns and will help you to pick up all sorts of subtle messages, which students may not communicate explicitly.

As we, the language trainers/teachers/instructors/consultants of tomorrow become more in touch with our clients and as we become increasingly knowledgeable and professional, so our options will increase. Companies should begin to use us, not only for our English teaching skills but also for any other skills we might have to offer. As language 'experts', not only will we be asked to provide English courses, we may also be asked to sit in on meetings, proofread correspondence on an ongoing basis, translate – if we are able to – and advise on a whole range of non-verbal cross-cultural problems. Our job can only become more interesting in a world which is becoming increasingly international and, therefore, increasingly dependent on effective communication skills ... as long as we continue to adapt!

The challenge of improving communication in the world's workplace is well worth taking up. Teach Business English – so as to help to lay the groundwork for a world in which people are better able to communicate (through the lingua franca of English). It can be extremely satisfying, thanks to the ever-present link with real-life needs. If taught with a sense of responsibility, Business English classes can make a small but important contribution to increased global understanding.

If you have any comments or questions about this book, you can contact Sylvie Donna at the following e-mail address:
sylvie.donna@profilesolutionsinternational.com

Recommended reading

Needs are very individual and books are constantly being published, not to mention CD-ROMs, etc.! Speak to your local publishers' reps to find out about titles which may be of interest or simply browse in your local bookshops. This list provides a starting point for those wanting to follow up on some of the areas introduced in this book. Titles are listed alphabetically by author. Don't start at the beginning of the list because that wouldn't be fair to the Ws of this world!

Collett, P. 1993. *Foreign Bodies: A guide to European mannerisms.* London: Simon & Schuster Ltd.
An entertaining but informative book about cultural differences in Europe. Covers values as well as non-verbal behaviour.

Deal, T. and A. Kennedy. 1988. *Corporate Cultures*. Harmondsworth: Penguin.
Provides a useful introduction to what corporate cultures are and how they affect workplaces.

Ellis, M. and C. Johnson. 1994. *Teaching Business English*. Oxford: Oxford University Press.
Especially useful for real newcomers to the field, giving very basic definitions and guidelines.

Gower, R. and R. Walters. 1983. *Teaching Practice Handbook*. Oxford: Heinemann.
A key text for general EFL teachers with useful step-by-step instructions for some basic techniques, such as elicited dialogues.

Handy, C. 1993. 4th edition. *Understanding Organisations*. Harmondsworth: Penguin.
A useful core text which gives an insight into issues affecting companies.

Lewis, M. 1993. *The Lexical Approach: The State of ELT and a Way Forward*. Hove: Language Teaching Publications.
An antidote to what you might hear some EFL teachers say! Useful for helping you consider broader issues.

Lewis, M. (ed. Hill, J.) 1997. *Implementing The Lexical Approach: The On-going Debate*. Hove: Language Teaching Publications.
Develops the ideas originally presented in *The Lexical Approach*

and describes how the lexical approach works in practice. It includes exercises and activities.

Madeley, J. 1999. *Big Business, Poor Peoples: The impact of transnational corporations on the world's poor.* London: Zed Books.
Written by an experienced journalist, this book provides important background information about certain business practices which you may find yourself discussing with students.

McCarthy, M. 1991. *Discourse Analysis for Language Teachers.* Cambridge: Cambridge University Press.
A good introduction to discourse analysis, which is an essential focus of study for anyone wanting to teach 'real' language, not merely the somewhat odd language of the classroom.

Mead, R. 1990. *Cross-cultural Management Communication.* Chichester: Wiley.
Gives an insight into this potentially difficult area, which is an essential part of Business English teaching.

Micklethwait, J. and A. Wooldridge. 1996. *The Witch Doctors.* London: Heinemann.
Provides an overview of management theories and gurus.

Mole, J. 1997. *Mind Your Manners: Managing Business Cultures in Europe.* London: Nicholas Brealey Publishing.
An introduction to some not-so-obvious cultural differences in Europe.

Mullins, L. J. 1996. *Management and Organisational Behaviour* (4th edition). London: Pitman Publishing.
A useful volume, which should help newcomers to business find out about many key concepts and historical developments.

Richards, J. C. and T. S. Rodgers. 1986. *Approaches and Methods in Language Teaching.* Cambridge: Cambridge University Press.
Provides an insight into EFL's recent history and the rationale behind some common methods.

Ricks, D. A. 1993. *Blunders in International Business.* Oxford: Blackwell.
A fun read which might help you to introduce some humour into your classroom!

Robbins, H. and M. Finley. 1997. *Why Teams Don't Work: What went wrong and how to make it right.* London: Orion Business.
An award-winning book which provides an insider's view of teamwork problems. Useful reading because so many Business English students have to function effectively in teams.

Recommended reading

Schiffrin, D. 1994. *Approaches to Discourse*. Oxford: Blackwells.
An essential text for anyone wanting to consider words as they operate in real life, i.e. as part of real communication, rather than simply nuts and bolts which make up sentences.

Scollon, R. and S. Wong Scollon. 1995. *Intercultural Communication*. Oxford: Blackwells.
Provides useful insights into some common problem areas in communication between East and West.

Scrivener, J. 1995. *Learning Teaching*. Oxford: Heinemann.
A sensitive, useful text which is essential reading for those new to English language teaching.

Skehan, P. 1989. *Individual Differences in Second Language Learning*. London: Edward Arnold.
Food for thought which is extremely relevant to the Business English context, where small classes make individualised programmes a real possibility.

Stevick, E. W. 1980. *Learning Languages: A Way and Ways*. Rowley, MA: Newbury House.
Detailed descriptions of some silent way and CLL classes in action.

Tannen, D. 1995. *Talking from 9 to 5*. London: Virago.
Essential reading for anyone wanting to gain an insight into how women's and men's communication might differ in a working context.

Underhill, A. 1994. *Sound Foundations*. Oxford: Heinemann.
A useful guide to teaching pronunciation with lots of tips and useful ideas.

Waterman, R. 1994. *The Frontiers of Excellence: Learning from companies that put people first*. London: Nicholas Brealey Publishing.
Commonly read by managers, this is one of the core texts on management approaches.

Weir, C. 1993. *Understanding & Developing Language Tests*. Hemel Hempstead: Prentice Hall.
Introduces some basic concepts of testing. A useful supplement to this book's section on testing.

Weir, C. and J. Roberts. 1994. *Evaluation in ELT*. Oxford: Blackwells.
A detailed analysis of evaluation procedures, which are useful for those genuinely trying to improve their language programmes.

Useful addresses

1 Professional associations

International Association of Teachers of English as a Foreign
Language (IATEFL)
3 Kingsdown Chambers, Whitstable, Kent CT5 2FL, UK
Tel: +44 1227 276528, Fax: +44 1227 274415,
E-mail: iatefl@compuserve.com, Website: http://www.iatefl.org
Note: IATEFL has a special interest group for Business English – the
BESIG (Business English Special Interest Group).
Japan Association of Language Teachers (JALT)
JALT Central Office, Shamboru dai-2, Kaweseki 305, 1–3–17
Kaizuka, Kawasaki-ku, Karagawa 210, Japan
National Centre for English Language Teaching Research (NCELTR)
School of English and Linguistics, Macquarie University, Sydney,
NSW 2109, Australia
Teachers of English to Speakers of Other Languages (TESOL)
1600 Cameron Street, Suite 300, Alexandria, VA 22314–2751 USA

2 Business-related information

London Stock Exchange
Information and Press Department, London EC2N 1HP, UK,
Tel: +44 20 7797 1000/1372/ 3306, Telex: 886557,
Website: http://www.londonstockex.co.uk
US Information Agency
301 4th Street West, Washington DC 20547, USA

3 Publishers

BBC books and audio cassettes:
Available from Oxford University Press
BBC Training Videos
Woodlands, 80 Wood Lane, London W12 0TT, UK
Blackwells Publishers
108 Cowley Road, Oxford OX4 1JF, UK

Cambridge University Press
  ELT Marketing Department, The Edinburgh Building, Shaftesbury
  Road, Cambridge CB2 2RU, UK, Tel: +44 1223 325819,
  Fax: +44 1223 325984, E-mail: eltmail@cup.cam.ac.uk,
  Website: www.cup.cam.ac.uk
  USA: 40 West 20th Street, New York, NY 10011–4211, USA,
  Website: www.cup.org
  Australia: 10 Stamford Road, Oakleigh, Melbourne 3166,
  Australia
Edward Arnold
  338 Euston Road, London NW1 3BH, UK, Tel: 01235 400403 (UK)
  or +44 1235 400400 (International trade),
  Fax: +44 20 7873 6325, Website: www.arnoldpublishers.co.uk
Gower Publishing Ltd
  Gower House, Croft Road, Aldershot, Hampshire GU11 3HR, UK,
  Tel: +44 1252 331551, Fax: +44 1252 344405,
  E-mail: gower@cityscape.co.uk
Heinemann
  See Macmillan Heinemann ELT
Intercultural Press Inc
  16 US Route One, PO Box 700, Yarmouth, ME 04096, USA,
  Tel: +1 800 370 2665 or +1 207 846 5181, Fax +1 207 846 5181,
  E-mail: interculturalpress@internetmci.com,
  Website: http:// www.bookmasters.com/interclt.htm
Language Teachers' Development Training Books
  Contact: Pilgrims Language Courses, 8 Vernon Place, Canterbury,
  Kent CT1 3HG, UK
Language Teaching Publications (LTP)
  114a Church Road, Hove, East Sussex BN3 2EB, UK,
  Tel: +44 1273 736344, Fax: +44 1273 775361,
  E-mail: LanTeaPub@aol.com
Longman
  See Pearson Education
Macmillan Heinemann ELT
  Macmillan Oxford, Between Towns Road, Oxford OX4 3PP, UK,
  Tel: +44 1865 405700, Fax: +44 1865 405701,
  E-mail: elt@mhelt.com, Website: www.mhelt.com
McGraw-Hill
  Director of Special Sales, McGraw-Hill, 11 West 19th Street, New
  York, NY 10011, USA
  In Asia: McGraw-Hill Book Co, 60 Tuas Basin Link, Singapore
  638775, Tel: +65 863 1580, Fax: +65 862 3354, Telex: McGRAW
  RS36791, E-mail: phillip_ang@mcgraw-hill.com,
  Website: http://www.learner.org

Nelson
  Nelson English Language Teaching, 100 Avenue Road, London
  NW3 3HF, UK
Newbury House
  Newbury House Publishers Inc, Rowley, MA 01969, USA
Nicholas Brealey Publishing
  Nicholas Brealey Publishing Ltd, 156 Cloudesley Road, London
  N1 0EA, UK
Open University Press
  Celtic Court, 22 Ballmoor, Buckingham MK18 1XW, UK
Oxford University Press
  English Language Teaching, Great Clarendon Street, Oxford
  OX2 6DP, UK, Tel: +44 1865 556767, Fax: +44 1865 267633,
  Telex: 837330 OXPRESG, Website: http://www.oup.co.uk/elt
Pearson Education
  for former Longman/Phoenix ELT/Prentice Hall Regents books
  Sales Dept, ELT Division, Pearson Education, Edinburgh Gate,
  Harlow, Essex, CM20 2JE, UK, Tel: +44 1279 623623,
  Fax: +44 1279 431059, E-mail: elt@pearsoned-ema.com,
  Website: www.pearsoned-ema.com.
  USA: Pearson Education, 10 Bank Street, Suite 900, White Plains
  NY 10606, USA
Penguin Books Ltd
  Bath Road, Harmondsworth, West Drayton, Middlesex, UB7 0DA,
  UK, Tel: +44 20 8757 4000, Fax: +44 20 8899 4099,
  Telex: 933349, Website: www.penguin.co.uk
  USA: Penguin Books USA Inc, 375 Hudson Street, New York,
  NY 10014, USA
  Overseas orders: Export Sales Dept Penguin Group, 27 Wrights
  Lane, London W8 5TZ, UK, Tel: +44 20 7416 3000
Phoenix ELT
  See Pearson Education
Prentice Hall Regents
  See Pearson Education
Thames TV
  Seymour Mews House, Seymour Mews, Wigmore Street, London
  W1H 9PE, UK
Thorsons
  Harper Collins Publishers, 77–85 Fulham Palace Road,
  Hammersmith, London W6 8JB, UK
Training Services
  Brooklands House, 29 Hythegate, Werrington, Peterborough,
  PE4 7ZP, UK, Tel: +44 1733 327337, Fax +44 1733 575537,
  E-mail: Tipton@trainingservices.demon.co.uk

Video Arts Group Ltd.
  Dumbarton House, 68 Oxford Street, London W1N 0LH, UK
  Tel: +44 20 7637 7288, Fax: +44 20 7580 8103,
  Website: www.videoarts.co.uk, E-mail: info@videoarts.co.uk
Wiley
  John Wiley & Sons Ltd, Baffins Lane, Chichester, West Sussex
  PO19 1UD, UK

4 Mail order of materials

Alta Book Center
  14 Adrian Court, Burlingame, CA 94010, USA
BEBC
  ELT Mail Order, 15 Albion Close, Parkstone, Poole, Dorset
  BH12 3LL, UK, Tel: +44 1202 715555, Fax: +44 1202 739609,
  E-mail: elt@bebc.co.uk
Biblos
  Fl Bldg 1–26–5 Takadanobaba, Shinjuku-ku, Tokyo 160, Japan
KELTIC Bookshop
  25 Chepstow Corner, Chepstow Place, London W2 4TT, UK
Language Book Centre
  555 Beaufort Street, Mount Lawley, Western Australia 6050

5 TV & radio

BBC English Radio
  Bush House, The Strand, London WC2B 4PH, UK,
  E-mail: bbc.english@bbc.co.uk, Website:
  http://www.bbc.co.uk/worldservice/BBC_English/index.htm
BBC World Service (television)
  BBC World Service Television Ltd, Woodlands, 80 Wood Lane,
  London W12 0TT, UK

6 Examining bodies

ARELS (Association of Recognised English Language Schools)
  2 Pontypool Place, Valentine Place, London SE1 8QF, UK,
  Tel: +44 20 7242 3136, Fax: +44 20 7928 9378,
  E-mail: enquiries@arels.org.uk, Website: http://www.arels.org.uk

Educational Testing Service (Graduate Record Examination Board)
Educational Testing Service, PO Box 6155, Princeton,
NJ 08541–6155, USA, For GREB Tel: +1 800 808 0090 for update
info or +1 609 771 7243 (outside the US) to order materials,
Website: http://www.gre.org. For GMAT publications
Tel: +1 800 982 6740 (Department G35), Fax: +1 609 406 5090,
Website: http://www.gmat.org
International Certificate Conference (ICC)
Holzhausenstr. 21, D–6000 Frankfurt 1, Germany,
Tel: +49 1540 0547, Fax: +49 1540 0538
Language Training Services
LTS Training & Consulting, 5 Belvedere, Lansdown Road, Bath
BA1 5ED, UK
London Chamber of Commerce and Industry (LCCI)
London Chamber of Commerce and Industry Examinations Board,
Marlowe House, Station Road, Sidcup, Kent DA15 7BJ, UK,
Tel: +44 20 8302 0261, Fax: +44 20 8302 4169 /
+44 20 8309 5169 Publishing Dept: Athena House, 112 Station
Road, Sidcup, Kent, DA15 7BJ, UK
Pitman Qualifications
1 Giltspur Street, London EC1A 9DD, UK, Tel: +44 20 7294 2471,
Fax: +44 20 7294 2403,
Website: http://www.city-and-guilds.co.uk/pitman
Trinity College London
16 Park Crescent, London W1N 4AP, UK, Tel: +44 20 7323 2328,
Fax: +44 20 7323 5201, E-mail: info@trinitycollege.co.uk,
Website: http://www.trinitycollege.co.uk
University of Cambridge Local Examinations Syndicate (UCLES)
Marketing Division, 1 Hills Road, Cambridge CB1 2EU, UK
Tel: +44 1223 553311, Fax: +44 1223 460278
University of Oxford Delegacy of Local Examinations
Ewert House, Ewert Place, Summertown, Oxford OX2 7BZ, UK
Tel: +44 1865 554291, Fax: +44 1865 510085

Glossary of terms

As well as terms from this book which may not be widely known worldwide, you will also find here terms commonly used in Business English and the related world of EFL.

If and when you encounter terms to do with business or the students' speciality, simply refer to your course materials for clarification and/or ask your students. As well as giving students an opportunity to practise their spoken English, this will enable individuals to contribute to lessons in a meaningful way. If students don't know the meaning and you are unable to find any information in course materials, ask students to check the meaning themselves (with bosses or in a library) before their next class. Although it is helpful if you also check these unknown terms in your own reference materials (e.g. in Business English dictionaries or similar – contact the publishers listed on pp. 333–336) you are primarily a language teacher so you don't need to know all the jargon in advance!

accuracy a term which usually refers to grammatical accuracy in ELT
approach a teacher's overall way of teaching
appropriacy the extent to which a given phrase (or word, etc.) is appropriate in a situation
authentic materials materials extracted from real-life situations, not written specially for the classroom
backchaining a drilling technique in which the phrases at the end of an utterance are drilled first; the whole utterance is gradually built up as earlier phrases are added to later ones
backchannelling the process by which a listener uses sounds or phrases (e.g. *Uhu, I see*) to give feedback to a speaker to show attention, interest, agreement or understanding. See: NOISY LISTENING (p. 153) and HUMAN CHATS (p. 166)
BEC Business English for Commerce, the UCLES examination available in levels 1, 2 and 3
board: a blackboard or whiteboard
CAE Certificate in Advanced English, a high level general English exam offered by UCLES, which is between FCE and CPE in terms of standard

cc an abbreviation – standing for 'carbon copy' – used on business correspondence to indicate that a copy is to be sent to somebody (whose name will follow this abbreviation)

CCSE Certificates in Communicative Skills in English, a general English exam offered by UCLES at four levels, which is intended for students whose focus is communicative competence, perhaps because they intend to live in Britain short- or long-term

CEIBT Certificate in English for International Business and Trade, the advanced two-level examination for Business English students run by UCLES; the tasks included in the exam are both relevant and practical in orientation

CELTA Certificate in English Language Teaching to Adults (replaced CTEFLA and COTE which were for native speakers and non-native speakers of English, respectively)

Cert TEB Certificate in Teaching English for Business, different qualifications offered by LCCI and UCLES for teachers with little or no experience of teaching Business English

choral drill the procedure whereby a teacher asks a whole class to repeat a word, phrase or sentence simultaneously. *Also see:* mumble drill, substitution drill, transformation drill

classroom procedure the way the teacher proceeds in class at a given time

CLL Community Language Learning; *see* pp. 104–105

closed pairs pairwork in which each student in the class has a partner and works together with this partner, often practising speaking; *also see* pairwork and open pairs

communicative (usually of language practice) involving real communication

Community Language Learning a methodology described in detail in *Learning Languages: A Way and Ways* (Stevick, E. W. 1980. Rowley, MA: Newbury House) and in brief on pp. 104–105

conventions the generally accepted format, layout and abbreviations used in business correspondence (e.g. letters, faxes, memos)

core material the main material used on a language course

corporate culture the particular way of doing things, the beliefs and values in a particular company; the 'culture' of that company

COTE Certificate for Overseas Teachers of English, the UCLES exam previously taken by inexperienced non-native teachers of English; now replaced by CELTA

course objectives the aims or targets of a specific programme of study

CPE Certificate of Proficiency in English, a high level general English exam offered by UCLES; students passing this exam are often considered proficient enough in English to take a university course

CTEFLA Certificate in Teaching English as a Foreign Language to

Adults, the UCLES exam previously taken by inexperienced native teachers of English; now replaced by CELTA

CUP Cambridge University Press

deep-end exercise an activity which makes students feel they have been thrown in at the deep end of an imaginary swimming pool in terms of what they are capable of doing; in other words, the exercise will require them to do a task which they are likely to find difficult, without preparation or preliminary practice; this type of exercise is often used to establish what needs to be studied in a specific area; see DEEP ENDING (p. 78) and DEEP-END RECORDED MEETING (p. 205)

DELTA Diploma in English Language Teaching to Adults (replaced DTEFLA and DOTE which were for native speakers and non-native speakers of English, respectively)

detail question a question (about a text or listening) which checks students' understanding of a key detail

Dip TEB Diploma in Teaching English for Business, a qualification offered by LCCI and UCLES for teachers with some experience of teaching Business English

discourse a chunk of speaking or writing which is complete in itself (e.g. a dialogue or fax)

discourse elements the individual elements which contribute to make a piece of speaking or writing 'discourse', i.e. the elements which give the discourse coherence

discourse stress the particular stresses (in terms of pronunciation) which might be required because of the context of a word or phrase within its discourse context

discrete language items separate, decontextualised language items

DOTE Diploma for Overseas Teachers of English, the UCLES exam previously taken by experienced non-native teachers of English; now replaced by DELTA

drilling the class technique where a teacher asks students to repeat words, phrases or sentences. *Also see:* choral drill, substitution drill, transformation drill

DTEFLA Diploma in Teaching English as a Foreign Language to Adults, the UCLES exam previously taken by experienced native teachers of English; now replaced by DELTA

DTP Desk Top Publishing – a type of computer software

EAP English for Academic Purposes

EFL English as a Foreign Language

ELT English Language Teaching

Enc. enclosures, a term used at the end of business letters to indicate that things have been enclosed with the letter, e.g. a cheque or a price list

ESL English as a Second Language

ESP English for Specific Purposes (or English for Special Purposes)

exponents the language required for a particular function (e.g. *How would it be if we were to ...* ? for making suggestions

exposure the process by which students are 'exposed' to English – through reading or listening; the term may suggest that students do not explicitly study the language

extensive course a course conducted over a fairly long period of time

external relating to events outside a particular company or organisation; external correspondence means letters, reports, faxes and e-mail passed from one company or organisation to another

FCE First Certificate in English, an intermediate level, general English exam offered by UCLES which is between PET and CAE in terms of standard; it is widely recognised in many countries and may be a requirement for many jobs

feedback spoken or written comments given by the teacher or learners to evaluate performance

filler an activity which fills a short gap between other activities in a lesson

foreign language a language which a student learns after his or her mother tongue, usually not for the purposes of living in that country (cf. second language)

formulaic language phrases which are often used as 'formulae' in particular situations (e.g. *What can I do for you?*, *I look forward to hearing from you soon*); considered in detail by Michael Lewis 1993. *The Lexical Approach: The State of ELT and a Way Forward*. Hove: Language Teaching Publications

function language used to achieve something, e.g. 'giving advice' or 'making requests'; teaching and practising functional exponents is often considered more useful than teaching aspects of grammar which often seem to have no immediate practical usefulness

functional exponent the language which performs a particular function (e.g. *If I were you, I'd ...* for giving advice, *Could I ...* ? for making requests or *Perhaps we could ...* for making suggestions)

functional syllabus a syllabus which focuses on and suggests a teaching order for functions

gapfills texts with gaps which need to be completed by students

genre the type of writing or speaking suitable for a given situation (e.g. a menu or memo)

gist question a question about a text or listening which checks students' understanding of overall meaning or context

GM General Manager

GMAT Graduate Management Admission Test

grammar structures such as tenses (e.g. the present simple), aspect (progressive and perfect), as well as all the other parts of language which can be analysed as a system

groupwork a class activity where a group of students work together

Human Resources the modern term for the Personnel Department; it is often Human Resources which organises and oversees in-company language programmes

IATEFL International Association of Teachers of English as a Foreign Language; *see* p. 333 for address

IELTS International English Language Testing System, an English exam offered by UCLES, which is taken by students of any level wishing to study in the UK, Australia or New Zealand

in-company within a company or for a company; on company premises

information gap a 'gap' of information (or opinions) between two or more people which forces them to communicate – other parties have the necessary information

in-house within a school (i.e. on school premises); within the same organisation

input language which is presented to students to be learnt

intake what a student actually learns or internalises

intensive course a course conducted over a short period of time

internal relating to events within a particular company or organisation; internal correspondence means memos, reports, faxes and e-mail passed round within a company often from branch to branch

internal agenda a person's unstated but private intentions or objectives, which may well be in conflict with their professed objectives

intonation the way the voice rises and falls as a person speaks

KET Key English Test, the lowest level general English exam offered by UCLES

L1 a student's first language (or mother tongue)

L2 (L3, L4, etc.) the second (third or fourth) language a student learns

LCCI London Chamber of Commerce & Industry

learner-centred a class or teaching approach in which the learner is the centre of attention

learning style the approach a particular learner adopts in order to learn

lexical syllabus a syllabus which focuses on and suggests a teaching order for lexis

lexis vocabulary – individual words, phrases and whole, formulaic expressions; the word 'vocabulary' has a more limited meaning

MBA Master's in Business Administration

MD Managing Director

metalanguage the language a teacher uses in class, typically to give instructions or make comments to students; contrasted with the language which is being presented in class

methodology the system of methods used in class which reflects an underlying theory of how learning takes place

model a good example of speaking or writing provided to students in the form of a written or spoken text (e.g. a fax or telephone conversation on tape)

model-mentoring an approach recommended in this book which involves giving students models of language before asking them to produce it and then allowing students to practise; during this practice phase the teacher acts as a mentor, rather than as a teacher. See: MODEL-MENTORING (p. 101) and also MODEL-MENTORED DIALOGUES (p. 103), MODELS THROUGH LISTENING (p. 102) and MODELS THROUGH READING (p. 100)

multinational corporation a company with offices in many different countries (e.g. Procter & Gamble); also known simply as a 'multinational'

multi-strand syllabus a syllabus which focuses on and suggests a teaching order for a range of items; parallel strands of the syllabus may consist of structures, functions, notions, pronunciation practice, vocabulary items, skills practice sections and cultural focus points

mumble drill the process whereby a teacher asks several students to simultaneously repeat a word, phrase or sentence several times, in their own time; the teacher usually gestures with circular hand movements to indicate that students should repeat the word, phrase or sentence repeatedly in their own time and encourages all students to participate through eye contact and other gestures

needs analysis the process by which a student's or company's language needs are analysed before or during a course

negotiated syllabus a syllabus which is negotiated with students either at the beginning of a course or on an ongoing basis

non-verbal factors factors which affect communication, excluding words, i.e. facial expression, body space, timing, etc.

notional syllabus a syllabus which focuses on and suggests a teaching order for notions

notions areas of language, such as 'language to talk about size and dimensions' or 'language to talk about increases and decreases'

objective marking marking which does not involve the opinion of the individual examiner; for this to be the case, there has to be a limited range of answers which are clearly 'right' or 'wrong'; most marking is necessarily subjective and involves the professional judgement of the marker

OHP overhead projector

OHT overhead transparency, used with an OHP

OIBEC Oxford International Business English Certificate

open pairs pairwork in which two students in the class work together (e.g. practising a dialogue) across the room so that the teacher can check that individuals are using language correctly and so as to demonstrate an exercise to the rest of the class before beginning closed pairwork. *Also see:* closed pairs, pairwork

OUP Oxford University Press

pairwork a class activity where two students work together, as a pair

parameters the characters, setting and background to a situation in which communication takes place, e.g. the person writing a memo, his or her position and reasons for writing and his or her relationship with the recipient of the memo

performance area an area of language use, such as telephoning, negotiating or meetings

performance skill the skill of being able to cope with a particular performance area

PET Preliminary English Test, a low level general English exam offered by UCLES, which is between KET and FCE in terms of standard

phatic communion conversation which takes place merely to 'oil the wheels' of relationships, e.g. *Good to see you again!, How are you?, How are things going?*

phonemics a system for transcribing pronunciation which is an adaptation of the IPA (International Phonetic Alphabet); often used in EFL; see the chart on p. 81

placement the process by which students are allocated to classes or levels

presentation a pre-planned, structured talk, given to large or small groups (or even to individuals) in formal or informal settings; usually aims to inform or persuade

procedure see classroom procedure

productive skills speaking and writing

pronunciation the process of producing sounds which includes the production of individual sounds (often written in phonemics in EFL), stress (word stress, sentence stress and discourse stress) and intonation

Q&A a question and answer session following a formal presentation

R&D Research & Development, a department within a company

Re regarding or reference; used in the subject line of memos, letters and faxes

receptive skills listening and reading

Ref. reference

reference material any material to which reference can be made for information, e.g. dictionaries or resource books

reflective listening an approach to listening which involves the listener 'reflecting' back what he or she thinks has been said so as to check that he or she properly understands, typically using phrases such as *So you mean … , You're saying that … , You want me to … . See:* TRIO REFLECTIONS (p. 218), CLARIFYING QUESTIONS (p. 220),

ROLED SUMMARIES (p. 227)

register the particular style of writing appropriate in a given situation or profession, e.g. the legal profession

role-play the process whereby people act out the parts in a particular situation; particularly useful for helping Business English students practise relevant language

second language a language which a student learns after his or her mother tongue, often for the purpose of living in another country; in the USA this term is used to refer to both the learning of a foreign and a second language, whereas it tends to be used only to refer to immigrants' learning of a 'foreign' language in Britain

second language acquisition the term used to refer to the process of learning a second or foreign language

SEfIC Spoken English for Industry and Commerce

self-study study which takes place by the student working alone, with or without the additional support of a teacher

sentence stress the stress placed on individual syllables in words when they occur in sentences; note that these stresses may be different from stresses placed on words when pronounced in isolation

Silent Way a methodology which involves minimal teacher-talking; described in detail in *Learning Languages: A Way and Ways* (Stevick, E. W. 1980. Rowley, MA: Newbury House) and in brief on pp. 105–106

skills the four areas of language to be developed, i.e. listening, speaking, reading and writing

skills work practice which focuses on developing the four skills. *Also see:* skills, above

spoken discourse a spoken text (i.e. piece of language) which is complete in itself, in that it has internal coherence, e.g. a chat to a visitor or a presentation

stress *see:* word stress, sentence stress, discourse stress

structural syllabus a syllabus which focuses on and suggests a teaching order for structures

structure an area of grammar, e.g. the present simple, the verb 'to be', gerunds, etc.

style a particular way of speaking or writing in a given situation, especially informal vs. formal

subjective marking marking which to some extent depends on the opinion of the individual examiner; since most marking in ELT needs to be subjective (if tasks are to be realistic) subjectivity must be reduced by the use of carefully developed marking criteria

substitution drill the process whereby a teacher repeatedly gets individuals or a class to repeat sentences; in each repetition one word is substituted by the students after cues are given by the teacher; often used to give students practice repeating key grammatical structures. *Also see:*

choral drill, mumble drill, transformation drill

supplementary material material which supplements the core material used on a course

syllabus a programme of study which selects items for study and suggests an appropriate teaching order. *Also see:* functional syllabus, lexical syllabus, multi-strand syllabus, negotiated syllabus, notional syllabus; structural syllabus

teacher-centred a class or teaching approach in which the teacher is the centre of attention

TEFL Teaching English as a Foreign Language

TESOL Teachers of English to Speakers of Other Languages

TESP Teaching English for Specific Purposes

time-line a line which shows how language relates to time; the following time-line illustrates the use of the present continuous for temporary activities:

Past   NOW   Future

time–results ratio the balance between the time invested and the results achieved in consequence; a good time–results ratio means an activity which involves minimum investment of time for excellent results, in terms of student progress

TOEFL Test of English as a Foreign Language

TOEIC Test of English for International Commerce

Total Physical Response a methodology which involves students responding physically to verbal cues given by the teacher or another student (e.g. *Stand up!, Pass that to Pierre!*)

TPR Total Physical Response

transformation drill the process whereby a teacher repeatedly gets individuals or a class to repeat sentences; in each repetition one word is changed by the students, after cues are given by the teacher; often used to give students practice repeating key grammatical structures. *Also see:* choral drill, mumble drill, substitution drill

TSE Test of Spoken English. *See:* p. 316

TWE Test of Written English. *See:* p. 316

UCLES University of Cambridge Local Examinations Syndicate

UODLE University of Oxford Delegacy for Local Examinations

voice range the extent to which a person's voice rises and falls when they speak

warmer an activity which starts a lesson

word stress the stress placed on individual syllables in words

written discourse a written text (i.e. piece of language) which is complete in itself, in that it has internal coherence, e.g. a letter or an e-mail message

Bibliography

Adamson, D. 1991. *Starting English for Business*. Hemel Hempstead: Prentice Hall.

Badger, I. and P. Menzies. 1993/1994. *The Macmillan Business English Programme: Pre-Intermediate*. London: Macmillan.

Barnard, R. and J. Cady. 1993. *Business Venture 2*. Oxford: Oxford University Press.

Brieger, N. and J. Comfort. 1989. *Early Business Contacts*. Hemel Hempstead: Prentice Hall.

Brieger, N. and J. Comfort. 1990. *Social Contacts*. Hemel Hempstead: Prentice Hall.

Brieger, N. and A. Cornish. 1989. *Secretarial Contacts*. Hemel Hempstead: Prentice Hall.

Collett, P. 1993. *Foreign Bodies: A guide to European mannerisms*. London: Simon & Schuster Ltd.

Comfort, J., R. Revell and C. Stott. 1984. *Business Reports in English*. Cambridge: Cambridge University Press.

Cotton, D. and S. Robbins. 1993. *Business Class*. London: Nelson.

Deal, T. and A. Kennedy. 1988. *Corporate Cultures: The Rites and Rituals of Corporate Life*. Harmondsworth: Penguin.

Edge, J. 1992. *Cooperative Development*. Harlow: Longman.

Ellis, D. G. and B. Aubrey Fisher. 1994. *Small Group Decision Making*. Singapore: McGraw-Hill.

Ellis, G. and B. Sinclair. 1989. *Learning to Learn English: A Course in Learner Training*. Cambridge: Cambridge University Press.

Ellis, M. and C. Johnson. 1994. *Teaching Business English*. Oxford: Oxford University Press.

Gower, R. and R. Walters. 1983. *Teaching Practice Handbook*. Oxford: Heinemann.

Handy, C. 1993. 4th edition. *Understanding Organizations*. Harmondsworth: Penguin.

Jones, L. and R. Alexander. 1996. *New International Business English*. Cambridge: Cambridge University Press.

Lannon, M., G. Tullis and T. Trappe. 1993. *Insights into Business*. London: Nelson.

Lewis, M. 1993. *The Lexical Approach: The State of ELT and a Way Forward*. Hove: Language Teaching Publications.

Bibliography

Lewis, M. (ed. Hill, J.) 1997. *Implementing The Lexical Approach: The On-going Debate*. Hove: Language Teaching Publications.

Lindenfield, G. 1996. *Self Motivation*. San Francisco: Thorsons.

Littlejohn, A. 1994. *Company to Company*. Cambridge: Cambridge University Press.

Madeley, J. 1999. *Big Business, Poor Peoples: The impact of transnational corporations on the world's poor*. London: Zed Books.

McCarthy, M. 1991. *Discourse Analysis for Language Teachers*. Cambridge: Cambridge University Press.

McCormack, Mark H. 1995. *McCormack on Negotiating*. London: Arrow Books Ltd.

Maley, A. and A. Duff. 1975. *Sounds Interesting*. Cambridge: Cambridge University Press.

Maley, A, and A. Duff. 1979. *Sounds Intriguing*. Cambridge: Cambridge University Press.

Matthews, C. 1987. *Business Interactions*. Hemel Hempstead: Prentice Hall.

Matthews, C. and J. Marino. 1990. *Professional Interactions: Oral Communication Skills in Science, Technology and Medicine*. Hemel Hempstead: Prentice Hall.

Mead, R. 1990. *Cross-cultural Management Communication*. Chichester: Wiley.

Micklethwait, J. and A. Wooldridge. 1996. *The Witch Doctors*. London: Heinemann.

Mole, J. 1997. *Mind Your Manners: Managing Business Cultures in Europe*. London: Nicholas Brealey Publishing.

Mosback, G. and V. Mosback. 1976. *Practical Faster Reading*. Cambridge: Cambridge University Press.

Mullins, L.J. 1996. *Management and Organisational Behaviour* (4th edition). London: Pitman Publishing.

O'Connor, P., A. Pilbeam and F. Scott-Barrett. 1992. *Negotiating*. Harlow: Longman.

O'Neill, R. 1993. *Longman English Works 1*. Harlow: Longman.

O'Neill, R. 1994. *Longman English Works 2*. Harlow: Longman.

Parry, M. and L. Weller. 1980. *Getting Through*. Harlow: Longman.

Revell, R. and S. Sweeney. 1993. *In Print*. Cambridge: Cambridge University Press.

Richards, J. C. and T. S. Rodgers. 1986. *Approaches and Methods in Language Teaching*. Cambridge: Cambridge University Press.

Ricks, D. A. 1993. *Blunders in International Business*. Oxford: Blackwells.

Robbins, H. and M. Finley. 1997. *Why Teams Don't Work: What went wrong and how to make it right*. London: Orion Business.

Schiffrin, D. 1994. *Approaches to Discourse*. Oxford: Blackwells.

348

Scollon, R. and S. Wong Scollon. 1995. *Intercultural Communication*. Oxford: Blackwells.

Scrivener, J. 1995. *Learning Teaching*. Oxford: Heinemann.

Skehan, P. 1989. *Individual Differences in Second Language Learning*. London: Edward Arnold.

Stevick, E. W. 1980. *Learning Languages: A Way and Ways*. Rowley, MA: Newbury House.

Tannen, D. 1995. *Talking from 9 to 5*. London: Virago.

Underhill, A. 1994. *Sound Foundations*. Oxford: Heinemann.

Viney, P. and J. Curtin. 1994. *Survival English*. Oxford: Heinemann.

Waterman, R. 1994. *The Frontiers of Excellence*. London: Nicholas Brealey Publishing.

Weir, C. 1993. *Understanding and Developing Language Tests*. Hemel Hempstead: Prentice Hall.

Weir, C. and J. Roberts. 1994. *Evaluation in ELT*. Oxford: Blackwells.

Wilberg, P. 1994. *Business English Assessment*. Hove: Language Teaching Publications.

Wilberg, P. and M. Lewis. 1990. *Business English: An Individualised Learning Programme*. Hove: Language Teaching Publications.

Woolcott, L. 1992. *Business Review*. Harlow: Longman.

Alphabetical list of procedures

Alphabetical list of procedures

Index

Index

Index

Index

Index

Index

Index